Claude Reignier Conder

Heth and Moab

Explorations in Syria in 1881 and 1882

Claude Reignier Conder

Heth and Moab

Explorations in Syria in 1881 and 1882

ISBN/EAN: 9783337245962

Printed in Europe, USA, Canada, Australia, Japan

Cover: Foto ©Andreas Hilbeck / pixelio.de

More available books at **www.hansebooks.com**

HETH AND MOAB.

Explorations in Syria in 1881 and 1882.

BY

CLAUDE REIGNIER CONDER, R.E.,

AUTHOR OF 'TENT WORK IN PALESTINE,' 'JUDAS MACCABÆUS,'
'A HAND-BOOK TO THE BIBLE,' ETC.

*PUBLISHED FOR THE COMMITTEE OF THE PALESTINE
EXPLORATION FUND.*

New Edition.

LONDON
ALEXANDER P. WATT,
2, PATERNOSTER SQUARE.
1889.
[*All rights reserved.*]

TO THE

RIGHT HON. THE EARL OF DUFFERIN, G.C.B.,

This Volume

IS VERY RESPECTFULLY DEDICATED BY

THE AUTHOR.

PREFACE.

In this volume Captain Conder gives the more popular results of his short but most interesting and valuable campaign in 1881-82. The history of the expedition, its promising commencement, and its untimely end, have already been related in the pages of our 'Quarterly Statement' and elsewhere. While he was waiting for the arrival of his instruments and his surveyors, Captain Conder utilised the time by taking a journey north in search of the long-lost Kadesh, the sacred city of the Hittites: what he found, and how he found it, is here told. As soon as his instruments were landed he made preparations for the Eastern Survey. This was to have been commenced in the north, but there was fighting among the Druses, which made it impossible for a party commanded by an English officer of Engineers to work in the neighbourhood. Accordingly, Captain Conder attempted the eastern side by way of Moab. How he set to work without a day's delay, how he was ordered back by the Turkish officials, and how he succeeded, while being forced out of the country, in securing the survey of 500 square miles, may also be learned from these pages. Efforts were made through the kind offices of Lord Dufferin at Constantinople, to obtain the Firman necessary for the resuming of the work, but they were unsuccessful. Captain Conder returned home in June, 1882, and began at once upon the preparation of his memoirs. He was interrupted by the Egyptian war, during which he served on Lord Wolseley's staff. On his return home he was invalided with typhoid fever, but returned to us in May in order to finish his memoirs.

I have only to add that Captain Conder is, in this work, as in his 'Tent Work in Palestine,' solely responsible for any identifications proposed, topographical theories, and conclusions.

JAMES GLAISHER, F.R.S.,
Chairman of the Executive Committee.

CONTENTS.

CHAPTER	PAGE
PREFACE	v
I. KADESH ON ORONTES	1
II. 'THE LAND OF THE HITTITES'	36
III. THE LAND OF PURPLE	75
IV. THE LAND OF SIHON	106
V. THE LAND OF AMMON	156
VI. MOUNT GILEAD	178
VII. RUDE-STONE MONUMENTS	196
VIII. SYRIAN DOLMENS	246
IX. SYRIAN SUPERSTITIONS	276
X. THE BELKA ARABS	314
XI. ARAB FOLK-LORE	357

APPENDIX.

SCRIPTURE GAZETTEER OF EASTERN PALESTINE	377
NOTE ON THE MOSLEM RELIGION	381
INDEX	394

HETH AND MOAB.

CHAPTER I.

KADESH ON ORONTES.

THE evening of the 1st of April, 1881, found me once again in camp in Syria, after an absence of more than five years spent in work at home. Lieutenant Mantell and I had reached Beyrout on the 29th March, and were about to avail ourselves of the time which must elapse before the arrival of our companions and heavy stores, in endeavouring by a rapid march to reconnoitre as much as possible of Northern Syria, especially with the hope of fixing the site of the great Hittite capital, which Egyptologists had been so long seeking in vain, and which had been variously placed at Antioch, at Homs, or in the middle of the long lake near the latter town, now called Baheiret Kotcineh.

Our tents were pitched on the heights near the village of Kareiyeh, beside the Damascus road, and thence we looked out north on one of the most beautiful and extensive views in Syria. Immediately before us was the great gorge of the Nahr Hamana, with a grey foreground of bare rocky slopes. Beyond the river Lebanon rose ridge behind ridge towards the snowy back of Sannin—the central point of the picture. Precipices and crags: a stream fed by gleaming waterfalls several thousand feet below: a mid distance of ruddy brown and dark indigo formed by the red rock and the dusky umbrella pines which stood out like great mushrooms along the ridges: grey and purple cliffs beyond, here and there crowned with villages and hemming in that wonderful theatre of crags whence the sacred Adonis pours from its cave at Afka, the shrine of the mourning Venus: further off again the spurs of Sannin, flecked with snow, and the main ridge 8,500 feet above the sea: such were the details of the picture, which increased in depth of colour as the purple shadows lengthened and the wonderful glow of the Syrian sunset smote the barren mountains. On the right a tawny and dome-shaped summit stood out against the sky, bearing the name of 'Church Mountain,' from the ruined chapel to which the superstitious Maronites yearly repair to pay their vows. On the left the town of Beyrout was seen spread out among its mulberries and dark pines on the spit of red sand. The streams were all full, but the vines were not yet in leaf, and Lebanon looked cold and barren indeed. The white road meandered like a snake up the mountain slopes, in glaring contrast with the general colouring. As the sun set the patches of vapour spread faster even than the long shadows; and the broad dark effect of colour was swallowed up for a time in the hill mists, until the electric moonlight, which is so marvellous in Eastern lands, changed the whole scene to one of yet more fairy-like unreality. It is a view which never fails to charm the traveller. In the depth of the next winter Sannin looked yet grander in the gloom of the great storm as witnessed from St. George's Bay. In the early summer of 1882 the vine-clad slopes and the rugged precipices of Afka looked equally picturesque, while the white line of the Troados in Cyprus lay like a cloud on the horizon of the motionless sea.

The scenery of the great plain between Lebanon and Anti-Lebanon I have before endeavoured to describe. The plains were on the occasion of our present visit green with young corn, the hog's-back of Hermon was white with snow, and as we descended into the Bukei'a magnificent thunder pillars rose into the blue heaven above the castellated crags of the Anti-Lebanon; and a great flash of lightning was followed by the endless roll of the thunder reverberating from ridge to ridge and cliff to cliff.

From the flourishing town of Zahleh, picturesquely perched on the stream above the poplar beds among the russet hills, we went on to Baalbek, and here encountered the first symptoms of those vexatious difficulties with which we were destined to struggle for the next fifteen months. A travelling order was necessary, that we might obtain the required guards through the somewhat disturbed regions of northern Lebanon : for the Druzes were gathered in open revolt in the fastnesses south-east of Damascus, and the unwilling soldiers marched against them were deserting in great numbers, and were scattered over the country, pursued by the irregular mounted police. This order the Consul obtained for us, but his Highness the Waly (Hamdi Pasha) had heard of our arrival, and intimated that he had strict orders not to allow any kind of survey or reconnaissance work to be undertaken by Europeans of any nationality, unless newly authorised by the Sultan himself. This was a pleasant message indeed to be received by those who had been commissioned to continue the survey of Palestine east of Jordan on the same method and with a degree of accuracy equal to that of the Western Survey: it was a change of attitude towards Englishmen and English work on the part of Turkey which we had been unable to appreciate in England : for in the old days our difficulties had arisen from the inertness of government and from passive obstruction, whereas we were now destined to contend with active interference, with acute suspicion and stupid fear of the unknown intrigues, attributed to us all the more because we insisted on the purely antiquarian character of our mission and on the well-established reputation for fair dealing which the Society may claim in Palestine. Even our travelling order was delayed as long as possible, and we started without it from Beyrout. We were obliged to wait three days for it at Baalbek, and the letter sent to Beyrout to give information of this delay took eighteen days to travel a distance of fifty miles, and only arrived after our return.

At length, on the 6th April, we turned our faces to the little-visited district between Baalbek and Homs, and left the great ruins escorted by two irregular horsemen, and an infantry guard of honour of four, who presented arms and expected a gratuity for so doing. And who could refuse a few shillings to men who had perhaps fought so bravely against hope in the Balkans, and who were now not merely unpaid and unclothed, but even reduced almost to starvation, unless they could keep themselves alive by civil employment or by robbery?

The road leads northwards by Nahleh ('the torrent'), with its ruined temple on the southern cliff of the stream, by Yunin and Resm el Haddad ('the tracing of the boundary'), across the deep 'Valley of Shepherds,' through the dry and monotonous district of rounded hills, white, brown, and tawny, of chalk and marl, lying at the western foot of the Anti-Lebanon. On the east a rough limestone ridge, on the west the broad plain, with here and there a clump or row of poplars; and dusky Lebanon beyond, covered with dark mastic scrub, and rising in a second ridge of tawny naked rocks to the snowline. In the middle of this plain stands a solitary pillar, which is called 'Amûd el Benât— 'Column of the Girls,'—and is traditionally connected with a channel of water rising at it and fed by the Lebanon lakes. Visiting the pillar a year later, it seemed to me possible that, in common with one near Acre, it may have been erected in its present position as a place of penance for one of the followers of St. Simeon Stylites, who, in the fifth century, imitated throughout northern Syria the life of their master, who died, it is said, on his pillar east of Antioch in 459 A.D. The idea of his penance was not original, for the hermits of India and Egypt had long before invented a similar symbolic self-torture; but the practice became popular among the early Christians of Syria, and it is difficult to see with what other object solitary pillars are likely to have been erected so far from any main road or ruined town.

At noon we reached the little village of Lebweh, and halted by the springs issuing from the bare slope to the east of the village, which stands on a mound by the open valley with a few poplars, and on the north side foundations of an ancient building —perhaps a temple.

Lebweh, though now a poor village, was a fortified town in the twelfth century, and is mentioned in the Antonine Itinerary (about the second century of our era); but it is doubtful whether it can be connected with the Biblical Leboa (Num. xxxiv. 8; Ezek. xlvii. 15) so often mentioned in connection with Hamath, and once with Zedad. The question is, however, of considerable interest in regard to the boundary of the Israelite and Hittite dominions, and is thus connected with the immediate subject of the present chapter; it demands, therefore, a moment's attention.

The northern boundary of the Land of Israel, as defined in the Pentateuch (Num. xxxiv.), ran from the Great Sea to a certain Hor-ha-Har, or Mount Hor, quite distinct from that near Petra, and possibly connected by name with the Khar or Har, by which title the Phœnicians and their land are designated on early Egyptian monuments. Thence the border passed by the 'entrance' of Hamath (Liba Hamath) to Zedad, apparently the extreme point. From Ziphron and Hazar Enan ('the enclosure of the springs') it went eastwards to Shepham, and thence down to Riblah east of Ain. This account is hard to follow, because Riblah alone is fixed, being the village of the same name which we passed subsequently north of Lebweh. Zedad has with some probability been placed south-east of Riblah and east of the Anti-Lebanon ridge at the Jacobite village, Sadâd; and the 'entrance' of Hamath is possibly the same as the place called Liboa Zedad in another passage (Ezek. xlvii. 15). It is generally supposed that the broad plain which extends from south of Homs to Hamath is intended. Hazar Enan appears to have been the western border of the Damascus region (Ezek. xlvii. 17), and in this latter passage the boundary of the Holy Land is drawn through Hazar Enan from the sea (or from the west), and thence described as follows: 'And the north (Tzephon) northwards and the border of Hamath.'

The position of Hazar Enan is thus of great importance, and the best suggestion which has been offered is that the site is to be found at 'Ain el 'Asy, one of the principal sources of the Orontes, and close to the present north-west limit of the Damascus district. In this case the curious expression, 'the north northwards,' is easily explained, for Strabo tells us that the Orontes was called Typhon (that is Tzephon, 'the north' or 'the hidden'), perhaps, because it flows northwards. The modern name el 'Asy, 'the rebel,' is perhaps connected with the idea of the ancient Typhon or Set, the enemy of the Egyptian Osiris. The passage in Ezekiel may possibly be rendered 'Hazar Enan and the Orontes northwards,' and in this case it is not difficult to define the line, which follows the Orontes to Riblah, where the broad Hittite plain expands from the narrower vale of Cœlesyria (the 'entering in' to the Hamath region), and thence the border may be traced east to Zedad, and southwards to Damascus. The Lebanon is entirely excluded, and is, indeed, not mentioned in defining the boundary, for it was no doubt already in the hands of a strong Semitic race, the Phœnicians, with whom the Kings of Israel were in league, while in the time of David and Solomon at least the plains of Hamath were ruled by the Hittite Princes.

It is true that a border so drawn does not agree with the Talmudic view which places the northern Hor at Mount Amanus, the modern Alma Dagh, north of the Orontes; but this opinion has little critical importance, and the Rabbinical boundary does not agree with the Book of Joshua or with the conquests of David. Sidon, Afka, the Amorites or 'hillmen' of Lebanon, the Giblites or Phœnicians, the mountaineers of the Anti-Lebanon, or of Hermon even, and of the hills above Tyre, remained unconquered when Joshua died (Joshua xiii. 4—6); but in David's time the Syrian conquests were extended to include Damascus and all Syria to Hamath, with Berothah (possibly Beyrout, though this is often denied), and even as far east as Euphrates. At whatever time the boundary thus described was drawn, even Ezekiel does not mention Lebanon as destined to form part of the Holy Land, although that goodly mountain was promised earlier to Israel. The line is one which appears to be the naturally historical boundary between the Hebrews on the south, the Phœnicians on the north-west, and the Hittites on the north, while, as we shall see later, the wanderings of Joab were bounded by the vicinity of Riblah on the north, and did not include any part of Lebanon beyond Sidon.

It is not easy very definitely to fix the position of Mount Hor in Lebanon, but it is quite possible that Sannin itself is intended, and it is probable that the Litâny, flowing from Baalbek to Tyre, is practically the real old mountain boundary between the Hebrews and the Phœnicians.

To return to the springs of Lebweh, the most southern sources of the Orontes, it is possible that the name may have a connection with the Hebrew Leboa, although the position has no great geographical value, for the modern meaning—'a lioness'— is not the probable origin of the word.

From the springs we pushed on, having always in sight the great monument of the Kamû'at el Hirmil about to be described; and passing by the villages of Neby 'Othmân, 'Ain, and Fikieh with its flourishing Christian settlement, its stream, orchards, and well-built houses, we mounted the bare marl slope which leads to Râs Baalbek, a village on the edge of the plain, with a fine spring and rows of poplars.

On the following day we diverged westwards to visit 'Ain el 'Asy (where, as I have above mentioned, Hazar Enan may perhaps best be placed), together with the hermitage of Mar Marûn and the monument of Kamû'at el Hirmil. The stream from Lebweh runs gradually down northwards, until at 'Ain el 'Asy it is in a gorge about 300 feet deep, of yellow limestone, arid and rocky, the slopes dotted with wild olives and stunted firs. The rugged Lebanon rises on the west, the flat plain extends eastwards above the gorge. The stream, two or three yards wide, is fringed with brambles. In a recess to the east, under a rocky cliff, is a deep green pool, welling up from the earth and shaded by a large plane-tree on its northern brink, from the branches of which luxuriant creepers hang down over the water. Two caves for cattle are scooped in the tawny cliff, and little springs issue under the rocks on the north and south. The pool is about ten yards north and south, by twenty yards east and west, full of fine cresses and fringed with osiers. Such is the real birthplace of the famous Orontes, which rushes northwards to the long lake of Koteineh, and thence to the gorge of Hamah, and through the marshes to the plain of Omk, where, turning west by Antioch, it joins the Lower Kara-Su, and flows past the oleander and myrtle groves of Daphne to the open bay of Seleucia, under Mount Casius, where it forms the true boundary of Syria, the border between the Arab and Turkish populations.

A bright stream from the 'Asy pool flows some fifty yards to join the Lebweh current, and more than doubles the volume of the Orontes. Following the right bank of the stream, we saw beneath us the gleaming river rushing over its rocky bed, breaking here and there over rapids, and winding in a green meadow, about a quarter of a mile wide, with a few fruit gardens and wild olives, all walled in by barren rocks, in a gorge some 400 feet deep. Two miles from the pool, in the eastern cliff, is the hermitage of Mar Marûn, the founder of the Maronite sect.

This hermitage, perched 300 feet above the bright river on which it looks down, is not unlike the original cave of St. Saba in the famous Judean monastery. A gallery in the rock, forty yards long, leads to chambers of various sizes cut in a precipice about fifty feet high at the top of a very steep slope. The entrance is defended by a loopholed wall, the loops round-headed; but there is a pointed arch below the gallery, and the masonry appears to be mediæval. The traditional Maron lived in the fifth century, and is said to have had his eyes put out in this cave by a certain Nicola; but the real founder of the Maronite sect, if he ever inhabited this den, lived at a much later period, and the earliest mention of the cave is found in the works of Abu el Feda.

Climbing over the white bare chalky slopes east of the river for another three miles, we reached the interesting and conspicuous monument called Kamû'at el Hirmil, which had been in sight even before reaching Lebweh. It has been visited and described by Vandevelde and Robinson, and was discovered by Dr. Thomson in 1846. Traditionally it is the tomb of a Roman Emperor, and architecturally it would seem to belong to that famous period of Syrian art, the age of the Antonines, when Syria and Peræa were covered with magnificent buildings, cities, temples, and tombs.

The Kamû'a stands on the crest which divides the basin of the Litâny from the plains of Homs, and here we caught our first view of the lake which was the object of our journey. The northern plain, twenty to thirty miles wide, stretched away to Homs and to the shining sheet of water some twenty miles off. The little island mound could easily be distinguished in the lake, and a larger mound, black and prominent, was seen beside the Orontes, south of the sheet of water; this was the Tell Neby Mendeh, which we afterwards discovered to be the real site of Kadesh on Orontes. On the north-east, Riblah with its poplars stood low beside the river, which has a very tortuous course after leaving the ravines near the monument. To the north-west, beyond the stream, the prosperous-looking white houses of the village of Hirmil stood on the slopes of Lebanon, amid gardens and orchards. Lebanon itself sinks gradually from the white cedar summit, 10,000 feet above the sea, towards the valley of the Eleutherus, which divides it from the Nuseireh mountains. On the east was the rich green plain, with the tall mosque tower of Jusieh, Zer'a also and Kuseir; and beyond rose the rocky Anti-Lebanon; on the south the dome of Hermon might easily have been seen, but for the grey haze of the southern breeze. It was a fit site for a great monument, and perhaps once witnessed the battle for the possession of Syria.

The Kamû'a is a block of solid masonry, thirty feet square and seventy feet high, in two orders, each with a cornice and flat corner pilasters, surmounted by a pyramid. On the walls are bas-reliefs, which represent the hunting of the deer, the bear, and the wild boar. The masonry is limestone, but the basement is formed of three steps of hard black basalt. There are numerous tribe-marks cut by wandering Arabs on the sides of the monument, but, as in the case of other Roman monuments beyond Jordan, there is no inscription to tell the date or ownership of the structure.

The swell on which the Kamû'a stands consists of basalt, and the barren down to the north, treeless and covered only with scanty grass, low shrubs, and thorny bellân, is dotted with the camps of Turkoman nomads similar to those of the Bedawin. Blocks of hard black stone, covered with grey or orange lichen, are strewn over the surface, and it is clear that these downs rising out of the rich lower plain can never have been more than a pastoral district. The most curious feature of the scene, however— and one which I am as yet unable to explain—is the existence of what appear to be innumerable barrows or graves of great size, covering the swelling ground round the Kamû'a for at least a mile in either direction. These structures consist of flat piles of basalt stones, six to ten feet in length, and about a yard broad and two or three feet high. Some occur in rows; some crown the hillocks; some are on the slopes. They are not oriented, nor arranged in any particular order, and with them occur circles and enclosure walls of basalt, placed generally in the hollows and constructed of small stones. We afterwards noticed similar stone-heaps on the shores of the lake of Koteineh, and they may perhaps prove to be only Turkoman graves, for the Arabs east of Jordan bury the slain hastily in a similar manner, by merely piling stones on the corpses; but at the moment these rude stone monuments were wonderfully suggestive of the scene of a great battle round the central rallying-point at the Kamû'a.

Over the barren basalt downs our course was next directed to Riblah, the most northern point visited by the great Robinson. Before reaching the village, we found traces of an aqueduct crossing the plain east and west, and probably once fed by the waters of the Orontes. The channel was formed by walls of mud, and craters resembling dens of gigantic ant-lions appeared to show where access had been made to a covered waterway beneath. These mud aqueducts, which are not used in Palestine, occur throughout the plains of Homs, and supply the city gardens from a great distance. They are of interest, because it would seem from the Egyptian sculptures that they existed also in Hittite times, resembling those used by the Assyrians and the Egyptians.

Riblah is a large mud village with a group of poplars, well built, in the middle of the plain, on the right bank of the river. It is said to be entirely inhabited by Christians; but although famous in Semitic history for nearly thirty centuries, it possesses no antiquities, and owes its importance mainly to its ford and its surrounding corn-lands.

The inhabitants were busily employed in making bricks (libben) of sun-dried mud and straw. They are a sturdy race, with eagle-like profiles and short projecting beards, which, with the thick under-lip, gave them a decidedly Assyrian cast of countenance. It was most interesting to contrast these Semitic agriculturists with their Turkoman neighbours; for in this mixture of races—the Semitic tillers of the plains and the Turanian shepherds on the downs—we find a condition of society precisely parallel to that which existed in this very region when Rameses the Great attacked the Turanian Hittites and their bearded Syrian allies. The gaily dressed women, tattooed with blue all over their hands and faces, the older ones with grey hairs dyed red in henna, were baking bread in the dome-shaped ovens built up of disks of camel-dung nearly two feet in diameter and three inches thick, which form a conspicuous object in the village. Even the tombs are of mud and straw, neatly modelled, with a short pillar at each end; and in this remote district, far from the influence of European ideas, we might imagine ourselves transported back to the times of the earliest Semitic civilization, and might have seen without surprise the war-chariots of Kheta Sar sweeping over the broad flat plain.

From Riblah we rode on again to Kuseir ('the little tower'), a large village, half Moslem, half inhabited by Greek Catholic Christians. This is the seat of government, and we underwent the tedious civilities of the Kaimakam and the Bishop, who were suffering from 'strained relations,' due to the disappearance of a Christian girl carried off by the agents of the Moslem Sheikh. Our arrival was as usual supposed to have a political meaning, and no doubt the simple inhabitants thought that the English Government had heard of their troubles and sent officers to report on the facts. We avoided political conversation as far as possible; but we could not help hearing the often-reiterated assurance, which was repeated throughout Syria whenever possible, that Christian and Moslem alike would welcome the European Power to which in their despair they turn to save them from the Turk.

On the morning of the 8th of April we rode out westwards to the dark mound of Neby Mendeh, near which, in enumerating the names of the district, a peasant on the evening before had casually mentioned a ruin called Kades. The unexpected sound struck my ear suddenly, and the situation was not at all that in which I had supposed Kadesh on Orontes to lie, but there could be no doubt of the genuineness of the name; and it has since been ascertained that many other travellers had found the ruin Kades on the same spot, but without recognising the importance of their discovery, a fact of which I was not at the time aware. My attention had been directed towards the discovery of the great city of Kadesh on Orontes early in 1880, and several friends had kindly endeavoured to provide the funds necessary for an expedition during that year; but I had always supposed the island in the lake of Koteineh to be the real site, and was at first very unwilling to believe Kadesh to have stood at Tell Neby Mendeh. There is, however, no better guide to identification than the discovery of an ancient name, and whatever may have been written concerning the migration of sites, we have not as yet any clearly proven case in which a Semitic indigenous title has wandered away from the original spot to which it was applied for geographical or religious reasons.

For those who have not closely followed the process of Egyptian and Hittite archæology during the last twenty years, it will be convenient here to explain briefly the reasons which give so much interest to the discovery of Kadesh on Orontes, and which led to the conclusion that the true site has at length been found. The Kheta or Hittites are mentioned as early as the time of the 18th and 19th

Egyptian dynasties as a warlike race of Northern Syria, allied to many other tribes in resisting the onward progress of the Pharaohs. At Megiddo they encountered Thothmes III., and Kadesh, their southern capital and sacred city, was first attacked by that great monarch, who established an outpost at the foot of Lebanon. The most famous conflict between the Egyptians and the Hittites occurred, however, during the reign of the celebrated Rameses the Second, or Miamun, of the 19th dynasty. This monarch made an expedition against Kadesh in 1361 B.C., and his exploits are recorded in an epic composed by the court poet, Pentaur, while the subsequent treaty of peace, which was engraved on a silver plate, is also inscribed on the outer wall of the temple at Karnak. On the walls of the Ramesseum at Thebes is a picture of Kadesh, and again at Abu Simbel, not far north, is a battle picture containing 1100 figures, and measuring 57 by 25 feet. From these contemporary records it is possible to draw very definite conclusions concerning the situation of the town.

The history of the Egyptian attack appears to be as follows. Leaving Thebes, Rameses marched along the coast to the Lebanon, and crossed over to the Hanruta, or Orontes. The Hittites gathered a formidable confederacy, including Phœnicians, Mesopotamians, and tribes from Asia Minor. 'The vile chief of the Kheta, with many allies accompanying him, lay in ambush to the north-west.' The Egyptian army was near a place called Shabatuna, on the border of the land of the Amairo (possibly Amorites or 'hillmen'), and Kadesh itself is in the same account said to have lain 'on the western bank of Hanruta,' or Orontes. The poem gives a very hyperbolic account of the courage displayed by Rameses, who, being far in advance of his army, was apparently reconnoitring the district north-west of Kadesh, having been deceived by the statements of Hittite prisoners, who represented the enemy as being far away north, near Aleppo. The Kheta passed over a ditch on the south of the town and surprised the Egyptian monarch in rear, but in spite of the surprise and of the confusion into which the van of his army was thrown while advancing (apparently) from the south to his aid, Rameses fought his way out of the trap, and the 2,500 chariots of the Hittites and their allies were driven back, and fled, seized with panic, to the Orontes, in which many of their men were drowned. Kadesh was assaulted next day, but the Hittites at once submitted and signed a peace.

The sculptures at Abu Simbel represent this great battle; but, as is common in such representations, more than one episode is shown simultaneously on the bas-relief. Kadesh appears as a walled city at a point where the Orontes widens considerably. Rameses charges the Hittites from the south (such being the deduction from the fact that the text states that he followed the west bank of the river), and the defenders of the city are seen falling into the stream and endeavouring to cross it. On the opposite bank the Prince of Aleppo is being held head downwards by his followers, who are endeavouring to recover him after dragging him out of the water, and an element of caricature seems here to be introduced, as in many similar representations in Egyptian pictures. Other forces are crossing the river north of the city, and the previous episode of the reconnaissance of Rameses on the north-west of Kadesh is represented on the spectator's right. Fighting seems also to be going on east of the city, but whether this belongs to the first, second, or third epoch of the story is not clear. The victory is commemorated in a second picture beneath, where a third figure of Rameses is portrayed seated on his chair of state.

In the picture of the Ramesseum Kadesh is seen surrounded on all sides by a double ditch with bridges on the east and west, but the bas-relief is unfortunately injured close to the city walls on the spectator's right. In this picture the Hittites and their allies are represented as distinct races with different kinds of weapons. The one race is bearded, the other beardless, and in the Abu Simbel picture the Chinese-like appearance of the Hittites, who have long pig-tails, is very remarkable. They are a light red colour, with high caps. Kheta Sar, the Hittite King, is elsewhere represented with curled hair and beard, and on certain bas-reliefs with Hamathite or Hittite inscriptions figures appear with curled slippers, like those common once among the Turks, and shown on Assyrian monuments as distinctive of Armenian tribes.

The peace which was concluded between Kheta Sar and Rameses was consolidated by the marriage of the latter with Ramaur Nefru, the daughter of the former. The document is of value as throwing light not only on the civilization of the period, but also to a certain extent on the question of the Hittite nationality. The names of the Hittites here recorded do not appear to be Semitic; but on the other hand their Gods, including Baal, Ashtoreth, and Set, are those which were adored by Syrians, Assyrians, and Phœnicians. A thousand war gods and a thousand goddesses are invoked by the Egyptian signatories. Set of Aleppo, Set of Daphne, Set of Orontes, and six other Sets are called to witness by the Hittites, with many Ashtoreths. The mountains and the rivers of the Kheta land are addressed as divinities, with the mountains and rivers of Egypt, the wind and the clouds. In this interesting tablet we are thus allowed a glance at the beliefs of the Hittite race, and find them worshipping local deities having a generic name (like the Madonnas of Italy), with mountains and living water. Their princes had many war-chariots, and scribes accompanied them to record their actions. Their infantry fought in regular ranks, and among their allies the learned have recognised the inhabitants of the island of Aradus, the Mysians, possibly also the Trojans, the Cyprians (according to Brugsch), the Dardanians, the men of Carchemish (now Jerabis), of Aleppo, of Diblath, of Kinnesrin, of Asshur, of Pethor, and of Mesopotamia. It was, in fact, a confederacy of all Syria and Chaldea, of Phœnicia and Asia Minor, to withstand the growing power of the 19th Egyptian dynasty.

The study of Hittite antiquities has of late attracted great attention, and has been especially elucidated by Professor Sayce. The Hamathite inscriptions, though discovered by Burckhardt early in the century, have only of late years been copied and studied. Professor Sayce has pointed out many striking resemblances between their symbols and those of the Cypriote syllabary. Similar characters have been found also on seals of the time of Sargon and Sennacherib, and inscriptions in the same text have now been recovered at Aleppo, at

Jerabis (or Carchemish), at Ibreez in Lycaonia, and on the statues near Karabel and Smyrna, once known as representing Sesostris and Niobe respectively. All these texts have been published by the Biblical Archæological Society, and have the remarkable peculiarity (in common with the old wooden hieroglyphics of Egypt) that even when the stone used is a hard basalt, the letters are all in relief.

Bas-reliefs also occur in Asia Minor, with or without inscription, which are evidently the work of races akin to the Hittites. One of them is in the valley of Karabel, north of Ephesus: a second south-west of Angora, on the old road from Armenia to Lydia, representing warriors with the Phrygian cap and peaked boots, spears and quivers. The walls of the fortress on which these figures (each nine feet high) occur are built in polygonal masonry. Fifty miles east of the Halys another bas-relief shows us a procession of gods in Phrygian caps, and goddesses in mural crowns, treading on lions and leopards, with a two-headed eagle and winged sun disc, as in Assyria. This sculpture has ten lines of inscription in characters like those of Hamath.

To apply the name of Hittite to all these monuments is perhaps premature. The Hittites were one among many tribes belonging to a great race, the headquarters of which seem to have been in Asia

Minor or Armenia. It attained to power at an early historic period, and established sacred capitals at Carchemish on Euphrates, and Kadesh on Orontes, both of which are now known. Their extension southwards was checked at the battle of Megiddo, as early as 1600 B.C., and their strength was broken by the rise of Babylonian power in the eighth century B.C. In the Bible we find Hittites as far south as Hebron in the time of Abraham; but in the eleventh century, B.C., the Hittite princes are mentioned only in Northern Syria (1 Kings x. 29). Northern Syria is the 'land of the Hittites' in Joshua (i. 4); and on Egyptian monuments we find mentioned as early as Seti I. 'great chiefs of the Rutennu, whom his majesty brought from the land of the Kheta.' Ruten, or Luden, is Syria in the decree of Canopus, and thus the Hittites are found not in Asia Minor, but in Aram, where lay their cities Aleppo, Tibhath, Kadesh, Hit, and Pethor.

Hittite princesses were found in the harem of Solomon, and the Hittite Uriah was one of David's champions. 'Kadesh of the Hittites' is the true rendering of the words which have been corrupted into Tahtim Hodshi in our Bibles (2 Sam. xxiv. 6), and their land thus bounded the conquests of David, and the wanderings of Joab and of the census-takers who were with him. This Kadesh is also probably the Cadytis of Herodotus (iii. 5), a city of the Syrians of Palestine, which he estimates to have been not smaller than Sardis.

The name is radically connected with that of the Kodeshoth, or 'holy women,' devoted as Nautch girls to the service of Ashtoreth, who probably had her shrine here, as at Tripoli, Jerusalem, Kadesh Naphtali, or Kadesh Barnea—wherever, indeed, a Kadesh or 'holy' city existed, from Syria to Gades in Spain.

A bilingual inscription (in Hamathite and Cuneiform, for instance), is sorely needed to give the key to the new language yet unread; but as there are many unexplored sites in Asia Minor where monuments of this class are awaiting examination, we cannot but hope that the riddle will still be read. It will in the end probably be found that the Hittite and the Accadian (or mountaineer from the north) come of one stock, akin to the old dark Turanian race which the Semitic Assyrians subjugated in Chaldea; and the pigtails of the Hittites seem to point to their kinship with the Mongols and Tartars —the oldest, perhaps, of existing Asiatic races.

The recovery of Kadesh is a contribution to the study of this interesting old tribe, the eldest of the sons of Canaan. It was thought that the island in the lake of Koteineh was the probable site of Kadesh, because this lake is called Bahret Kades by Abu el Feda, who lived not far north of its shores;

but it should be remembered that there is no mention of any lake in the Egyptian historic account of the city, though the river is marked with the name Hanruta on the bas-reliefs. The enlargement of the stream is out of all scale if it is intended to represent the Koteineh lake, which is six miles long and two broad; and as there is no mention of any boats or rafts, while the defeated Hittites are shown endeavouring to swim across the water and even to drive through it, we may fairly conclude that an enlargement of the Orontes stream only is intended. It would certainly have been a hopeless attempt for men encumbered with arms to endeavour to swim nearly a mile from the shores of the Koteineh lake to the island in its midst, and had the city of Kadesh stood on such an island, rafts or boats would have been necessary for the attack, and the Hittites would clearly not have submitted merely on seeing the line of Egyptian chariots arrayed helplessly on the border of the lake.

But in addition to this argument, we have the fact that the Koteineh lake depends for its existence entirely on the dam at its northern end. There can be no doubt that this dam is Roman work, for the character of mortar and of masonry so resembles the constructions of the Romans in other parts of Syria. According to the Talmud of Jerusalem and of Babylon alike (for there are two distinct passages, viz., T. B. Baba Bathra, 74 *b*, and T. J. Kilaim ix. 5), this lake, which was then called Yam Hemetz, or the 'Waters of Emesa,' was a reservoir, not natural, but constructed by Diocletian, no doubt in order to carry a high-level aqueduct, as at present, to the city of Homs or Emesa. There seems no reason why this statement should not be credited, and in speaking of Kadesh we may, I think, leave out of consideration altogether the lake of Koteineh, and confine our attention to the Orontes at that site where the ancient name of the Hittite capital survives unchanged.

From this preliminary sketch of the subject we may now proceed to a consideration of the newly found site of Kadesh.

It has been pointed out that the name was long ago discovered by Thomson, and has been mentioned by several subsequent travellers; but as they were unaware of the historical importance of the site, its identification remained unsuggested until 1881, when we found the name Kades well known as applying to ruins on the south slope of Tell Neby Mendeh. To us the recovery of the name was an unexpected revelation, for my original wish was to explore the island in the lake further north, and I had consequently overlooked the accounts given by Thomson and others of the site of Tell Neby Mendeh. A visit to the spot, however, convinced me that the ancient name, as in all other cases, had stuck to the original site, and that no such migration, as is commonly suggested by those who find ancient names in positions not in accord with their own theories, had taken place in this instance any more than in others.

The name of Neby Mendeh, or Mendau (as Robinson heard it), is also interesting. He is said locally to have been a son of Jacob: but his name recalls the Egyptian Mentu or Mando, the war-god whom Rameses himself is represented by Pentaur as invoking in his attack on the city.

The great mound of Tell Neby Mendeh is from 50 to 100 feet high, and about 400 yards long. A modern Arab village of stone and mud occupies the centre, and the shrine, which is unusually large, is on the higher part to the north-east. The dome shines with whitewash; the walls are of basalt masonry; beside it, stretching to the extremity of the mound, is a cemetery of Moslem tombs, some of stone, others of mud, but all correctly oriented. East of the village are the high conical ovens built of round cakes of camel's dung, which are common in this part of the country.

Looking down from the summit of the Tell, we perceived that the site was surrounded with water, just as in the Egyptian representations of Kadesh.

The Orontes flows east of the Tell, and is

dammed with a broad flat bulwark of masonry, part of which at least is modern, since a stone with a Greek inscription is built in. Above this dam, which is opposite the higher part of the Tell, the river expands into a wider reach than usual; the average breadth of the stream is perhaps not more than 30 feet, but the dam is about 25 yards long, and the wide reach, or lakelet, is about 50 yards across, fringed with rushes. The water is taken from the upper side of the dam to feed a little modern mill.

On the opposite, or western and northern sides of the Tell, runs a separate stream called el Mukâdîyeh, flowing from a spring called et Tannûr ('the Oven'), which is at some distance to the south-west. The brook is fresh and rapid, full of fish, and flowing through gardens where it joins the Orontes below the dam. Dr. Thomson visited the place in 1846, and states that a ditch, cut across south-west of the Tell, once joined the Orontes to the upper part of the Mukâdîyeh stream, in such a manner as to make the mound an island surrounded on all sides with water. On the west there is a second channel or aqueduct, between two earthen banks, flowing parallel to the natural stream of the Mukâdîyeh, and thus the double moat of Kadesh, as seen at the Ramesseum, appears to have its modern representative. Two small foot-bridges, each of a single arch, span these streams, just as the western bridges on the bas-relief lead out from the Hittite fortress.

On the south-west, just south of the Mukâdíyeh stream, is another small mill, rudely built of basalt chips, and beside it a travelling juggler was amusing the peasantry with the antics of his bear. The mill is called also 'mill of Kades;' and the ruins of an ancient city are here visible in the ploughland at the south-west foot of the Tell. A wall of alternate courses of brick and limestone was first found, and further south the foundations of a monument called the Kamû'a, which perhaps once resembled the Hirmil monument already noticed. On the west side of the stream we found the fragment of a statue rudely executed, apparently once a seated figure with a long robe. The block was of marble, and four feet high. It may have been Roman or Byzantine in origin.

West of the mill there are sarcophagi standing on a floor of rubble mixed with coarse chips of pottery. The natives stated that some twenty tombs exist beneath. Beside the Kades mill are several well-cut column shafts, and three very large blocks of basalt.

The brick and stone-work wall is of a style exactly resembling that of the old walls of Stamboul which were built in Byzantine times. It is probable that the existing ruins on this side of the old mound are those of the Roman town called Laodicea ad Libanum, or Laodicea Scabiosa, first a Roman colony, afterwards a bishopric. This city was founded apparently by Seleucus Nicator (300 B.C.), and was allowed the 'jus Italicum' by Severus (193—211 A.D.); it is noticed by Ptolemy, Polybius, Strabo, and Pliny, and shown on the Peutinger Tables. Its site was identified by Robinson at Tell Neby Mendeh, from the measured distances and other indications in the ancient accounts.

Of Hittite antiquities we found no traces, though we sought them even within the sanctuary of Neby Mendeh. But already, in 1846, Dr. Thomson found the natives breaking up ancient columns at this spot, and the work of destruction at an inhabited site goes on with frightful rapidity. Excavations on the sides of the Tell might lead to the discovery of such slabs and bas-reliefs as are found in other Hittite towns facing the slopes of the great mounds.

The view from the Tell is a fine one. On the north-east, about four miles distant, stretches the calm lake with its little island mound, and to the left of this is the pass which separates the Lebanon from the Anseiriyeh range—a high saddle of dark basaltic rock. The mounds of Shômarîn and Koteineh, with the square enclosure of 'Noah's Ark'—hereafter to be noticed—are also visible; and the broad plain towards Homs is sown with similar great Tells rising from the flat arable lands. The fortress of Homs can be seen bearing about 47° north-east, and on the south, Riblah and the Kamû'at el Hirmil. The ranges of Lebanon and Anti-Lebanon bound the view; and there is little else to note on the spot, for the neighbourhood is almost bare of trees, and consists mainly of corn-land.

Here, then, standing on the acropolis of the sacred Hittite fortress of Kadesh, we could in imagination see enacted at our feet all the episodes of that battle, famous more than thirty-two centuries ago, yet so forgotten that neither Robinson, Thomson, Burton, Drake, Porter, Wright, nor any other visitor, had been aware of the importance of this prominent site. We might picture the serried ranks of the Egyptian infantry advancing northwards, with the light chariots yoked each to its pair of horses, and hung with quiver and shield. We could see the adventurous Rameses, with his scanty following, coming down from the rougher land into the open plain north-west of the city, and the host of the Turanian warriors concealed behind the river and by the great Tell itself. We might almost hear the cries of the wild Hittites dashing over the bridges in their chariots to intercept the incautious monarch, their long pig-tails floating behind them as these red-booted and mustachioed princes, with their cloaks swelling in the wind, urged on their steeds. The dark beards and eagle noses of the Semitic allies, with their shawl-headdress, so like that of the modern Arab, contrast with the Tartar-like mien of their Turanian masters, and with the slimness of the Egyptians. The clash of the opposing chariots is hidden by clouds of dust from the corn-lands. The first brigade of Ra, the god of light, gives way before the Hittite charge; but Rameses, calling aloud to his father, Ammon, to help him, rallies his hosts, and the panic-stricken Syrians flee. The Prince of Aleppo falls into Orontes, and is dragged out by his men, who, on the opposite bank, vainly strive to recover him by holding up his feet to let the water run from his mouth. The stream, the ditches, and bridges, the distant mountains, are before us as of yore, and all the stir and wild energy of the Abu Simbel battle-piece seem to rise at once before the eye of the imagination.

CHAPTER II.

'THE LAND OF THE HITTITES.'

DESCENDING from the Kadesh hill, we proceeded northwards to examine the lake of Kotcinch and its island, and passing by the little village of 'Ârjûn, we came, after a ride of two miles, to the Sefinet Nuh, or 'Ark of Noah.' This is an earthen enclosure about 300 yards square, with mounds at the angles, as though indicating corner towers. The ditch outside we estimated to be 40 feet deep and about the same width; the building lies with its angles to the cardinal points; the interior plateau, which is now plough-land, rises above the general level of the plain.

At Ârjûn is a Roman milestone, so that we are clearly on an old Roman road from Emesa to Laodicea Scabiosa; but this curious enclosure can hardly be a Roman camp. The tradition attached probably indicates the antiquity of the monument, and perhaps its religious character. It has lately been noted by Assyriologists, that whereas Egyptian monuments have almost invariably their sides in the direction of the cardinal points, the Assyrian buildings and pyramids have generally their angles so directed. It is possible, then, that the *Sefinet Neby Nûh*, or 'Ark of Noah,' near Kadesh, might, if excavated, yield antiquities either Hittite or Assyrian. It is very curious that an earthen enclosure should be called an ark; but in Persia we have the legend of Yima's walled garden, which escaped the winter floods. The Hebrew *Tebah*, like the Egyptian *Teb*, was a coffer or box, rather than a boat, and the Hebrew word for Noah's ark, Moses' cradle, and Joseph's coffin is the same. The legend of Noah's ark at this spot is clearly connected with the Tannûr south of Kadesh, for the Tannûr or 'Oven,' according to the Korân, was the crevice from which the flood issued, and which again swallowed its waters. Clearly there was once a flood legend at Kadesh, but it is most probably to be compared with that of the sacred cleft beneath the Temple of Hierapolis further north, and with the holy lakes which adjoined Phœnician and Philistine temples at Aphek or Accho or Ascalon, not less than the temples in Egypt.

Leaving Noah's Ark, we rode west to the shores of the lake, which we reached about a mile below where the Orontes enters it on the south. The east shore of the lake is flat, shelly, and shingly, bordered with rushes and with coarse turf; the plough-lands extend across the plain to the east. The mound called Tell el Baheirah rises as an island about three-quarters of a mile from the eastern shore, and the lake is about six miles long and two miles wide. The island is laid out in gardens, and no traces of any ancient building are visible from the mainland. It is cultivated by the peasants of the neighbouring shores with the mattock, but no ploughing is there possible, because these primitive people have not a single boat. As we sat on the shore we saw strange figures standing erect, and apparently gliding, pole in hand, over the little waves which were raised by a fresh western breeze. Each naked figure was in reality balanced on a diminutive raft, made of two inflated goat-skins. These little rafts, resembling some still used on the Euphrates, are unmanageable in the wind, and of course liable to be upset when the water is rough. They moved very slowly over the lake, and where the water was shallow the sailor propelled his vessel with the pole. We might almost fancy that we had stepped back into pre-historic times, among a people who wore no clothes and had not learned to make a boat; or that we were among the savages of South America and Polynesia. To reach the island it would have been necessary either to swim all the way against the wind, or to wait till a raft was built somewhere to the south-west of the lake; but there seemed to be no special reason for visiting the island, which is called only Tell el Baheirah, or 'The Mound in the Lake,' and is said by the natives to have nothing on it except a Mezr'ah, or 'sowing place,' a hamlet of a few modern huts inhabited during the season of cultivation.

The three black rafts were blown far down the lake as we looked. The children from Shômarin, Mudhân, and Hauzal—villages near the lake— drove goats, sheep, calves, and donkeys to drink its clear water; and a chattering group of blue-robed women came down to do the family washing. On the west beyond the lake was the black saddle to which Lebanon and Casius die down on south and north. The great Crusading Castle, now called el Hosn, was visible commanding this pass on the north side. The lake itself extended north-east, with a great mound, called Tell Koteineh, at its further end, and a smaller one (Tell Shômarin) on its eastern shore. A few plover, and some grey water birds with black wings and red feet, were flapping over the waves; and on shore the hoopoes had already arrived, and a few of the 'little pilgrims' or 'fathers of luck,' as the white storks are affectionately called in Syria. The swallows were also skimming in the bright and cloud-piled sky; the scarabeus was rolling his ball; the orange-tip and painted-lady and Apollo butterflies were swarming in the open. The blood-red anemone was in flower, with the little pink vetch, the moon-daisy, and purple orchid.

Following the eastern shore of the lake, we reached our tents, pitched at the end of the great dam, and were thus able to examine it at leisure. Here were white chalk cliffs 20 to 40 feet above the shore line, while opposite, on the north-west, the black basalt comes down to the water's edge. A strong breeze now blew the green and turbid water towards the dam, tossing the surface of the lake into tiny breakers. A flock of six white pelicans were slowly skimming up against the wind. On the east, we looked across the flat plain, with ruddy soil and green corn, to Anti-Lebanon, whose furthest chain was broken into several fine peaks, one of which was still streaked with snow. The great Tells, which are perhaps Hittite towns yet unexplored, stood out against the northern horizon, and furthest of all a dusty hillock, crowned by a white dome, marked the vicinity of the old Sun Temple of Emesa. The villages of Sidd, Ikmeim, and Koteineh are from one to three miles from the dam; and the great aqueduct between high mud banks runs hence from the lake to the city of Homs or Emesa. Looking southwards across the water, which shines in the sinking sun, one sees the black island and the black Shômarin mound, with dusky Lebanon crowned with snow. Above the mountains were huge piles of cumulus, and in the foreground the black masonry of the basalt dam, against which the waves, which elsewhere break on a rushy shore, were beating hard and sending up clouds of spray, while the water poured down with a rushing sound in many cascades through the broken sluices and over the ruined masonry. The sun set, the breeze abated, but the flock of pelicans was still slowly sailing away up the water.

On the morning of the 9th, after a dip in the lake, we proceeded carefully to examine the dam. It is about half a mile long, built V shaped up stream, like a starling below a bridge pier. The breadth at the top is 25 feet, but it is thicker below, the courses being stepped back from the bottom on the lower side. It is constructed of coursed rubble, of basalt chips set in hard cement, white, but mixed with pottery and with charcoal. This mortar is always found in Roman work in Syria. The rubble was originally faced with a small basalt ashlar, which has also a very Roman appearance.

The difference of level thus attained we measured carefully, and found to be 10 feet, so that before the dam was made the Orontes would have had a fall of about 20 inches in the mile. This represents a flow like that of the Thames; but as the bottom of the lake, where examined, was found to be always very flat, such a difference would most materially affect the original breadth of the stream, which probably ran between banks, as it does both above and below the present lake. Excepting perhaps towards the south, the sheet of water may be said to owe its existence entirely to the dam.

The north-west end of the dam is marked by a little tower, Crusading, or more probably Saracenic, and at this end there are buttresses to strengthen the dam on the down-stream side. We found a Greek inscription on a block of basalt, five feet long, built above the eastern door sideways. It seems to have been a tombstone, possibly Pagan, with an age and an entreaty for prayer.

We walked as far as possible along the dam, trying to reach a high piece of masonry resembling a pillar in its centre, but were stopped by the stream rushing through a broken sluice, which could not be passed with safety.

Below the dam there are ruins on both banks of the river, and about half a mile further down there are mills. The village called es Sidd ('the dam') is said to have been moved from these ruins further east — probably because of the great engineering works falling into disrepair, and the region below becoming marshy. There are remains of ancient channels for irrigation leading from the dam, and the aqueduct to Homs issues from the south-east end of the same. On the west and south is a great field of basalt, and the tents of Turkoman shepherds are placed near the lake on the west shore.

A little shrine, now ruined, appears to have existed below the dam on the left bank of the river. Here we found five shafts of basalt $2\frac{1}{2}$ feet in diameter, and a stone cut out into an arch 3 feet in diameter, now forming a Mihrab facing south. Close beside it is a modern-looking tomb of mud and stone, hung with votive rags on stakes stuck into the top. Around it are the little piles of stones which Moslem pilgrims erect, and it is called ' Jeriyet 'Aly,' or the slave of the Imâm Aly Ibn Abu Taleb. This early convert of the Prophet has become a mythical hero, and the tomb of his slave is probably the site of a little temple, perhaps built by Diocletian when he constructed (as the Rabbis tell us) the dam which makes the lake of Koteineh. These notes will perhaps suffice to show that though satisfied that we had already found Kadesh, we did not fail carefully to examine the lake and island where formerly the city was supposed to have existed.

From the dam we rode about ten miles to the city of Homs, the ancient Emesa, a place of 20,000 inhabitants, including Moslems, Greeks, and Greek Catholics (or Melchites); it has a wall measuring about a mile and a half in circuit, but the citadel on the great mound to the south-east was blown up by Ibrahim Pasha. This city, known to Pliny as Hemesa, and mentioned also by Strabo and Ptolemy, is in the Talmud called Hamatz, and said to have been the city of the Zemarites (Gen. x. 18), which is probably a mistake. It became famous in Roman times as the native place of the extravagant Bassianus, who called himself 'Priest of the Sun God,' and Elagabalus (or 'God of the Mountain'), and became Emperor in Rome in 219 A.D., being soon slain, and succeeded in 222 A.D. by Alexander Severus. Strange, indeed, must have been the condition of society when the proud Italian race allowed their national divinities to be set aside by this effeminate Syrian; and when senators and populace alike looked with approbation on the procession of the black conical stone from Emesa, when in sweeping Oriental garments Elagabalus paced backwards in front of his idol, accompanied by the dancing girls, who were direct descendants of the old devotees of Ashtoreth. Nor was the sun priest content till he had married his obelisk to a goddess and erected two shrines in Rome which outshone all former temples, although the foreigner and his foreign sun-emblems were tolerated but four years in Italy.

The long Greek inscription now found in the 'Mosque of Light,' in the city itself, is perhaps connected with this famous episode, and the name of the mosque suggests a connection with the old sun temple; but whether this famous temple stood on the same site or on the great mound beyond the walls must be at present uncertain. The inscription may here be given, as an error has crept into the version published from my notes. It is more correctly given by Waddington, as follows:

Κυκλοτερης κοσμοιο τυπος βασιλευς εκο (μισσεν)
Εθνεα παντα εχοντα σοφαις φρεσιν ηνιοχ (ευων).*

Whoever may be the King of the world in question, it seems probable that Constantine fixed on this same site for a great basilica which he built in Homs; and tradition says that John the Baptist's head was here buried, although his body lies at Samaria, and according to others his head on Mount Ebal, or in the mosque at Damascus. Such sites are certainly rather distant from the gloomy fortress east of the Dead Sea where he was executed.

Homs fell to the Crusaders when by bribery they had taken the impregnable Antioch, and when the imminent failure of the expedition had been averted

---

* This is rendered by Dr. H. Hayman:

'The King (who is) the round image of the universe won over
The peoples having all things by driving a chariot with skill.'

This would no doubt apply to the Sun God of Emesa.

by this very doubtful success, and by the miracle of the spear so opportunely discovered. From this city, which they reached up the Orontes valley, they passed down to the coast at Arka and Tripoli, thus avoiding the rugged Lebanon, and thence they marched to the plains of Lydda on their way to Jerusalem. In 1281 the Saracens defeated at Homs the Mongol descendants of the old stock to which the Hittites belonged, and Ibrahim Pasha took the city from Turkey before his final defeat by the English at Acre. If ever a railway should run from Tripoli to Damascus and Aleppo, Homs will be near the junction; but at present it is one of the least visited, and consequently most Oriental, of Syrian cities.

Approaching from the south past the green mound called Tell Bâba 'Amr, the dusty hillock of the citadel first appeared on the right, with fragments of its shattered walls. Towards the left rose several minarets, and on the west of the city are beautiful fruit orchards, with shady orange-groves, figs, lemons, pomegranates, and poplars, enclosed in mud walls as at Damascus. Here Mrs. Digby had once a pleasant palace, as well as at the more southerly capital. The city walls next appear of black basalt masonry with round towers, evidently belonging to the best Arab period—the fourteenth and fifteenth centuries. The streets within are fairly paved with basalt, and many of the houses are of the same material, with flat mud roofs. Thus, as Damascus may be called a brick city, Jerusalem a limestone town, Aberdeen a grey granite city, Homs has the distinctive character of being a black town of basalt. The numerous minarets, the long narrow bazaars, the poplars, recall Damascus; but Homs is even more purely Oriental than the Syrian capital. The pale merchants in snowy turbans, the water-carriers, sometimes with the green turban of a Hajji or Sherîf, the dusky Bedawin in lambs'-wool jackets, stained red on the outer side (the wool being inside), Circassians with silver daggers and black Astrakan caps (perhaps like those of the Hittites), and with innumerable cartridge-cases on the breast of their long coats, the blue and check-patterned izars and black face-veils of the women, all form a picture of true Eastern character, unspoiled by the flaming advertisements of Cook, or the gaudy Levantine imitation of western art and architecture. In such cities fanaticism still has a home, and the Sokhta and the Derwish still scowl at the Christian. Yet there are upwards of 7,000 Christians of the Eastern Churches in Homs, of whom 1,500 are of the Melchite sect—that curious heresy founded apparently on the old Ebionite Church of Pella, and perpetuated by the early conversion of the Beni Ghassan Arabs, whose Queen was the famous Zenobia.

The town is full of fragments of Greek and Arab inscriptions, and of coins and gems, among which I found an almost unique Greek coin of Emesa, with the head of the tower-crowned goddess on the obverse, while little gnostic cornelians and garnets are common as in other parts of Syria.

We left the city on the 11th, and climbed up the hill of the Kal'ah, or fortress, where is a little shrine, called, apparently, Mes-haf Othman, although Meshaf may only mean the 'place destroyed' by Muhammed Aly. There was once a very fine sloping scarp to this fortress, 60 to 70 feet high on all sides, of black basalt masonry, with a fosse outside. On the top are remains of the walls and casemates, and a granite pillar shaft. The diameter of the mound is supposed by Porter to be 300 yards. The view extends north as far as Restân, and gives a good idea of the city. North of the fortress, outside the town walls, are remains of a Roman tomb, which is mentioned by all travellers. It has brick arches, and remains of mosaic on its walls, but does not appear to be of great antiquity or importance.

The 'Mosque of Light' is evidently an ancient basilica of three aisles, with a courtyard on the north. The capitals of the pillars in the colonnades are of early Byzantine character; but the eastern apse appears to have been entirely destroyed. Our entrance, though sanctioned by the courteous Governor, caused grumbling among the Moslems. We, however, copied the Greek inscription above given before leaving.

Here, at length, we were obliged to turn once more south, although I felt sorely tempted, had time allowed, to go on to Restân, Hâmah, Aleppo, Carchemish, and Antioch; for it was a disappointment not to bring back a new Hittite inscription, especially one from the borderland, where their country marched on David's kingdom.

These inscriptions are probably the oldest monuments in Asia, and may almost vie with the Egyptian records. The Hâmah stones are, it is true, no longer at that city, for I found them, in 1882, in the Constantinople Museum; but there is at least one such text at Aleppo, and others may be hidden in the great mounds of the land of the Hittites. The emblems already known have the most curious forms. Thus, for instance, a head with the finger raised to the mouth (like Harpocrates), occurs four times on the Hamath stones, and again on one from Carchemish, while birds, and heads of cows and antelopes, open hands, and hands with daggers, are accompanied by knives like those which form hieroglyphic signs, with a rod and two rings, a kind of fleur-de-lis, or a horse-shoe. Many of the symbols resemble the good-luck marks of ancient races; but others are clearly connected with the Cypriote characters. It seems as yet, however, hopeless to expect these texts to be read, until a bilingual example shall be found; and when that lucky find occurs, a new chapter in Asiatic history may be opened for our reading.

Our return route was to be by the valley of the Eleutherus to Tripoli, as I was anxious to get an accurate idea of the military advantages and disadvantages of this line, and of the possibility of constructing a railway from Homs to the best harbour on the Syrian coast, which is acknowledged by all the coasting captains to be that at Tripoli.

Homs is only about 1,500 feet above the sea, and is fifty miles from Tripoli. The pass west of the Koteineh Lake is somewhat higher, but does not probably exceed 2,000 feet. The rise of the line would be about 2,000 feet in rather more than 30 miles, or about 70 feet in the mile; but it is hardly correct to state (as Commander Cameron has done), that there is no engineering difficulty to be encountered, for the district west of the lake consists entirely of very hard black basalt, and the same formation occurs in the pass north of Lebanon—the valley of the Eleutherus river. There is also a kind of crater immediately west of the high saddle, measuring some five miles across. Thus considerable cuttings would be necessary, and would have to be blasted through the hard rock. This would very greatly increase the expense of the line, and it is not by any means clear that a better system for railways would not be to make parallel lines along the coast and along the plains east of Lebanon, with a cross communication up the valley of the Orontes, by Antioch from the Bay of Seleucia and the Gulf of Alexandretta (which I afterwards visited), inland to Aleppo, and across to the Euphrates. The Sharon railway to Egypt, and a line from Damascus into the Hauran, would be part of this system, with a probable cross-communication from Acre, through Tiberias and under Hermon, to the capital. But let it not be hoped that such lines will ever be laid down while the Turks hold Syria, for, while on the one hand any European scheme is regarded with not unnatural suspicion, it is, on the other hand, certain that they consider their hold on the country to be greatly strengthened by the difficulty of communication. The Turk is not blind to the advantages of science. He has adopted, and uses very extensively for Government purposes, the electric telegraph, which he is now extending to Mecca. But he has no wish to see new hopes and new ideas roused among his subjects by Western teaching, and he fears the complications and sometimes unjust claims which follow the spread of European enterprise, and the sinking of European capital in public works in Asia.

As a military road the line from Homs to Tripoli still possesses those advantages which led to its being chosen by the Crusaders, and which induced the unfortunate Midhat Pasha, when last he was Governor of Syria, to commence the highway, which we found complete all but the bridges—a very unfortunate deficiency in any road. Along this road we journeyed to the basalt moors west of the Lake of Koteineh, by miserable black hamlets, with fields of thin stunted barley. There must be some 500 square miles in all of this hard rock, which stretches south, as we have seen, to Kamû'at el Hirmil.

Crossing the saddle we came in view of the broad crater called el Bukei'a, which is dotted with fine clumps of oak, and covered with Arab or Turcoman encampments. Of our baggage difficulties and our adventures with the fat Pasha of Tripoli it is not necessary here to speak, for many of my readers will have undergone such troubles, and all will have read of them *ad nauseam*. After much difficulty, due to the impression that we were political emissaries, we obtained a new escort, and set forth from the Anseireh village of Hadîdeh, on the 12th of April, to visit the magnificent castle of el Hosn, which frowns from the hillside north of the valley of the Eleutherus—now called Nahr el Kebîr.

The crater, or low plain, where the river gathers its head-waters, was extremely boggy, and hard to cross; but we were well repaid by finding so perfect a specimen of Crusading work rising on steep cliffs above a little village. The very battlements of the great round towers and the great oak gates studded with iron are still in place, and the machicoulis overhanging the posterns. Entering the southern gate, we rode up a long vaulted passage, the hoofs of the horses clattering on the cobble pavement under the dark tunnel, and thus reached the inner courtyard, partly occupied by a beautiful Gothic chapel with windows of delicate tracery. On the south wall of this little church, close to the door, is a mediæval inscription, which is strangely suggestive of the proud humility of the old Knights, and which is still fairly legible in beautifully incised Gothic capitals.

'Sit tibi copia
Sit sapientia
Formaque detur
Inquinat omnia
Sola Superbia
Si comitetur.'

'May wisdom, wealth, and beauty be with thee,
But Pride spoils all, should she accompany.'

So reads the text; but wisdom, beauty, and riches have long since passed away from the land, and only the evidence of pride and power is left in this huge stronghold of the Frank.

On the south-east one can still see where the great breach was once made in the outer line of ramparts, although the Moslems built it up again with smaller masonry when they had gained possession. Small Arab huts are built against the chapel, which is inhabited and partly hidden by these poor modern hovels.

We ascended several of the great towers, and obtained an extensive view. Lebanon and Anti-Lebanon, Kadesh and its lake, the Mediterranean, and the tower of Safita (once the stronghold of the Nuseirch chief, Ism'aîl Kaïr Bey), are visible, with many villages, and rounded basalt hills sinking towards the green sea plain and the yellow beach. Among the names collected I find Tell Hettch, which is no doubt named (as are Hatta in Philistia, and Kefr Hatta above Lydda) from the old Hittite race; but perhaps the most interesting view was that to the north, where, in a narrow valley at the foot of the steep mountains of the Assassins (or Nuseirch), can be seen a white monastery with a red-tiled roof. It is called Deir el Ahmeirch ('The Red Convent'), and is consecrated to St. George. Pilgrimages to the spot are recorded as far back as the seventh century, and its vicinity is known as Abil el Kuds, 'the Holy Meadow.' About a mile lower down the ravine is the 'Ain el Fuwâr, or 'bubbling spring,' which is the source of the old Sabbatic river. The water rises in a cave about six yards long and two yards wide, with a deep clear pool. At intervals of from four to seven days a rumbling sound is heard in the mountain, and torrents of water flow from the cave and from the rocks around, and continue for five or six hours to pour down the valley. The usual interval is four days, but sometimes only two, and in 1822, when Aleppo was destroyed by earthquake, there is said to have been no flow at all for a year.

Such intermittent springs are not very rare in the limestone mountains of Syria. We have an example in the Virgin's Fountain (Bethesda) at Jerusalem; and the plain of Kefr Kûk, in the Hermon district, is annually converted into a lake by a sudden flow from under the mountains. The Nahr Sebta, or 'River of Rest,' as the stream just described is called, is the Sabbatic river of the ancients, which Josephus (7 Wars v. 1) mentions as visited by Titus. He correctly states the interval as being seven days, but Pliny (H. N. xxxi. 11) got hold of the story incorrectly, and makes the river observe the Sabbath (as the Bordeaux Pilgrim in 333 A.D. says of the Jerusalem spring), running for six week days and resting on the seventh.

The name of the river is no doubt ancient, and due to an observation of its periods of intermission; but some archæologists have sought to connect it with the Shabatuna mentioned in the account of Rameses' advance on Kadesh. It appears, however, that the name Shabtûn still applies to a valley south of the site of Kadesh, and this fits better with the topography of the battle.

Tradition states that a Christian prince here lost his daughter, who was to have been married, but on her wedding procession was carried off by an Arab chief. This legend, related by el Wakîdi, still survives perhaps, half-remembered, at el Hosn, where the inhabitants tell us a princess was shut up by her father to prevent her marriage; but it is no doubt only a variant of the old legend of Danae, which is found all over Asia.

Kal'at el Hosn was called Hosn el Akrad (Kurds' Stronghold) in the Middle Ages, and also Crac des Chevaliers, a name which, like that of Kerak in Moab, seems to be derived from the Syriac word for a 'fortress.' In 1180 it is found in possession of the Knights Hospitallers, and it surrendered in 1271 to the irresistible Bibars. On the south-west there is a bas-relief, with two lions and an Arabic inscription belonging to the time of the Moslem restoration of the fortress.

The masonry of the Crusaders is here, as everywhere else, drafted with a boss, which is left rustic in exterior walls, but finely finished in the interior. It is a very common mistake to suppose that such masonry was found and re-used by the mediæval architects, but we have now good evidence to show that it was actually cut by the Gothic masons, as in Cyprus also and elsewhere. Indeed, so far from drafted masonry indicating Jewish or Phœnician builders, we have no evidence whatever that these nations ever used it, though we know that Greeks, Romans, Byzantines, Crusaders, and Arabs, all drafted their stones. The Jerusalem temple-walls, and those at Hebron, give no contradiction of this supposition, for they are in all probability Herodian imitations of Greek or Roman work. Here at Crac we find masonry drafted, yet dressed with the peculiar Gothic diagonal dressing, and, moreover, marked with masons' marks. We find pointed arches with the keystone cut out to form the point, and yet drafted as are the remaining voussoirs.

The masons' marks are of considerable interest, and the subject has now been carefully studied in all parts of Syria. They are distinctive of the Crusading work of the twelfth and thirteenth centuries, and are found on all the best finished stones in the walls of such buildings, but especially on interior walls. The same mark is found in places separated by hundreds of miles, and in English cathedrals and Persian palaces no less than in Crusading castles or churches. The same mark is used in buildings which differ in date by more than the lifetime of a single man; and I have found all the letters of the alphabet, save Q, which seems to indicate that the masons were French or Italian. *X* is doubtfully found, and so curiously enough is *D*; but the marks are not merely letters, for many very interesting signs also occur. Among these more suggestive marks may be noted the 'Solomon's Seal,' or five-pointed star; 'David's Shield,' or the double triangle, giving six points; the lituus, or crozier; the fish, the cross, the trident, the arrow, the fleur-de-lis, the hammer, and other well-known emblems of good luck. The two first are Indian caste marks, as is also the trident: the letters of the Slav alphabet, dating earlier than the ninth century, are also in many cases exactly like the Norman masons' marks; and several of the masons' marks, found by Ouseley on the old palace of Saaditalat, near Ispahan, are the same as those copied in Syria, including the cross, the arrow, the hour-glass, the trident, and the square.

No doubt in some cases a letter was put on the stone by way of claiming its workmanship—as, for instance, at Rosslyn, where such a mark is found on the famous ''prentice's pillar,' no doubt cut by that proud mason to mark his own work; and this perhaps accounts for the marks being always on the finest stones. There is evidently no indication intended of the position for which the stone was destined; but in many cases it seems pretty clear that the signs were intended as charms to secure good fortune to the building, just as the hand or the

'Shield of David' is now painted in red on doors and walls by the Moslem masons in Syria.

But to return to el Hosn, which is perhaps, with exception of the magnificent stronghold of Kerak, in Moab, the best preserved of Crusading fortresses, though in size, perhaps, inferior to the great castle at Banias and to others. El Hosn, or Crac, was one of a great group of castles which defended the frontiers of the principality of Antioch, and it commanded the pass from La Chamelle (as Homs was then called) to the coast. Mont Ferrand lay to the north-east, and Chastel Blanc to the north-west, while others above Antioch, and at Turbessel, near Carchemish, marked the north borders, where the principality marched with the domains of the Count of Edessa.

While gazing on these enormous fortifications, we become aware of the length of time necessary for their building, and realize the long period during which a settled Frankish rule endured in Northern Syria. We are too apt to think of the first Crusade as a mere raid, and to forget how three generations of Franks succeeded one another even in Southern Palestine, while Antioch remained in their hands as late as 1268 A.D., or nearly a century after the fall of the southern kingdom after the defeat of Hattîn, in 1187 A.D. Acre was not taken till 1291 A.D., and the names of the Casales round it, as recorded in the Cartulary of the Holy Sepulchre, show how extensive were the possessions of the Church, and of the Orders of Hospitallers and Teutonic Knights in the thirteenth century.

No sooner had the country been seized, than castles began to be built. Toron, in Upper Galilee, is apparently the oldest, dating from 1104; but Montreal (at Shobek), far south-east of the Dead Sea, was erected by the King of Jerusalem in 1115. The prosperity succeeding the taking of Tyre in 1124 gave an impulse to architecture, and specially to the erection of churches. The Castle of Ernuald was erected in 1134, and Gibelin (Beit Jibrîn) in the same year. Blanche Guard (or Gath), and Ibelin (Yebnah), defended the country against incursions from Ascalon after 1144. Mirabel (Râs el' Ain) was built five years later, and Darum, on the Egyptian frontier, in 1170. Beauvoir (above Beisân) is a fine example, commenced in 1182, and probably the latest before the great defeat at Hattîn. The western advance from Damascus was barred by the great line of strongholds in Upper Galilee, extending from Banias to Acre, and including Belfort, Hunin, Château Neuf (at the Huleh), Toron (or Tibnîn), and Montfort (el Kurein), while on the sea coast Castel Pelegrino, Tanturah, Cæsarea, Arsuf, Kakon, and Plans formed a line whereby men travelled to Toron on the Jerusalem road (now Latrûn), and so passed safely to the Holy City. To say nothing of numberless churches and minor fortresses, such an enumeration of huge strongholds, each requiring unlimited labour for several years to construct, bears witness to the energy of men who had walked, be it remembered, from France or Germany to Jerusalem. Each fortress stood a siege before it fell to the Moslem, and each was long the centre whence law and justice emanated to a contented population of Syrian serfs. The second and the twelfth centuries were the great building epochs in Palestine, and neither Jew, Hittite, nor Phœnician has left such marks on the country as have the Romans of the Antonine period or the Crusading Franks.

The Assizes of Jerusalem show by what just and wise rule the kings and princes of the twelfth century gained willing submission from the Moslem serfs. The coins struck with a cross on one side and Arab letters on the other, bear witness to the trade which was carried on between Christians and Moslems, as do the treaties giving mutual facilities for hunting on their lands signed by Frank princes and by the Sultans of Damascus and Aleppo. In the height of their power the Franks made the wild Assassins, and the Bedawin even, pay annual tribute, and raised a native body of horse called Turcopoles, under European officers. There were no ideas of representative government in those days, yet the native peasant was judged by his Moslem peers, as was the baron by a court of his equals. Each fief supplied a certain quota of knights, of yeomen and of bourgeois men-at-arms. The Casales, or feudal villages, inhabited by Greeks, Turks, Syrians, whether Christian or Moslem, were divided into gastines, and each gastine into so many ploughs (like the modern feddân, or yoke). The population was classed as lieges owing military services and of Frank origin, and as villeins or serfs, not obliged to fight—an idea surviving in the Christian immunity from conscription in Moslem lands in our own times.

The downfall of this great system was due not to discontent of the conquered, not even to the energy of the Arabs of Damascus and of Egypt, or of the Kurdish Saladin, but to the rapid degeneracy of the conquering race, especially when not annually recruited by pilgrim settlers from Europe.

Foucher, of Chartres, already speaks of the mixed marriages with Syrian, Armenian, and Arab baptized beauties; and William of Tyre draws a gloomy picture of the immorality and luxury of the third generation, especially of those *pulani*, as they were called, who were the offspring of such unions. Well might the old moralist warn the inhabitants of Crac of pride which preceded their fall; and in later times no doubt these great walls witnessed many an unholy revel, many an act of tyrannous cruelty, instead of the stern but impartial justice of the first strong generation. The accusations which are recorded against the Templars—their secret initiation, their adoration of 'a certain cat,' and of the mummy-like Baphomet, with charges yet more horrible of trampling on the Cross, of eating a newborn child (as also Jews and Gnostics were said to have done), and of general infidelity and immorality —are no doubt exaggerated; but we may thence conjecture how, when fanatic enthusiasm had cooled, and when constant intercourse with the natives had broadened the views of the knights, some, at least, were attracted by the mysticism of Derwish initiation, or by the surviving Gnosticism of Syria, and fell gradually into philosophic scepticism, thinly veiled beneath the cloak of the great Orders of the Temple or St. John.

The associations of the fortress have led us into a considerable digression, and we must now continue our journey down the valley of the Eleutherus, where the railway, 'without engineering difficulty,' is still unmade. On the right is the Nuseireh mountain, the old Mons Bargylus, which was inhabited by the Assassins; on the left, Jebel Akkâr, the furthest point of Lebanon. Thus far Jonathan the Hasmonean pursued the army of the Seleucidæ; and in this region dwelt the Arkites (at 'Arka), the Zemarites (at Sumrah), the Arvadites (in the island er Ruâd), with Hamathites and Hittites. After a long ride we gained our camp at 'Arka, close to the coast and to the old city of the Arkites. We had accomplished thirty-five miles in the day, but the night's rest was broken by the storm, which drove us to the hospitable house of M. Blanche, the French Consul at Tripoli. At this city we remained till the 16th, visiting the harbour and the Derwish monastery, and gaining many interesting hints from the studious and scientific Frenchman, whose contributions to the information published by Brugsch and Renan have hardly, perhaps, been acknowledged as they should have been by those authorities.

Tripoli is a well-built and picturesque town, standing on either bank of the river Kadîshah, which, perhaps, retains its older name of Kadesh. There are fine gardens stretching down to the port (Mînet Trâblus), where is a district town, more than a mile and a half distant. The river here flows nearly north; the castle on the left bank is south of the town, and the Derwish monastery is up the glen further south on the same side. The mosque of el Beidawy (an old church, it is said, of St. Anthony of Padua) is two miles to the north, and has a pond of sacred fish in its courtyard. The population is estimated at 17,000 in the town, and 7,000 in the port, including Moslems, Greeks, Maronites, Melchites, and Jews. There are eighteen churches and twenty mosques, and a trade in silk, in fruit, in sponges, and in soap is carried on under the usual advantages of Turkish rule.

The modern history of Tripoli begins with the Seleucid monarch, Demetrius I., and the Crusaders took the city in 1104, when Count Raymond of St. Gilles built the castle and called it Mount Pilgrim. His name survives in the Moslem title Sinjil applied to the fortress, as at his camp, called also Sinjil, on the road from Jerusalem to Shechem.

Count Raymond is said to have been buried at Tripoli, and M. Blanche informed me that many years ago some aged Janissaries survived in that castle, who knew of a tomb there which may be found some day to be that of the great Crusader. At present the castle is a convict prison, Midhât Pasha having removed the criminals here from Acre: exploration is therefore not allowed, nor would it be pleasant, if indeed safe.

The old church of St. John is now a mosque, but the sacred fishpond preserves the memory of an older divinity—of Atergatis, the Venus who rose from the sea, the patroness of all Kadesh cities, who has yet her fishpond in Acre, and who was adored by Hittites and Phœnicians, as well as at Jerusalem and Ascalon. The streets of Tripoli are fairly paved, the Khan and bazaars, with great piles of soap, are prosperous, the women are plump and pretty, and in

1881 Mr. Austen, an English engineer, started a tram from the port, which we found working and affording endless amusement to the natives. Whether it continues to amuse them and to pay, I have not since heard.

The port is said to be the best on the Syrian coast, better even than Haifa, or than the gusty gulf of Alexandretta, or the shallow bay of Suweidîyeh. A tongue of sand and rock runs out, as at Tyre or Sidon, with a great reef towards the north-west, breaking the force of the waves. The roadstead is, however, shallow, not exceeding eight fathoms, and the old mole from the reef is destroyed above water. The boatmen of the port are said to differ in physiognomy and dialect from the landsmen, and are, indeed, almost Phœnicians. They still call the Eleutherus *el Afros*, though the peasantry know it only as 'the Great River.'

Turning eastwards, we see the town rising on a low hill above its orchards, with their cactus hedges, and backed by the steep Lebanon, veiled in mist. The river, about twenty to thirty yards wide, is spanned by two bridges, and is very rapid. One of the bridges in the middle of the town is flanked by little shops, resting on wooden brackets, so that when passing along the street the visitor is unaware that he crosses the stream.

Following the gorge of this sacred river, past

orange gardens, and vineyards between cactus hedges, and under the dark-brown walls of the castle built on the foundations of the old Mount Pilgrim, we reached the white monastery of the Malawiyeh, or Dancing Derwishes, an order recruited from among the respectable shop-keeping class, its members only distinguishable by the high cap of light brown felt, in shape a truncated cone, sometimes wound round with a green turban. There are at Tripoli twenty Derwishes in all, and the monastery is their club, to which they resort every Friday to dance.

The revolutions of this sect have been often described, but a few notes respecting the symbolism and character of the dance may perhaps not be considered superfluous. On Friday, 15th April, we witnessed the ceremony, which takes place in the Liwân, or arched chamber, opening to the air on the north, with a spectators' room on the east, and a gallery above this for the musicians. We were courteously greeted in the Diwân, a separate building to the north, with a view over the lovely gorge with its rushing stream, and were then assigned places close to the wooden railing on a level with the parqueted floor where the Derwishes dance. The male Moslem spectators had a gallery on the south, and all the children of Tripoli, Christian and Moslem, seemed to be scrambling behind us.

A poor member, or lay brother, was in charge of the floor, which was swept clean. He allowed none of the spectators to smoke, and even took away the children's sweetmeats, for the solemnity of the ceremony is quite equal to that of any rite in a mosque or a Christian church. Barefooted, he paced the floor, and most good-naturedly he chid the young men and children. Opposite to us, in a gallery behind a thick wooden lattice, we could distinguish white veils, while a few fingers, tipped with henna, were at times thrust through, and other women looked down from windows in the dome above.

About 2.15 P.M., twelve Derwishes entered, barefooted, followed by the Sheikh. They were good-looking men of all ages, one of the number being quite a child. They had their conical hats on, and long cloaks, beneath which they held the skirts of the white dancing-robe. Eight of the cloaks were black, one green, and others grey, perhaps indicating degrees of initiation. They stood round the floor, facing south-west, and in this corner a sheep-skin rug, dyed blue (the sacred colour in Tripoli), was placed on the floor. All but the Sheikh and one other were barefooted: the latter was an old man, who wore kid boots with a soft sole. They stood with the great toe of the right foot placed over the great toe of the left, the legs being close together. This is a very ancient attitude of contemplation in India and elsewhere.

The Sheikh, who came last, was an ugly fat man, with a snub nose; he had a green turban round his hat, and wore a russet-coloured robe of fine stuff, with very long loose sleeves, which covered his hands, crossed in front. All the ring were now standing, holding up their skirts under their robes, the eldest member to the left of the Sheikh, who stood on the sheepskin, and the rest in order of age. They had washed their feet, and their beards were well trimmed, so that there was no touch of wild or grotesque appearance in their mien, such as is to be remarked among the wanderers of other orders.

Silence was enforced on the native crowd, and the Sheikh, having bowed to the south-west, stepped on the rug with heeled boots, and faced his followers. The whole thirteen then prostrated themselves, with their foreheads against the floor, and afterwards sat down in Oriental fashion, their arms folded under their cloaks. A single voice was then heard chanting in the gallery above us, and the Sheikh, still seated, recited a prayer, his hands raised with the palms to the face and the fingers upright. The twelve then kissed the floor, and a hymn, invoking 'Aly and other Moslem saints, was sung from the gallery.

The soft music of a flute was next heard, and the Sheikh rose, and followed by the rest, one by one they solemnly perambulated the floor three times against the sun. Each in turn bowed to the blue rug, then took two long strides past it, and turning back, bowed to the Derwish who followed. The walk of all was a sort of gliding motion, the feet sliding or dragging along the foor.

The towâf, or perambulation, completed, the cloaks were removed by the owner of the green cloak, and eight Derwishes stood ready to dance in white dresses tight fitting to the body, but with a full skirt to the ground, the hem heavily weighted with lead. The dress of one, who afterwards danced in the centre (and who had been the keeper of the floor till the rest arrived), was green, of a dull tint. The dancers stood with one foot on the other as before, and with the arms crossed on their breasts, the right above the left. The first to the Sheikh's left turned to bow to that dignitary, and then raised and kissed his right hand, while the Sheikh appeared to breathe on his brow; and, thus inspired, in perfect silence he began to revolve in an orbit against the sun, and spinning also against the sun on his own axis. The seven others followed until all eight were in motion, revolving slowly round the room without ever coming in collision or losing their relative position. Their long robes gradually expanded into discs, or cones, and their hands were slowly raised to the shoulder, and then carried outwards until the arms were nearly horizontal, the right hand having the palm upwards and the left downwards. The head was at times reclined almost on the right shoulder, the eyes half-closed, and the appearance not unlike that of a mesmeric trance. The motion was due to turning on the sole or heel of the left foot, the right being brought round in front. If the reader will try, he will soon find how much practice is required to attain to such even motion as was necessary to keep in position.

The whole eight moved twice round the orbit in about six or seven minutes, and the number of revolutions of each dancer on his own axis we calculated to be about two hundred. During the dance the oldest Derwish moved slowly among the performers, and seemed silently to criticize their style. The Sheikh stood on his carpet reciting a whispered prayer, with a troubled air suggestive of mesmeric concentration, though this may have been merely a fancy. The musicians in the gallery sang in discordant voices, and with accompaniment of tambourine, tabor, and flute. At length, the second revolution complete, the tambourine gave a sharp clash, and all the dancers stopped, although one or two gave a few extra turns in their places. It should be noticed that the green-robed dancer had gradually moved to the middle of the ring, where he remained spinning as a centre, with seven satellites. The time of the music was about that of a slow waltz, and the revolutions thirty to the minute.

The dance having been arrested, the performers remained in their original positions with crossed arms. They stood quite still, perspiring a little, and panting, but not more exhausted than a European after a waltz, and apparently free from giddiness. A long chant was sung by a single voice in the gallery, and then, after a rest of a few minutes, they began again as before, dancing round the central green-coated member. A third dance followed a second interval, and then the eldest Derwish gave over and received his cloak. The rest performed a fourth time, each dance consisting of two complete revolutions in the orbit. After the last round one member appeared much exhausted. They prostrated themselves, kneeling with their heads on the floor, which they kissed, and the Sheikh then uttered a prayer. They then received their cloaks from the green-coated member, and all stood up in place. The senior kissed the Sheikh's hand, and then stood on his right. The next kissed the hands of both, and stood again to the right, and the others followed in order, each kissing the hands of all his superiors, so that the boy of about thirteen years of age kissed the hands of twelve seniors; each superior also appeared to kiss or breathe on the forehead of the inferiors, who saluted him, and thus at length they were all drawn up, facing north, with the Sheikh on the left. Another prayer followed, concluded by a general Amen, which sounded like the buzzing of a swarm of flies disturbed suddenly, and then in order they walked slowly out, the Sheikh in front, and put on their slippers and dispersed. It was about 3.15 P.M., so that the whole ceremony lasted just an hour.

During the ceremony a sweetmeat fell on the floor, and was removed by the boy at a silent sign from the Sheikh. A black cat also strayed into the circle, and received a gentle hint from the toe of one of the Derwishes; but the reverent decorum of the proceedings was never broken, and not a sound save that of prayers and music was heard.

This ceremony was far more interesting and suggestive than any ordinary *Zikr*, such as is seen in any Syrian town, when the circle of performers repeat the formula 'No God but God,' until they fall foaming at the mouth. It contrasts with the fury of the Howling Derwishes at Stamboul, who tread on sickly children laid at their feet, and with the disgusting eating of scorpions and snakes by the Bedawi sect in Damascus, who tread on coals, or, like Hindu fanatics, endure the bath of fire poured from a brazier on their heads. We could not doubt that the ancient dance we witnessed was that of the Cabiri, the seven 'great ones,' or planetary gods revolving round the green centre of the terrestrial globe. The Malawîyeh are a sect of Persian origin and considerable antiquity, the richest and best recruited of the Derwish orders, whose mosque at Konieh, in Lycaonia, contains the tomb of Hazret Moulana, their original leader. Sacred dances and symbolic processions are so common in India that it may be from an Aryan rather than a Semitic source that the ceremony is derived, but the perambulation of sacred shrines is apparently mentioned in the Old Testament itself as a religious ceremony performed by a Hebrew prophet: while the *towâf* at Mecca is a procession round the shrine said, even by Moslem writers, to be symbolic of the movements of the heavenly bodies. The dance can now be only witnessed in Syria at Tripoli, and at Damascus, as well as at Konieh in Asia Minor. The modern performers have possibly lost all tradition of the original meaning, and regard it only as a sacred duty.

CHAPTER III.

THE LAND OF PURPLE.

THE road from Tripoli to Beyrout is one so little known to tourists that it will perhaps be not too hackneyed a subject for description, and the reflections roused by a visit to Phœnicia, and an examination of one of the finest collections of Phœnician antiquities, forms an instructive sequel to the exploration of the Hittite country.

Four miles south of Tripoli is the site of Marina, where a cliff, covered with fresco, exists above a ledge or platform of rock, in which are sunk several graves. This place seems to have been a hermitage, where the monks or hermits were also buried, and the frescoes, judging from the character of the inscriptions, would belong to the twelfth or thirteenth century. They originally told the whole legend of a certain abbot, with a representation of the Annunciation, and another of St. George. They have been rudely painted over at a later period with Greek frescoes and larger inscriptions, the names of John, of Demetrius, and of the 'Mother of God' being legible above the smaller lettering. The rock is thus a sort of palimpsest of mediæval times. Such frescoes are very rare in Palestine, and are becoming rarer; those at Kasr Hajlah in the Jordan valley, preserved in the Survey Memoirs, have since been entirely destroyed. At the ruined monastery in the Kelt valley there is another cliff, which once, like that of Marîna, was covered with cement and painted with frescoes left exposed to the weather. Votive lamps appear to be still burned at Marîna, and there is a monastery of St. James in the hills above.

Passing next Kalmôn, the Calamos of Pliny, we reach the great promontory of Râs Shakka, some fourteen miles from Tripoli. The country is here extremely rough, consisting of hard dolomite, which stands up in grey pillars like giants turned to stone. The promontory of Shakka rises above this formation in a bold white cliff, not unlike that at Dover, with a little sandy bay to the north. This is the old Theouprosopon, or 'face of God,' a northern Penuel, which, no doubt, was so named by Phœnician sailors on the western sea. Here, climbing up over the soapy marl, we take our last view of Tripoli, and descend into the picturesque gorge of the 'River of Nuts.' The ridge which ends in this cliff is called the 'Hill of Light,' probably because it shines so white over the wine-coloured sea; the ravine is commanded by a little fort on the crag in its midst, once a famous haunt of robbers, but now a station of the smart Lebanon police. Emerging through gardens beside the stream, we reach the shore again at Batrûn, nearly twenty miles from Tripoli, a little Christian town of two thousand souls. It is the Phœnician Botrys, founded in Nebuchadnezzar's time, earlier than Aradus, as a frontier fortress. The inhabitants were busy with their Easter cakes, and appeared to be chiefly Maronites.

On the 17th of April we rode from Batrûn thirty-five miles to Beyrout, under continual storms of rain and hail. The start was by the fitful light of the setting moon, as she broke through the dark velvet of the low cloud-banks. The silver streak across the sea, the black boulders in the foreground, the roar of the waves in the darkness, made a romantic scene, which slowly vanished as the pale light rose in the east, and the silver faded from the waters. The moon-shadows gradually disappeared as the light spread and the clouds became whiter; the queen of heaven hid for a moment in their banks, and emerged again pale and shadowy as by day, turned to stone by the glory of the Eastern monarch, as he suddenly peered over the dark mountains.

The inhabitants of the villages were all celebrating the Easter-tide in their churches, and we met hardly a soul by the way. At length, the shallow bay of Jibeil came in view, with an open beach and a town with walls perhaps some three centuries old. A castle stood high above the water, and, together with the Church of St. John towards the west, belongs to the twelfth century. Passing by a huge sarcophagus, which looks as if thrown up by the waves on the beach, we enter the famous, but half-deserted, town, and find the streets lined with great shafts of grey syenite from Egypt, some supporting verandas and trellises for creeping vines. Four miles to the south is the Nahr Ibrahim, the ancient sacred river of Adonis, which we found swirling rapidly, a reddish turbid stream, with broad margin of reeds and rushes. From the theatre of rocks at Aika, high up on Lebanon, with its groves and cascades, the sacred river plunges down its deep gorge and hastens to the sea. Jibeil, Aika, and Baalbek are almost in one line in the direction of the summer sunset and the winter sunrise, and not far east of Jibeil the old temple of Adonis was excavated by Renan, while Phœnician antiquities abound on every side.

Here, then, we find ourselves at the very centre of the Phœnician worship, the holy Byblos, the city of Adonis and Osiris. The great coffin by the shore might to the imagination be the one which, covered with sea-weed, was washed by the waves from Egypt, and stranded at Byblos. It held, says the myth, the mutilated body of Osiris, and it was made a pillar of the King's house till the faithful Isis, having vainly flitted over the Serbonian swamp, followed her lord to Phœnicia, and restored to life the limbs mangled by the dark northern Typhon. It was here that Philo, the sacerdotal recorder of Phœnician legends, was born, and already in Ezekiel's time (xxvii. 9) the Giblites, or men of the mountain, were famous as shipbuilders; and possibly in David's time, with the men of Tyre, as masons (cf. 1 Kings v. 18, margin).

Here, also, at midsummer, the women went out to the river to bewail Adonis ('their lord'), or Tammuz ('the Son of Life'), and feigning to find his head in the sea, or his infant form in a cradle of papyrus on the waters, rejoiced to celebrate his new birth. The cradle was fabled to come, like the coffin of Osiris, from Egypt, where the Alexandrian women had, with tears, committed it to the waves. Not only does Lucian tell us this, but a Phœnician scarabæus represents the ceremony, and in Isaiah (xviii. 2) we find the Egyptian land thus denounced: 'Woe to the land,' says the prophet, 'that sendeth ambassadors by the sea in vessels of bulrushes upon the waters,' and Procopius already perceives the true meaning of the passage.

At Afka, the ancient Aphek, named from the 'springs' (such being still the Syriac meaning of the word), stood till Constantine's time the shrine of the mourning Venus, with its booths for the Temple-consecrated women, who resembled exactly the votaries at Indian shrines, or in the fane of Anu among the Accadians. The image had her hands wrapped in her robe, and into the sacred spring by her temple fell every year the star or heavenly fire called Urania. Her votaries cut off their long tresses in grief for Tammuz, who, born from the 'bitter tree' (Amos viii. 10), which was torn open by the boar, was again slain at midsummer by the same boar, so that his blood dyed red the sacred river of Adonis, and the crimson anemone by its banks.

It was no cold maiden of the dawn like Athene who was here adored, but the great mother (Mylitta), who rises from the waters, whether typified by the moon, the planet, or the star Sirius—the queen of heaven and of men, who, treading on her shell, her tortoise, or her goat in Syria, becomes the bearded Venus in Cyprus and dwells in the conical stone. Coming from the Red Sea these hardy traders bore their goddess with them; and the myth of Tammuz, the feast of the 'sun-hiding' at the 'fulness of the year,' the weeping and rejoicing, the marriage of Ashtoreth to her lover, Dumzi, were all known in

Chaldea before the Mediterranean was reached. So also was that variant of the story, which represented Adonis (or Izdubar) as irresponsive to the love of the goddess, and the tale of the sad descent of Ishtar—the waning of the moon—when in hell she was shorn of her glorious apparel, but received power through the water of life to rise and live again.

Like most travelling and trading nations, the Phœnicians were, however, very sensitive to foreign teaching, and they took from Greece and Egypt as much as they gave. From Phœnicia, it is true, Greece first received the story of Venus and Adonis, the flood of Deucalion, the legend of Kadmus, the 'Eastern' man. The forms now known as those of the earliest Greek alphabet bear out the assertion of Herodotus that Greece owed her knowledge of writing and the sixteen Cadmean letters to Phœnicia. Dionysus, Heracles, Cybele-Cabira, Asklepios, Palaimon, Atergatis, and some even say Poseidon, were deities borrowed from Phœnicia by the Ionians; but in return the custom of circumcision was discontinued by the Phœnician sailors in consequence of Greek derision.

The connection of Phœnicia, the 'purple land,' with Egypt, dates back to the times of the eighteenth dynasty at least, when its inhabitants were known as Kaft, Khar (or Khal), and Fenek. The

Semitic Adonis had appeared as the sun-god, Aten, in Egypt, in the sixteenth century, B.C., when Ku-en-Aten established the cultus of his possibly Phœnician mother. Typhon ('the northern one'), Set (the Hittite god), Athor, the Istar of Babylon, the Ashtoreth of Gebal, were yet older members of the Semitic Pantheon imported into the cycle of the Osiris triad. But, on the other hand, the Phœnicians failed not to recognise in Horus and Osiris the same sun deities whom they called Tammuz or Adonis. Horus became Khar in their language, and Osiris was Asar. Phœnician temples to such gods were built of Egyptian granite, and scarabæi of Egyptian appearance are dug up on the shores of Gebal.

On a monument of the time of Ku-en-Aten's grandson we see these Phœnician traders bringing presents of horses, and 'vessels of gold, silver, blue-stone, green-stone, and all kinds of jewels,' and accompanied by little yellow dwarf slaves. They have the hook-nose and Jewish-looking under-lip and swarthy tint of the Semitic race, and wear no hair on the upper lip, but only beard and whisker. Some have their black hair long and thick, with a white cord bound round it. Some (probably priests) have shaven heads. Their dress is a white shirt, like that of the fellahin of to-day, with a coloured fringe ; their presents include great gold amphoræ, like those of early Ionian art, an ivory horn tipped with gold, and green vases with two handles, also very Greek-looking, which may be of bronze, or perhaps of malachite. A great vulture's head is also carried on a tray, evidently a symbolic representation, and one of the bearers has a cross suspended to his neck, as have also some of the Assyrian monarchs in the fifteenth century B.C.

A Phœnician bowl, dating from the eighth century before our era, was dug up at Olympia, and might easily be mistaken for Egyptian work. On its inside the history of the sun is told in four pictures for the four seasons. In the first we see two goddesses (Venus and Persephone, Isis and Nephthys), one standing beside the egg, one suckling the infant hero. The crescent holding the sun in its embrace is the sign of the season. The second tablet shows us the young hero attacking the lion, and the goddess still beside him. In the third he is weak and faint, while the goddess offers him (like Parvai) a cup of ambrosial drink. In the fourth the women rejoice with pipes, harps, and tambourines, at the approaching birth of the infant, who again appears as the bowl turns round and the year revolves.

From such legends we may understand how vivid was the realization of the sun myth among these dark, hook-nosed traders of the stormy bays beneath the frowning mountains; and their art tells us of a

wide trade, and of conflicting influences—that of the
Greek to the north, that of Egypt to the south, and
that of their native Chaldea on the east. At
Beyrout we were courteously invited to visit the
finest local collection of Syrian antiquities—that of
M. Péretié, who is since dead—and the Egyptian
and Indian appearance of the mirrors found at
various places on the Phœnician coast, of the
scarabæi and seals, was extremely striking, while
with these were discovered little statuettes of Greek
character, representing Venus in every attitude,
sometimes with armlets or collars of gold.

One of the scarabæi obtained by M. Péretié from
Byblos (Jibeil) was cut out of a fine amethyst, and
some of his bronze heads dug up on the same coast
were remarkable for their negro features. He
possessed also Palmyrene texts, Assyrian bricks,
bas-reliefs of figures resembling Isis and the god
Bes, from Palmyra, with coins of the Seleucidæ,
including one almost unique of the usurper Try-
phon, mediæval signets, a rude ivory idol, French
pistols of the seventeenth century from Diarbekir,
and Cypriote pottery.

The gem of this collection is the bronze plate
found at Palmyra, which represents the history of
the soul according to the belief of Assyrians and
Phœnicians alike. The tablet is crowned by the
tiger-like head of a demon, whose wings, long body,

and bird-like legs occupy the reverse side. He is apparently one of the evil Mas of the Accadians, and appears again on the front. On this side are represented first, with their respective emblems, the seven planets, as robed figures with beasts' heads, the right hand raised, the left lowered, as among the Derwishes in the last chapter. The corpse lies on its bier in the second line, guarded by two priests or genii, each with the fish head-dress of the priests of Ea—the creative god of ocean, who in the great Assyrian triad answers exactly to Vishnu in India and Poseidon in Greece. To the right the ghost (Utuk) passes safely to the cavernous abode of the blessed, while the evil demons, conjured by the priests, turn with lion-heads and birds'-claws to rend each other. Lowest of all Nin-ki-gal, the terrible queen of hell, suckling two cubs and holding two snakes, kneels on the 'death-horse' in her boat on the infernal river, where ghostly fish are swimming, and beside which ghostly papyri are growing. Followed by her dreadful husband, Mulge, or Moloch, the king of the nether regions, she approaches the offerings laid on the bank, and the hideous pair open the great jaws of their lion-heads to devour the dainties offered by surviving friends of the deceased.

The Phœnicians, once such favourites among archæologists, are suffering from the reaction due to the exaggerated importance previously attaching to their history. At one time they were credited with almost every antiquity which could not be otherwise accounted for. All drafted stones, whether of Greeks, Romans, Crusaders, or Saracens, were pointed out as having 'the Phœnician bevel,' though there is nothing to show that Phœnicians ever either bevelled or drafted their masonry. The great blocks at Baalbek are said to have been laid by them, although it does not appear why in this case the remains at Tyre, Byblos (Jibeil), or Sidon, are so much smaller in dimensions. As traders who explored the Mediterranean coast, founding Carthage and Gades and Marseilles, passing beyond the Pillars of Hercules, and long jealously guarding the secret of the tin islands on our coast, they were so celebrated that even the bronze celts of Norway and Denmark (pre-historic relics of early round-headed tribes), and the dolmens of Cornwall—nay, Stonehenge itself—have been said to be of Phœnician origin, though there is no evidence of their having ever settled in England, or having ever penetrated anywhere near the shores of the frozen Baltic.

Nearer home they have been confused with the Philistines, and credited with most of the antiquities of Southern Palestine; but science is gradually controlling such wild fancies, and reduces this energetic people to its proper limits. The Philistines were once also said to come from Crete, because they were Cherethites; but the Survey map shows us Keratiya, in Philistia, whence they were named. In the Bible they are called sons of Mizraim, or of Egypt, and Philistines, or Pelethites, 'emigrants,' as the word is said to mean, from Egypt. The Phœnicians cannot be said ever to have ruled any great distance south of Accho, for as far back as history goes Southern Palestine has belonged either to Egypt, to Israel, or to Assyria. Ptolemy and Pliny agree that the Crocodile river, south of Carmel, was the furthest limit of Phœnicia, as it was also of the purple fisheries, and they draw the north line at the Eleutherus, or at the island of Aradus, not much farther north. But Phœnicia had also her colonies, such as Carthage and Gades (in Spain), and Phœnician inscribed stones have been found at Citium, in Cyprus, at Athens, in Malta, and at Marseilles, as well as at Sidon. In Rhodes, Crete, Sicily, the Balearic Islands, Sardinia, Corsica, and the Cyclades, they were once powerful, and their mines remain in Samothrace as far north as Thrasos, and perhaps also in Cornwall. But the men who carved the Moabite stone and the Siloam tablet were no more Phœnicians, properly so called, than were those who hewed the Samaritan texts at Shechem, or struck the Hasmonean coins: for the Phœnician character is but one of a family of

Semitic alphabets, which includes those of Judæa, Palmyra, Moab, and Samaria.

However narrowly we may limit the Asiatic bounds of this stock of hardy sailors who were the first to learn to sail by the Pole-star, who crossed over from the Persian Gulf, as Herodotus tells us, and settled beside the bays and streams of the Mediterranean coast, there is no doubt of the antiquity of their race, and of the civilization of their best age.

Although the cosmogonies of Sanchoniathon are not traced before the fifth century (B.C.) in Phœnicia, his system is identical with that of Chaldea, and although the remains at Umm el 'Amûd are comparatively late, and the inscribed coffin of Eshmunazar even has been suspected of being much less ancient than formerly supposed, while Tyre is not mentioned in the Pentateuch, and Sidon only as peopled by sons of Ham; yet on the other hand the Kaft (who are known from the bilingual decree of Canopus to be the Phœnicians) appear as neighbours of the Hittites, according to the Egyptian monuments, as early as the fourteenth century B.C.

So much did their power increase in Egypt about this period, that in the time of one of the last kings of the nineteenth dynasty, a Phœnician named Arisu usurped for a short period the royal dignity. Dr. Brugsch believes that the sailors and fishers of

Lake Menzaleh are descendants of old Phœnician settlers, and the same may be said of the Neapolitan fishers, and of the modern Carthaginians.

The earliest Phœnician coins are only of the Persian period, and in the days of Antiochus Epiphanes a coin of Laodicea has the legend, 'Mother of Canaan,' the Semitic name, as Herodian states, of Phœnicia. It was by this title also that the Phœnicians of Carthage still called themselves in the time of Justin, the original meaning being only that of 'lowlander.'

The most southern purely Phœnician town yet known is now called Umm el 'Amûd, marked on the Survey south of Tyre. This I visited in May, 1881, but it had long since been ransacked by Renan. The remains were, however, not earlier than Greek times, although a Phœnician votive tablet to Moloch Astarte was unearthed, and a long text in eight lines, invoking a blessing from Baal, Lord of Heaven. In Greek times this site was known as Laodicea, and the old temple seems to have been consecrated to Hammon. Possibly this may be the town of Asher, called Hammon in the Book of Joshua (xix. 28).

The ruins here visible stand on a hill above the shore, and are half hidden by the copse. The Temple was apparently 100 feet wide and 180 feet long, with three walks and a peristyle. It faced north of north-east, and its pillars are only 18 inches in diameter. The tombs near the shrine on the north are entered from the face of the cliff, whereas Tyrian tombs are all sunk from above. The most interesting remains on the site are, however, those of two altars, which almost exactly resemble the so-called 'libation tables' of the Egyptians preserved in the Bulak Museum. One of these had an eagle carved on the side, the other was plain. The first was a block of limestone three and a half feet high and five feet by three feet at the top; it had two flat basins, a foot square and a few inches deep, sunk in the upper surface. The second was three feet high and two feet eight inches square, with a single basin of the same size as in the former. No doubt on these ancient altars, now tumbled over on the hill-side, libations to Ashtoreth were often poured before Alexander came to break the power of Tyre.

But if Gebal were sacred to the woes of Istar, not less holy was the great Temple of Hercules or Melkarth ('the City King') at Tyre; and it may not be superfluous here to add some results of a visit of several days' duration which I paid to Tyre in May, 1881, with a view of examining on the spot the startling conclusions which were reached by Renan, and which seemed to me to contradict all that we know of Phœnician and Syrian antiquity, especially in respect to the extent of the ancient city and the position of its necropolis.

The priests of Melkarth told Herodotus that Tyre was founded at a date representing 2750 B.C.; but Josephus makes it only as old as 1250 B.C. That the original city was on an island, joined to the mainland by the mole made during the siege by Alexander, is generally allowed; but the three points to be settled were the position of the Egyptian Harbour mentioned by Strabo, the site of the great Temple of Melkarth, and that of the ancient cemetery and of Palætyrus. On each of these points our visit seems to me to have thrown considerable light.

Although doubted by some recent writers, there can be no reasonable difficulty as to the Egyptian port. It exists on the south side of the double island on which Tyre was built; but in order to properly survey its limits, it is necessary that the explorer should swim or row out to what appears to be a natural reef bounding the port. The plan published in the appendix to the Survey Memoirs shows that the area of this southern harbour, formed by a great mole on reefs, is quite equal to that of the northern or Sidonian port, and although both are very small, there is no reason to suppose they were ever larger. The Tyre harbours have an area of about 12 acres each; but the great port of

Sidon is not more than 20 acres in extent. That at Cæsarea is 10 acres, and those at Joppa and Jamnia are even smaller. The Tyrian ships were no doubt small, but so were the Viking galleys, and so are the craft which cross the stormy German Ocean to our eastern ports. To the stout seamen of old the smallness of their vessels was not so evident as it is to ourselves, and thus the most famous harbours of the ancient world are so small that a single ironclad even could perhaps not have safely entered the ports of Tyre or Sidon even before they had been filled up purposely by Fakr ed Dîn.

As regards the Temple of Melkarth on the island, there seems to me also little reason to doubt that its site is marked by the ruins of the great Crusading cathedral. This edifice, though just outside the little modern town, is in the very middle of the ancient double island, and on the highest part. It is oriented curiously enough on the line of the hill of Neby M'ashûk on the mainland (the site of the Temple of Heracles Astrochiton), and inside its walls lies a magnificent monolith 27 feet long, forming a double pillar, like those found in the ruins of Jerâsh and in the angles of the Galilean synagogues, each half-column being three and a half feet in diameter. There are remains of a second similar shaft, and also of single pillars of syenite. Other red granite columns of similar dimensions have been taken away by the Crusaders, and built as thoroughbonds into their city walls, or thrown down to form jetties in the southern harbour.

Now the granite came no doubt from Egypt; but the column is of a style quite unlike any Gothic work in Syria. No other church of the twelfth century in Palestine has such a twin shaft, and its proportions are quite out of keeping with the small masonry of the cathedral walls, and with the white limestone capitals which seem to have been cut by the Crusaders to cap the granite pillars. Considering how constant was the Phœnician intercourse with Egypt, and how often the red and grey granite is found in Phœnician towns, we are justified in supposing it probable that these shafts belonged to the Temple of Melkarth, and that it was erected on this very spot, and directed to face the sacred knoll on the mainland to the east, where stood a shrine which, as the Tyrians told Alexander, was older than that on the island. Considering how constantly Christian churches were built on pagan sacred sites, reconsecrating at Rome, or even perhaps at Jerusalem and Bethlehem, the cave of Mithra or the hill of Venus, we need not wonder that the old church, said to hold the bones of Origen, and the mediæval cathedral which replaced it, each preserved in their time the memory of the site of Melkarth's granite fane.

The shrine of Neby M'ashûk, or the 'Lover Prophet,' stands conspicuous on its isolated knoll, east of the island, about forty feet above the plain. There is a perpendicular cliff beneath the little domed building on the east side of the knoll, and a palm stands beside the double dome. On the north side rude rock steps lead up the slope, and on the north-west are rock-sunk Tyrian tombs. The aqueduct from the south passes close by the south side of the hill, and a legend attaches to the spot of a cave full of honey in the hill, which appears, however, to be mythical. Clearly we have here also a Phœnician holy place with a Phœnician cemetery— no doubt the Temple of Heracles Astrochiton of the time of Alexander. So fascinating was this divinity, that every woman who saw him fell in love with him; but his wife is now buried beside him, and no doubt looks after his ghost.

M. Renan would apparently have us believe that Palætyrus, the city on the shore, stretched as an open suburb all along the coast from Râs el 'Ain on the south to the Kasimyeh river on the north, which would make a city one quarter the size of London; but all we know of Palætyrus is the statement of Strabo that it was twenty stadia south of Tyre, which points to the site of the fine reservoirs at Râs el 'Ain. The aqueduct thence is perhaps as old as Shalmanezer's time, for he cut off its supply in besieging the island, so that the defenders had only their cisterns to depend on. No doubt the cemetery of Tyrian tombs east of Neby M'ashûk is an old Phœnician necropolis, but it is quite unnecessary to suppose that the city of Tyre therefore extended to the hills. Those who were buried at this cemetery (called el Lawâtîn, or the 'lime-kilns') no doubt desired to be entombed as near as rock could be found to the temple at Neby M'ashûk; but it should be noted that the account of this site, given by Renan, is greatly exaggerated. The 'immense hypogees' are in some cases only quarry pits, never roofed; in others they are excavations for chalk or marl, used to make lime and for roofing houses. They are not old, for in some cases they have Tyrian tombs near their roofs, half broken away. Clearly, as at other sites, the quarrymen found it easier to enlarge the opening already existing in an old tomb-chamber, than to work the indurated face of the rock. The caves cannot compare with those at Beit Jibrîn, and their name seems rightly to explain their origin.

But if the Tyrians were not here buried, where (it may be asked) was their cemetery? This question we may, I think, now answer. They were buried on the island, where the modern cemetery now exists, south of the town. Tyrian tombs consist of a chamber with *kokim*, or tunnels for single bodies, running in from the walls—three or four on each side of the chamber, as in Jewish tombs of the earliest period; but there is an essential difference between the two, for the Jewish chamber was reached by a little door from one side, the entrance being cut in the face of a cliff, or steep slope. The Phœnician, on the other hand, like the Egyptian, sunk a shaft down from the flat top of the rock, and placed his chamber at the bottom, filling the shaft no doubt with stones, or covering it with a slab. Thus, while the Jewish tomb remains still recoverable, though rifled, the Phœnician is hidden as soon as a little rubbish has gathered over the rock. Curiously enough, we were able to prove this, and to show where one Tyrian, at least, was buried on the island, for in the cliff of the little bay in the south-west angle of the double island is a hole, and through this it is just possible to squeeze into a small cavern called 'the Champion's Cave,' about ten feet by eight, and eleven high. Looking up, we could see the shaft which was the original entrance, covered with flat slabs, which are hid beneath the soil in which the modern graves are dug. The champion's grave had been plundered by some former visitor, and only the place where his sarcophagus lay could be seen; but on the top of the cliffs, which are about thirty or forty feet high, a large sarcophagus is still lying. To prove our contention more completely, excavations in the cemetery would be necessary; but as single tombs are rare, and the site of any necropolis generally immutable in the East, we may fairly consider that this discovery indicates the site of the old Tyrian cemetery.

Such a suburb as M. Renan would have us suppose is not indicated by any existing ruins, and has no parallel in Syria. Jerusalem at its greatest, when its suburbs had run far north, beyond the second wall, only covered about 300 acres; and so narrow are the streets of Oriental cities, that large populations are huddled in very little space. Sidon, Ascalon, Samaria, Shechem—all ancient sites of famous cities by which it is possible to form a judgment—show us only a small area concentrated round some central stronghold in positions defensible before gunpowder was invented. There is no parallel to the huge Egyptian city of Memphis, in Syria, and Tyre on its island was no larger than Sidon or Joppa.

The almost complete disappearance of Palætyrus is easily accounted for. Josephus says that in 332 B.C. Alexander the Great used up its stones to build the great causeway whereby he finally joined the island to the main shore, and this great work, now hidden beneath an isthmus of sand, would easily have swallowed up an entire town.

Not, however, by its area, which cannot have exceeded about a hundred acres, must we judge the importance of the city of Tyre. The account of its trade given by Ezekiel (xxvii.), six centuries before Christ, shows how wide a range Phœnician commerce then embraced. The Grecian Archipelago sent its silks: Persia and Nubia, the Cimmerians, Ionia and Tarshish, the Moschi, the Armenians, were among its traders. The carbuncles of Syria, the spices of Yemen, the riches of Mesopotamia, were thither brought, with scented woods from India, no doubt forwarded by caravans along the old line from Iran: the wine of Helbon, the wrought iron from Asia Minor, the flocks of the Syrian Arabs, cedar from Lebanon, oaks of Bashan, or firs from the Hermon sandstones, all found a market at Tyre. Nay, even the 'souls of men' were sold by the Phœnicians, and a high price was paid by Egyptian nobles for male and female slaves from the land of the Khar, whether as private slaves or as servants in temples. But their glory was broken down by the Babylonian and the Greek, and though now a dull town with a population of 5,000 souls, Metâwileh and Christian, Tyre was found by the travellers who visited it early in the century a deserted ruin, a 'place for the spreading of nets in the midst of the sea' (Ezekiel xxvi. 5).

There is a remarkable passage in the same book of

Ezekiel (xxviii. 12), which seems perhaps to refer to Melkarth, the 'City King,' or Hercules of Tyre. 'Take up a lamentation upon the *King of Tyrus*,' it reads, 'and say unto him, Thus saith Jehovah Elohim; Thou sealest up the sum, full of wisdom, and perfect in beauty. Thou hast been in Eden, the garden of God; every precious stone was thy covering. . . . Thou wert the anointed cherub that covereth (or defendeth); and I have set thee so: thou wast upon the holy mountain of Elohim; thou hast walked up and down in the midst of the stones of fire.' The whole passage seems rather to point to an acquaintance with the symbolism of Tyrian Sun-worship, which it condemns, than to any mortal monarch.

In connection with this idea may be mentioned a very interesting gem belonging to Dr. William Wright, the Secretary of the Bible Society, and recently described by him, although without any attempt to explain its symbolism. It presents just that mixture of Egyptian and Assyrian features which is common on Phœnician seals (as, for instance, on that brought home by Prince Albert Victor of Wales in 1882). A human figure with a disc in his hand is flanked by a hawk-headed cherub on one side, and by a scarabæus on the other. The hawk is the emblem of Horus: the beetle is Cheper, the 'setting sun.' We have thus the group of three, which in Egypt represent the rising, mid-day, and setting sun. The inscription in Phœnician letters reads Ani or Aneh, which may be compared with the Assyria Anu, the eldest of the great triad of their Pantheon. If this explanation is correct, we find the rising sun represented as a cherub in Phœnicia, and have thus a remarkable confirmation of the suggestion just mentioned respecting the 'King of Tyre.'

Tyre ('the rock') was essentially a holy city to the Phœnicians. Here Ashtoreth was born, rising on her shell from the deep. Here fell her star or thunder-bolt on the island which it consecrated. Here, underneath the sea, were the two great menhirs called ambrosial stones, and believed to have divine souls, and these, though no man ever saw them, are shown on Tyrian coins. Here Heracles, who was but a local Adonis, reigned supreme. Here also his dog fished the first murex from the water, and its purple was seen to dye the dog's mouth, whence arose the prosperity of the city favoured by Melkarth. Here games were instituted in honour of the 'waking of Heracles,' or the new birth of Tammuz; and here the great temple rose with its pillar of malachite (or of verde antique), its never-failing altar flame, its white-robed priests, with shaven heads. Women were no doubt excluded from its precincts, as in the sister shrine at Gades, and swine forbidden to the votaries, in memory of the boar that slew the solar Tammuz, that same black boar which, under the name of Typhon, swallowed the shining eye of Horus in Egypt, where its flesh was equally abhorred by the Egyptian priests.

In the 'Valley of Figs,' south-east of Tyre, there is a tomb over which is a carving in relief, belonging probably to the later Phœnician period. Guérin (with less than his usual exactitude) speaks of it as a figure of a shepherd with sheeps'-heads in crowns round it. In 1881 I made a careful drawing on the spot. The bas-relief is surrounded by a projecting frame, and this measures two feet in height by one and a half feet in width. The figure, much defaced, represents a man in a long robe, and a sort of arabesque of vine leaves (mistaken for sheeps'-heads set in circles) runs up each side within the frame. To the left the vine springs from an amphora, to the right from a dog-like animal crouching at the feet of the figure. As he has no crook or other sign of his profession, it is rather bold to call him a shepherd, and the ornamentation resembles the work on Jewish tombs at 'Abûd, or on the lintels at Semû'a, south of Hebron. The rock on which the carving occurs measures six feet by four feet, and a tomb shaft is visible below. It appears to me more probable that the figure (unless, indeed, it be that of the person here buried) represents the Tyrian Hercules, with his dog at his feet. The vine is always intimately connected with such solar deities, as in the case of Dionysus, also a Semitic divinity.

But sterner rites were observed in time of trouble, of famine, drought, or siege, at Tyre. The Tyrians during Alexander's siege sought to appease their angry god by sacrificing a child, and in his infernal aspect the Moloch or 'King' of Tyrus no doubt often received such victims. Wherever the Phœnicians travelled, in Cyprus, Rhodes, Crete, and Sardinia, we trace this bloody rite. When, in the sixth century B.C., Carthage was founded as a colony of Tyre, human sacrifice and the rites of the Succoth Benoth became so prominent, that a yearly victim was offered there (as also at Laodicea) to Ashtoreth; and a brazen image (like that described in Tophet by the Rabbis) received the child in its scorching arms, whence it slid to the furnace within, as Diodorus relates. Even down to the time of the Proconsul Tiberius the custom held, until he hanged the priests of Carthage on the trees of their own sacred grove, as Tertullian tells us. Nor can we doubt the reality of these cruel facts when we remember that human sacrifice, according to Pliny, was only abolished in Rome in 87 B.C. The memory of such deeds yet lingers in the minds of the peasantry when they ignorantly accuse the Jews of annually slaying a Christian child at the Passover—

a calumny widespread in Syria, Asia Minor, and Egypt, even now. And whenever our imagination becomes enchanted by the myths of pagan systems, we should remember that their creeds were not always beautiful and poetic, but barbarously cruel and shameless.

What measure of independence was enjoyed by the petty Kings of Tyre and Sidon we cannot easily judge. Certain it is that the sea-coast was a high road for the armies of Egypt in the fourteenth century B.C., for the Dog River, north of Beyrout, still shows us three Egyptian bas-reliefs, including one of Rameses II., while six Assyrian sculptures indicate the return current from Euphrates, when the Eastern Monarchy became strongest. In the reign of Rameses II., also, we find the Mohar, or Egyptian tax-gatherer, driving his chariot from the land of the Hittites down the Tyrian coast, but whether he got any tribute, or was only a court messenger, does not appear. On their rocky island the Tyrians might remain safely shut up while an army passed along the shore, just as Joshua did not burn the 'cities that stood still in their strength' (xi. 13); but it is perhaps more probable that the Phœnicians were regularly allied to Egypt, at least after the time of the battle of Kadesh.

The pride of Tyre has fallen, yet the old race can scarce be said to be extinct. The sailors of Tripoli are still Phœnician in feature and dialect ; the sacred fish of Ashtoreth are preserved at Acre and Tripoli ; the votaries of the goddess were forbidden to eat fish at all, and even yet the so-called Moslems who make pilgrimages to offer gifts at these ponds jealously forbid that the sacred carp should be devoured. We no longer see the fish-like Oannes or Dagon, the lord of corn and of the plough (like the creative Ea in Assyria), carved at the wayside shrine, but his name is preserved in more than one Beth Dagon yet; and the dome of Neby Yunas, though now supposed to mark where Jonah was thrown up by the great fish, no doubt replaces a Tyrian temple of Hercules, who was swallowed alive by the whale, or of Dagon, half man, half fish. We no longer hear of Eshmun ('the eighth') as ruling the Cabiri, yet the symbolic dance of the planets survives, as we have noted in the last chapter. The name of Reseph of Egypt, Phœnicia, and Cyprus, the satyr-like husband of Anat, a 'thunderer' and a rain-giver, with deer's horns, is still commemorated at the town of Arsuf, as M. Clermont Ganneau points out, comparing him to Horus and Saint George, to which names hundreds of others, Semitic and Aryan, might have been added. The sacred trees and stone-heaps are still preserved, and the shrines stand as of old on the mountain-tops. The feasts of Hercules are said still to be celebrated at Tyre, and Thoth or Set, the 'pillar god,' common to Hittite, Egyptian and Phœnician, reappears as the Prophet Seth. We can indeed hardly claim for the modern native of the 'Purple Land' more than this, that while, on the one hand, he has lost in civilization, in power, and in wealth, he, on the other, no longer offers his children to a wrathful deity, nor sacrifices his daughter to consecrated shame.

CHAPTER IV.

THE LAND OF SIHON.

THE object of the present volume is to describe, not the difficulties encountered, but the results gained, during our explorations in Syria in the years 1881 and 1882; but it may here be noted that most anxious delays had to be encountered in consequence of the attitude of the Turkish Government, and that all that was done was accomplished in the teeth of the categorical refusal of the authorities to permit either Survey or any other kind of exploration. I, for one, do not feel disposed to condemn the Sultan's Government for so acting. They had seen such exploration secretly carried out by the Power they have most reason to fear in Northern Syria; they had just suffered the loss of the province of Tunis, suddenly wrested from their hands: they were aware that trouble (partly of their own making, it is true) was brewing in Egypt, and that French and Russian intrigue was rife throughout Syria. It was, then, not unnatural that they should regard with suspicion the long and familiar intercourse of an English party settled among the disaffected Arab tribes, or dwelling amid the rebellious Druzes. There is no doubt that it was a time ill-suited for scientific research, and, indeed, far more so than that during which the Western Survey was completed, for in 1877 we were in high favour at Constantinople, and, although war was being carried on in the Balkans, Syria was all the quieter in consequence, because great numbers of the able-bodied men had been transported to Europe, and in many districts only the elders, the women and children were left.

The more quietly we set to work, the more likely we should be to excite suspicion, and yet the only hope of doing anything at all lay in escaping for a time the vigilance of the Government. I soon found that spies had been set to watch our movements, and that there was no hope whatever of penetrating into the Hauran. Our best chance lay in Moab, but how to get there and stay there without its being known was the difficulty. The Damascus Government had received orders from Constantinople not to accept the old Firman, under which all the former Survey had been carried out, although it was not limited either in time or in powers; for regulations have been made since 1877 which limit the rights of explorers and place great difficulties in their way. These may be overcome in times when the British and Turkish Governments are on good terms, but not when English influence is as low as it was at Constantinople in 1882.

Fifteen years ago the Turks had only just gained a hold on the town of es Salt, east of Jordan, and the Arabs of Moab and Gilead were virtually independent; but now that there is a military post in the Hauran, and that the Governor of Nâblus annually levies taxes on the tribes as far south as Kerak, the state of the case is entirely 'different. Formerly a covenant with the chiefs of the Arab tribes was quite enough to ensure the protection of the traveller, as it still is under ordinary circumstances in districts like the Shammar or the Nejed, which are beyond Turkish influence; but the danger in our case was this, that the Turks have inaugurated a wily policy which most successfully holds the Arabs in subjection. They subsidize and protect the weaker faction in each tribe (for every Arab clan is split into at least two factions), and encourage it to thwart the plans of the opposition. Thus our presence was certain to be discovered sooner or later, through the jealousy of some Government creature among the Bedawîn; and, although the Turks themselves might have done nothing to endanger our lives or properties, there was a very real peril in the fact that an 'accident' sometimes occurs in a manner most convenient for the ruling power; and even if this had entailed no loss of life, it would have created an 'incident' which might have seriously prejudiced the future of Palestine exploration, and have brought down on the head of the leader of the expedition the displeasure of his superiors; to say nothing of the loss of valuable animals, instruments, and stores, which might have been carried off in a strong night raid by some tribe really incited to attack us by the Turkish Government, or of the claims for damages on the part of muleteers and others, which would clearly not have been paid by the Porte, or by the Bedawin either.

When it is noted that we only left Syria a few days before the Alexandrian massacres, and when we remember the lamentable fate of Professor Palmer and his companions, betrayed by an Arab Sheikh, and butchered in the heart of the desert by Bedawin set on probably by the creatures of the rebel Egyptian Government, it will, I think, be allowed that our mission was pushed to the utmost limits consistent with a regard for the safety of those whom I had the responsibility of leading, and who so faithfully followed me against their own judgment. Had a single member lost his life on that expedition, I should have had a heavy burden on my conscience for having led him into danger; and it is not always when things appear to be going smoothly, and Arabs are obsequious and Governors apparently asleep, that a small party of explorers is really most safe.

It was clearly useless to endeavour to hide from the Turks. They knew that our heavy luggage had passed the custom-house, and that an expedition had been organized to take the field. Accounts of public meetings in England find their way through English newspapers to the Turkish and Arab press, and articles relating to his dominions are said to be often translated specially for the information of the Sultan. His Highness Hamdi Pasha was warned to stop us by a telegram from Stamboul, and he was doing his duty when he not only refused to aid us, but announced that he could not even ignore us. Had we been merely commissioned to travel, the case might have been somewhat different; but our object was to survey, as before, and survey is one of the operations which the Turk regards with most suspicion and terror. A man with a map can go where he wants without a guide, and may thus pass through the country undetected. A map, then, is evidently an incendiary document, and, like a newspaper article or a book, it must not be allowed to escape Government supervision.

But if the Waly was conscientious, perhaps some of his subordinates might prove less vigilant, and a visit to a provincial Governor might possibly do good. I therefore waited on the Mudîr of Nâblus, who governs all the country south of the 'Ajlûn, and told him that though other travellers often went over Jordan without notice, yet, as we wished to stay some time, I thought it only courteous to call on him first and explain that we were old friends who wanted to see all the ruins at our leisure. His answer was very significant. 'Others,' he said, 'went at their own peril, but we should receive Government protection if our application was approved by the Sultan and our papers found correct.' A few days after, this most courteous of officials regretted, in a letter sent through our Consul, that he could not countenance our expedition.

Here, then, was a check; but not, as the Kurdish Governor supposed, a checkmate. I applied duly for a new Firman, and we settled down apparently to wait for it—which we might still be doing—but our real reason for waiting was that the Mudîr had gone over Jordan to collect the taxes, and that we should have fallen into his hands and have been at once stopped if we had crossed over immediately. As it was, the Turks were fairly thrown off the scent, and began to regard us with the usual contempt which attaches to the great company of European 'waiters for Firmans.' Meanwhile, I had determined to use against them their own weapons, and was in treaty with the greatest of their opponents, the bold and wily Goblân, of the 'Adwân Arabs, who represents the hopes of the patriotic or anti-Turkish party in Moab, and who is as much a favourite among the Bedawîn as he is detested by the Turks. Under his care we knew we might succeed for a time, for the Governor of es Salt, though belonging to the Kurdish colony of Damascus (fellow-countrymen of Saladin, who are so valuable to the Turks on account of their fierce determination), was at that time an individual not given to temperance, and quite under the control of his Christian secretary, who was willing enough to give us the benefit of ignoring us, or indeed of information concerning the doings of his superiors not unlikely to be useful.

So close was the game of 'hide and seek' thus run, that having obtained a faithful messenger to reach Goblân, we arranged a meeting with him at Jericho, and slipped over Jordan on the very same day that the Mudîr crossed over on his way back to Nâblus. Lieutenant Mantell and I went on this expedition with only a few natives, leaving our two assistants, Messrs. Black and Armstrong, and most of our tents *en evidence*, to amuse the officers who had suddenly found it delightful to come out daily to the 'Ain Yalo camp, where we had pitched. Our intention was to send for the rest as soon as our contract with Goblân was signed and sealed.

Thus at length, on the 17th of August, we met Goblân at Elisha's fountain, on the morning of a summer day, with a temperature of 100°—not the best of seasons for a camp 1,000 feet below sea-level in the stifling Jordan valley. Riding slowly on a bay mare, he approached with four mounted followers. His figure was not unfamiliar, for I had met him at intervals ever since 1873, but it is one remarkably striking at first sight. A tall, gaunt man, with a grey bronzed face, half-hidden by his shawl, one eye red and sightless from the swordcut which has furrowed all one cheek, and of which he is much ashamed, because it was a blow from an injured relative, and not a wound received in fair fight. His hair (as I saw accidentally one night) is long and silvery, and his beard quite white. His age is probably about seventy, though he either does not know it, or else conceals it, for he told us that he believed himself to be about forty. He wore a double Kufeyeh, the inner shawl black, the outer one black with gold embroidery. His shirt was white and clean, with a *kumbaz*, or long gown, fastened by a belt, with yellow and purple vertical stripes. The white sleeves of the shirt hung out beyond those of the gown, reaching to his feet, which were cased in loose boots of red leather, without any sock or stocking. Over all he wore a beautiful abba, or cope-like mantle, of broad white and amber-coloured stripes. This most picturesque costume was strangely at variance with the long lean figure, the red eye, the muffled voice, the thick obstinate nose, and the long gash on the bony, dusky cheek; but the hand, so apt to wield the lance, was as soft and delicate to the touch as a woman's, with white nails carefully trimmed.

Goblân is a well-known character, and has been mentioned by Warren, Tristram, and other explorers. There is a touch of romance about his history and character, which, although he is sordidly covetous and of an evil temper, yet elevates him above the sadly degraded level of his followers and kinsmen, who are quite spoilt by their intercourse with the western world. I do not believe that Goblân ever related the story of his life to a European, but it is well known. How he rode behind a stranger on a grey mare and speared him, being led away by his covetous desire of the beautiful beast. How the stranger proved to be a chief of the neighbouring tribe of the Sakhûr Arabs, and how a blood feud was thus commenced which yet remains unsettled. Strange indeed was the sensation of riding day by day with a man marked down for vengeance, and liable to be slain by any relative of his victim who might cross our path. Seated on the great cairn at Sâmik above the corpses of men slain in battle on the boundary of his tribe, Goblân pointed one day to the black tents of the Sakhûr a mile away, surrounded with feeding camels, and as we slowly took our angles with a great theodolite, he remarked quietly, 'If they knew I was here they would come and kill me.' On another day he and I were alone near the same border, when his quick eye perceived a train of men on camels. He pointed them out, and begged me to finish my mapping as soon as might be. Yet he would not leave me till I was ready, and as we retired three horsemen appeared in the distance and followed us. We put a precipitous gorge between us and them, and they called across, as did David to Saul at the 'Cliff of Division.' It was one of the relatives of his victim with two followers, and although, while slaying him, they would no doubt have left me quite unhurt, an Englishman could not have stood by to see his venerable guide murdered in cold blood on account of a deed done many years ago.

I am told that Goblân showed the same trustworthy courage when he accompanied Colonel Warren in Moab, at a critical moment, when an English lady was dying and could not be moved, but when the tents of his enemies were approaching nearer every day, and hemming in this outlaw, who, in his old age, lives with Arab foes on the south and east, and Turkish enemies seeking his life or liberty from the north and west.

Although I became disgusted with his grasping desire for ever a little more money, and his covetous craving for everything I possessed, I could not but feel a respect and liking for this aged ruffian. He was the best guide I ever met, and his manners had none of the rude familiarity of some of his followers. He was indeed a perfect gentleman, never intruding, except on business or by invitation, into my tent, outside which he lay on a sack every night. He was fond of tea, but could not make a cigarette, and, like most of his tribe, he never smoked. Many an interesting conversation I have held in the evening with Goblân, interrupted always by offers on his part to retire if I was tired or sleepy. He was faithful to us under very trying circumstances, when even his own tribe deserted him, and his brothers feared he was getting into trouble on our behalf. He disregarded the repeated summons of the Kurdish Kaimakâm at es Salt to leave our camp, partly, I must admit, because the pay was good, but also, I believe, because he had sealed a covenant with us and would not draw back. Once, indeed, he picked a quarrel with our headman about sixpence per diem, and threatened to leave us alone to get on as best we could, but even then, in the storm of a quarrel, with five voices going at once, I was able, by an appeal to his courtesy, to defeat his object, which was, I believe, to get an excuse for going back from his agreement. 'A chief of the 'Adwân,' I said, 'should not quarrel with servants,' and, by a compromise, which I was only too glad in reality to offer, I retained his services. One motive for finally retreating in face of the Turkish Government was, in my mind, a feeling of consideration for old Goblân, and even now I should hear with the greatest regret that the old outlaw had fallen a victim to his many enemies.

At the time of our expedition he was arranging for a new marriage, though he has sons and grandsons enough of all ages; but he had just been obliged to give up to the Mudîr of Nâblus a ring which was of great value, and a present from the Russian Grand-Duke Nicholas, when he went to Jericho, in 1881. There were two names Goblân could not bear to hear uttered, namely, that of the Sakhûr Arabs and that of the Turks. The Arabs of Moab regard this venerable outlaw as their natural chief in case of any outbreak against the Turkish Government, but he is not likely to risk his neck in such a cause unless he knows that European aid can be relied on. He is the most wily of the politicians beyond Jordan, and when, many years ago, his cousins of the Diâb branch (the elder division of the tribe) were induced by promise of rewards and honours to go up to Nâblus, Goblân counselled them not to do so, and refused to go himself. No sooner were they in the town than the treacherous governor seized them, and the old chief Diâb got his leg broken by the brutal soldiery who took him to prison. Only by heavy bribery did they escape, and Diâb was obliged to abdicate in favour of his son 'Aly Diâb, who is now a Turkish favourite.

Such, then, was our Arab ally, and although an acquaintance with the Belka Arabs has not raised my estimate of Bedawîn character, it is but fair to acknowledge that our success, such as it was, was greatly due to Goblân. Our treaty obliged him to furnish as guards and guides four mounted men, and he remained with us as a guest, and acted as my guide whenever I was out of camp. He led us to Heshbon, where we encamped on the 18th, and where Messrs. Black and Armstrong joined us. Here we remained until the 10th of September, and then, by Goblân's advice, moved a mile south to 'Ain Fudeili; for we were on the main route to Jerusalem, and a quarrel might have arisen with the Sakhûr, since a fight occurred just then, in the Jordan valley, between their tribe and the 'Adwân. The feeling, indeed, was very bitter, for in the May of 1881 a battle had taken place in which Satam, one of the Sakhûr chiefs, was slain by the 'Adwân. While at Heshbon we had some donkeys stolen by thieves from Kerak, but for these Goblân paid finally in part, asking me to make good the rest. His men captured an old grey horse, which he offered in exchange, saying it belonged to the thief's brother, The thieves were known, but Mujelli of Kerak said he would only restore the donkeys when we came for them, whether as a threat or as an inducement I never made out.

On the 20th September Goblân became very restless, and wished us to move south, which we were able to do, camping at the spring in Wâdy Jideid. On the night after we moved this distance of eight miles the Mudîr of Nâblus reached our old camp, and, to his disgust, found us flown. He sent an officer to search for us, who arrived on the 23rd, and said the Governor considered it too dangerous for us to work alone, and that Goblân was to be taken to prison if we had any fault to find with him. I understood what was meant, and sent back word that we were getting on capitally, and only begged to be left alone, but I doubt what answer the officer really carried, for our headman, Habib el Jemal, induced him, I have heard, to say he could not find us at all.

The reason of this pursuit was simple. The Hâj, or pilgrimage to Mecca, was on its way south, on the east side of the Moab plateau. The Arab chiefs went north to Kal'at ez Zerka, to greet the celebrated old Kurdish Pasha, Muhammed S'aid, who was in charge, and he noticed the absence of Goblân's familiar face. This was the opportunity for his enemies, the Sakhûr chiefs, and they were not slow to seize it, although I had promised to employ and pay them handsomely as soon as we left the 'Adwân country to cross into theirs. I had interviewed several of their chiefs, and all appeared settled, but hatred of Goblân or fear of the Turk seems to have made them decide to do us an ill turn. They therefore at once replied to the Pasha's question, 'Oh, Goblân is with the English captains, who are measuring the land;' and none who know the Arabs will suppose that such an answer was merely a stupid indiscretion on their part.

An explosion of wrath followed. Muhammed S'aîd reproached the Mudîr of Nâblus, and the latter fell on the luckless Kaimakâm of es Salt. Telegrams were sent to Damascus, and the country was raised against us, and of all this we became aware through friends, though Goblân never uttered a syllable to indicate that he knew all about it. We were thus discovered within a month after reaching Moab, but were not yet run to earth. Fortunately, the base was measured and the triangulation all arranged, so that work could be pushed on fast now; but only 100 miles of actual survey were as yet completed. We went at once south to Minyeh, and completed our labours to the border of the Hameideh; but having failed to make any satisfactory arrangement with this small and wild tribe, I determined to try and put the enemy off the scent by a march northwards ; and this succeeded for a little, for while we were hard at work at 'Ammân, the emissaries of the Salt Governor went to look for us in the south. At length, on the 7th of October, I was served with a peremptory order to suspend operations and leave the country. I at once replied, expressing extreme astonishment, and stating that I had referred the matter to the British Consul at Jerusalem and to the Waly. Thus we gained a few days while letters were sent, telegrams exchanged between Jerusalem and Damascus, and an answer despatched to 'Ammân. We all worked like slaves until the 20th, and I then moved to 'Arâk el Emîr. Here again we were summoned to desist, this time with great courtesy, the Governor of Nâblus sending word that 'nothing unpleasant was to be allowed to occur,' while at the same time Goblân was commanded to leave us at once. I became alarmed at this, because such words are sometimes intended (if the seal, for instance, on the letter be upside down) to be differently understood by the initiated. I therefore sent back word that we were going, but had not mules enough all to go at once. Mr. T. Black, being ill with dysentery, had returned to Jerusalem on the 16th, and we moved down on the 25th to Kefrein, in the Jordan valley, where we completed the Survey as far north as Nimrîn. Thus, although discovered four weeks after crossing Jordan, we did not finally leave Moab until the 29th of October, and during this period of eleven weeks we surveyed in all nearly 500 square miles, discovered 700 rude stone monuments, and obtained a volume of notes, plans, and drawings, while Lieutenant Mantell took forty photographs.

I am glad to think that the home committee approved of the general conduct of the expedition, and I was grateful to them for the confidence they showed. I should not fail also to state how well we were supported by our old friend, Consul N. T. Moore, C.M.G., at Jerusalem, although our position was one which could not be officially recognised, as we were, in fact, little better than outlaws making a raid in face of the Government of the land. Lord Dufferin's kind interest and endeavours on our behalf at Constantinople also merited our gratitude, and I could only have wished that it had been possible to remove the groundless, though natural, suspicions of the Sultan's Government as to our real object in exploring Moab. But archæological enthusiasm is not understood in Turkey, and we were thus forced for a time to suspend operations until happier days, when temporary suspicion of the old English friend shall have passed away, or when the Eastern Question shall finally have been settled.

The Eastern Survey will some day be completed,

for it presents no difficulty of formidable character in itself. The country, with its bolder features, its broad plains, its population more intelligent and willing than the Fellahin west of Jordan, can be more rapidly and easily mapped than the rugged hills of Judea, and there is but little danger to the explorer if favoured by the Government of the land. We may hope, then, soon to see a survey on the east not inferior to that of the west ; but the fatal year 1300 of the Hejirah, when all Syria and Arabia were excited by the news from Egypt, was certainly not a time fitted for scientific exploration in the wilds.

There was much fascination in the rough life in the desert among men who were accustomed to danger all their lives, but the Arab in time of peace and in time of war is not the same man, and while those who understand how to treat him may be quite safe in ordinary times, even those who have most influence will fail if they are pitted against an oriental Government, which is neither so stupid nor so supine at an important crisis as the Englishman is inclined to imagine. I need not, however, say more on this matter, for a memorable and most unhappy illustration of the fact is still fresh in our memories in Sinai.

From this long digression on the history of the expedition we may now return to consider the results obtained ; and in the present chapter the sites of

Heshbon, of Nebo, of Minyeh, and of Callirhoe will be considered, together with the plain of Seisaban, at the foot of the Moab hills north of the Dead Sea.

The general aspect of Moab is the same throughout. It is a plateau about 3,000 feet above the Mediterranean level, or 4,300 feet above the Dead Sea. The western slopes are generally steep. The lower formation is the Nubian sandstone, which represents our English beds lying beneath the Greensand, and which stretches south to Petra and the Arabah. Above this a dolomitic limestone, with bold precipices in some places, forms the upper part of the hills, and is capped with a soft marl full of flints, which rises on the north of Wady Hesbân above the general level. The dip of the strata is towards the Jordan valley, but it is not nearly as sudden as on the west side of the great chasm; for the Ghôr is clearly a gigantic fault, and the slopes on its west, which descend from the Palestine watershed, are very steep, with breaks or smaller faults in places parallel to the line of the valley, whereas on the east the strata are less contorted, and thus the sandstone shows along the ridges of Moab and Gilead almost to the sea of Galilee, as well as in the eastern cliffs of the Dead Sea shore. The levels of the Dead Sea tell the same tale, for they give soundings in some places of 200 fathoms on the east, while on the west the water is shallow.

The low white hills which project into the Seisaban plain on its north side are the counterpart of the hills round 'Osh el Ghurâb, north of Jericho, and are of a white marl, probably of post-tertiary formation. They lie unconformably against the sandstone, and mark the level of that great lake of post-tertiary times which once filled the plain of Jericho, and has now dwindled down to the present 'Sea of Lot.' The history of the various levels of this lake has been already briefly noticed in 'Tent Work in Palestine,' and M. Lartet and Canon Tristram have pointed out that the lake of the Eocene period had even then, perhaps, no outlet into the Red Sea (the Arabah having already a high shed south of the Dead Sea), as is supposed to be evidenced by the fresh-water character of the deposits and the absence of marine fossils. This, however, does not quite prove the absence of connection, but merely that the lake was not then salt, as it now is.

The general aspect of the Moabite mountains rising to the plateau is barren in the extreme. The sandstone varies from purple to a light tawny colour, and the ridges are divided by deep narrow ravines, far bolder than most of those west of the river. The limestone is grey and bare, sparsely covered with grass, and with the scattered retem bushes—the white broom which is called 'juniper' in the Bible, of which charcoal was made (Job xxx. 4; Ps. cxx. 4), and under which Elijah slept in the desert. One of these gorges will, I believe, be some day found to be the true Brook of Cherith, where the great hermit found refuge; for Cherith was 'in face of' Jordan, an expression which generally seems to mean 'on the east,' and certainly as yet no definite traces of Cherith have been found in the vicinity of Jordan on its west bank. In spring the rounded shapeless hills are covered with grass and wild flowers, and parts of the plateau are now sown with corn; but the number of trees in Moab might be counted on the fingers of one hand, and the district thus presents a remarkable contrast to that of Gilead, further north.

Another striking peculiarity of the land beyond Jordan is its fine water supply as contrasted with Western Palestine, especially with the upper lands of Judæa. The rain, falling on the plateau and on the Syrian desert further east, sinks through the chalk to the impervious limestone beneath, and running westwards along this bed, issues in fine springs about 500 feet below the level of the plateau. From these springs considerable brooks run down each gorge, even in the dry autumn, and form affluents to the Jordan, or deliver their waters into the Dead Sea itself. Nothing was more remarkable in Moab, when crossing from the Hebron mountains and the Mar Saba desert, than thus to find ourselves suddenly entering a 'land of streams'; but, as at

Damascus, it is only the immediate course of the stream which remains green, with rushes, reeds, and brambles, while the mountains above are as bare and colourless as though there were no water at all in the land.

The zoology of Moab combines features of that of the Judean hills with others of the desert fauna of Beersheba or Mar Saba. The vulture and the eagle occur with the pterocles or sand-grouse, which we found near Mâdeba. Bee-eaters and wild doves were common. The storks appeared migrating south in the end of September. Wild duck visited the 'Ain Hesbân, and the Greek partridge was common, though the smaller Caccabis Heyi was also found. The African brown-speckled kingfisher, and the common English species, both frequented the streams, and in the gorge of the Zerka M'aîn we found the beautiful grackle, a black bird with gold wings, first described by Canon Tristram near Mar Saba, and existing also in the Kelt valley, and further north in the gorges of the great Wâdy Far'ah below Nâblus. Four wolves came to our camp at 'Ain Fudeili, whereas the wolf is almost unknown west of Jordan, though I have seen one close to the river. Jackals and hyenas were of course common. The gazelle appears to be abundant on the plateau, and Goblân knew of the roebuck (probably, however, in Gilead), which he called *himri*; in the west, on Carmel, it is called *yahmûr*. He also knew the *bakr el wahsh*, or 'wild cow,' which he described as being the size of a cow (the cattle being small), with horns lying back on the head like a buffalo. It appears to be the bubale. The *bedn*, or ibex, also exists apparently in the gorges east of the Dead Sea, as well as on the west. Goblân's father once rode down an ostrich, but they never come so far west now, though the tribes in the desert, east of the Hâj road, sometimes capture one. The greyhound (*sluki*) and the falcon are still used by the Arabs to hunt the gazelle.

Our first camp at 'Ain Hesbân was one of the most bleak we ever pitched, but as the heat in the hills rose for many days to 108° in consequence of a scorching east wind from the eastern desert, while our companions experienced 118° in the shade in the valley below, we did not suffer save from the absence of shadow. The beautiful clear stream flows out of a cave, and forms a brook two or three yards wide running south. This, though shallow, has many fish in it, and reminded us of the 'fishpools' of Heshbon by the gate of Bath Rabbim (Cant. vii. 4), which gate we supposed might be the passage cut through the rocks at the top of the steep winding mountain-path from the stream to the city on the plateau above. The flat ground near the spring is covered with coarse turf, and is a favourite place for the 'Adwân camps. There are a few clumps of oleanders near the water, but the bed is clear and stony. Here all day long the grunting of hundreds of the Beni Sakhr camels might be heard, for they enter the 'Adwân territory when the tribes are at peace, as there is no water on the plateau, save in the tank of Zîza, and in a few small wells, until Wâdy Themed is reached on the south. Here, also, the blue-robed maidens of the Ajermeh, who are allies or tributaries of the 'Adwân, were filling their black goatskins packed on impossibly small donkeys. Here wild, half-naked boys drove sheep and goats to water with sounds like those natural to their charge. Here Ibn Faiz of the Sakhûr came to see us, and was introduced by Goblân as 'brother of Satam, whom my people slew this year,' a remark which he received with complete indifference.

Our first ride was to the 'Springs of Moses,' and to the range of Nebo along the lower road by Sûmieh. At Sûmieh and below 'Ain Hesbân are the mills, which were erected by Dhiâb of the 'Adwân in the year 1191 of the Hejirah, but there are much older remains in the valley, for its slopes are sown with dolmens, of which more hereafter. The ruins of a little monastery seem to have stood on a cliff south of the stream at Sûmieh, and there are sarcophagi beneath, and rock-cut wine-presses on the hills to the south. Thus, though now utterly barren, this vicinity was once cultivated. The site seems to fit that of Sibmah (Numbers xxxii. 28; Joshua xiii. 19), and the discovery of the wine-presses illustrates the prophecy of the ruin of Moab, wherein the 'vine of Sibmah' is mentioned (Jer. xlviii. 32; cf. Isaiah xvi. 8, 9). The study of Biblical topography becomes very interesting in this district, for forty towns of the old kingdom of Sihon are mentioned in the Old Testament, and of these at least twenty remained to be found when we entered the country. The border of Reuben and Gad also required to be defined. As, however, the Mishor, or plain, which was the lot of Reuben, was evidently the plateau called Belka at the present day, and as all the towns in the Jordan valley (excepting Beth Jeshimoth, or Sûweimeh, close to the Dead Sea) belonged to Gad, it seems best to fix Jazer, the boundary town, at Beit Zer'ah, north of Heshbon, the boundary valley being thus in all probability the present Wâdy Hesbân.

The name Moab is often applied to this district of the Mishor round Heshbon, although the Arnon was the old north border of Moab proper (Deut. ii. 36); but as the valley east of the Jordan and opposite Jericho is called the Plain of Moab (Numbers xxxiii. 48), while the later Prophets include all the cities near Heshbon as Moabite, there is no impropriety in extending the title as far north as Elealah; for it is evident that the sons of Lot gradually encroached on the pastures of Reuben, and extended the limits of the Moabite kingdom to the borders of Gilead.

Just above Sûmieh, on the north, is an extraordinary group of castellated crags called 'the Castles,' which we found to be entirely natural, though surrounded with dolmens. Rather higher up, at the bend of the valley, is 'Ain Fudeili, where Goblân has his summer camp, and here the flat ground south of the stream is called the Garden of Belkîs, a legendary queen of the Himyarites sometimes identified with Zenobia.

Riding southwards, we reached the so-called 'Springs of Moses,' which are under Pisgah, on the northern side. They are, no doubt, the ancient 'Ashdoth Pisgah,' or Streams of Pisgah, and the site is mentioned by Antoninus Martyr, in 600 A.D., as near Salmaida, and as called 'the Baths of Moses.' It is a most picturesque spot. The northern spring, rising in a shallow valley, pours its stream over a cliff some thirty feet high, down which hang long trailing creepers beside the water. The hollow below the fall is full of maidenhair fern, and a large wild fig grows up against the cliff. There are two cascades again lower down, and the rushing brook disappears in a narrow gorge, between tall canes and various shrubs. The contrast of this vegetation with the great blocks of limestone in the valley, the tawny hill above, glaring against the blue sky, without a tree or a blade of glass, is very effective. The southern spring, some hundred yards away, issues from a cave at the foot of a cliff, forming a fine clear pool with a pebbly bed, flanked by two aged wild figs, curiously gnarled and twisted, but with rich foliage. The stream breaks down hence in a rapid shoot to join the northern brook in the gorge. To the south a high mountain, quite bare, and of a drab-coloured limestone, rises steep from the valley with a ruined site on the sky-line. This is the town and ridge of Siâghah, the Pisgah of Moses.

The cliff of the southern spring has a cottage built on its lower edge, against a cave, and here we found, living with his family, a Greek Christian from Taiyibeh, near Bethel, who had fled, 'because of blood,' from the other side Jordan.

The ridge of Mount Nebo has been often described, and some have claimed to know the very spot on which Moses stood. Yet we were able to make one or two additions to previous discoveries, and as the view is of the highest interest and importance, a new description may not be considered unnecessary. The ridge runs out west from the plateau, sinking gradually; at first a broad brown field of arable land, then a flat top, crowned by a ruined cairn, then a narrower ridge, ending in the summit called Siâghah, whence the slopes fall steeply on all sides. The name Nebo, or Neba ('the knob,' or 'tumulus'), applies to the flat top with the cairn, and the name Tal'at es Sufa to the ascent leading up to the ridge from the north. Thus we have here three names which connect the ridge with that whence Moses is related to have viewed the Promised Land, namely, first, Nebo, which is identically the same word as the modern Neba; secondly, Siâghah, which is radically identical with the Aramaic Se'ath, which is the word standing instead of Nebo in the Targum of Onkelos (Numbers xxxii. 3), where it is called 'the burial place of Moses'; thirdly (and this was a new discovery of the Survey party), *Tal'at es Sufa* is radically identical with the Hebrew Zuph, whence Mizpeh and Zophim; it is the modern representative of the old 'field of Zophim' (or of views), in the form 'Ascent of Zuph.' The field of Zophim is, no doubt, the field close to the cairn of Nebo, and there are, indeed, few places in Palestine as well fixed as is this interesting ridge, whence Moses took his last look of the land he was not to enter. The name Pisgah is not now known, but the discovery of Zophim (cf. Numbers xxiii. 14) confirms the view generally held, that it is but another title of the Nebo ridge.

The view is much the same from Neba and from Siâghah, and I have thrice carefully noted it on separate occasions, although the autumn haze unfortunately always obscured some distant features of the view which are clear enough in the spring-time. Standing on the ruins of Siâghah (which are Byzantine and of no great interest) one sees down into the Jordan valley better than on the cairn of Neba, and the latter has the disappointing peculiarity that it commands no view at all to the east. The top is actually lower than the level of the great shed or western brink of the Belka plateau, and this ridge shuts out entirely the eastern view towards Mâdeba and sites further east. On this side the view only extends, therefore, a couple of miles, and on the south only four or five, for here another parallel ridge of equal height runs out from the summit called el Maslûbîyeh, although the peak of el Mureijib and the top of Tell M'aîn can be seen above.

On the north-east, the site of Heshbon appears on the edge of the Mishor plateau, with Elealah behind, and on the north the ridge of Neby Osh'a bounds the picture, entirely concealing Hermon and the Sea of Galilee. The view is therefore only extensive towards the western half of the circle, and the chief places were observed through our theodolites from both Neba and Siâghah. The northern half of the Dead Sea is visible, but the Lisân is concealed by the eastern ridges south of Nebo. On the west rises the water-shed of Judea and Samaria, while Bethlehem and Jerusalem and the molehill of Herodium can be clearly made out. The 'nest of the Kenite' appears on the south-west (Numbers xxiv. 21), and thence the ridge runs by Beni N'aim—whence Abraham saw the smoke of Sodom rising in the deep gorge—on to Olivet and Mizpeh (Neby Samwîl), while the cone of Taiyibeh (Ophrah) and the ridge of Tell 'Asûr (Baal Hazor) with its great oak-trees —remnants of an old 'enclosure' of Baal—are prominent objects. North of these again are Gerizim and Ebal, with the cleft between, indicating Shechem, and on the right Hazkîn, the lofty summit of 'Ezekiel's' mountain, and on the slope lies Bezek, where Saul numbered Israel gathered for the relief of Jabesh Gilead—a good deed which brought its own reward, since the men whose eyes he saved were those who rescued his body and that of his son from shameful exposure on the wall of Bethshan.

Tabor and the castle of Belvoir (Kaukab el Hawa) are said to be visible with the chain of Gilboa in clear weather, but as Carmel is only 1,700 feet high, and the ridge of Hazkîn 2,400 on an average, a very simple calculation shows that, even neglecting curvature, it would be necessary that Nebo should be 1,200 feet higher than Carmel, or over 3,000 feet above the Mediterranean, to allow of the place of Elijah's sacrifice being seen at all. The actual height of Nebo as now ascertained is only 2,643·8 at the cairn.

Returning south, the eye travels along the line of the lower hills and the Jordan valley. The mosque of Neby Mûsa (ignorantly supposed to be the site of Moses' tomb) is visible, as is the cliff of the Quarantania, with the dark groves round Jericho. The Sartabah peak towers above the Far'ah valley, and the black snaky line of this affluent (bearing to Jordan perhaps the waters of Ænon) is clearly marked. The Jordan itself winds like a great dusky dragon through the white valley, and the streams from the Jericho plain creep down to meet those which dash from the hills of Moab. The little island of Rujm el Bahr (the Cairn in the Sea) is visible off the north shore of the Salt Lake, whose calm oily waters sleep shining under the sun. This island is perhaps an old jetty, raised when the Crusaders or some other enterprising race sought to realize Ezekiel's vision of a Dead Sea made alive by traffic. The new Russian hospice at Erîha (Crusading Jericho) shines white in the valley, and the old brown fortress monasteries of Beth Hoglah and St. John on Jordan are now partly rebuilt, and entirely spoiled, by Russian money and monkish vandalism.

At our feet on this side Jordan we see the waters of Nimrim, flanked by tamarisks and oleanders, running by the mound whence they are named. Further south, the Scisaban plain expands, the Moab ridges receding to form a basin corresponding to the plain of Jericho. This is the old Abel Shittim, or 'Meadow of Acacias,' where the black tents of Israel were an offence to the sight of Balak standing where we now stand. The plain is yet covered with its thickets of the thorny sidr or lotus, and with the scattered 'oshîr, or 'apple of Sodom.' Just below us is the dusty mound of Râmeh, with bushes all round it, which look black rather than green. This is the old Beth Haran, and behind it is Kefrein, Goblân's winter home, with its hillock crowned by the tombs of his ancestors. Zoar, at our feet, is not distinguishable; but the tomb of Fendi el Faiz, the great chief of the Sakhûr, shines new and white. Coming from Nâblus he fell sick, and died within the territory of his enemies, the 'Adwân; yet, through the courtesy which Arabs never fail to show, he here lies peacefully in an honoured grave in Abel Shittim, the land of his foes.

Another tomb should also be noticed, namely, the Kabr Abdallah, shining on the sky-line to our north-east. Some have sought to connect this 'Servant of God' with Moses, whose sepulchre no man knoweth unto this day; but the idea is fanciful at best, for the tomb in question is apparently that of a Persian derwish, and has three more conspicuous monuments of the Ghaneimât Arabs beside it.

The general effect of the scene thus described is bare and colourless in the extreme. The distant grey ridge is hazy and tame in outline; the Jordan valley is white, with black serpent streams; the foreground is yet more barren. But we are looking on the scene, not, as probably Moses did, in early spring, when the hills were newly bathed, the sky blue, the luxuriant valley green; and we must not be led to express too unfavourable a judgment on the Land of Promise as he saw it from afar. The long reflections in the Dead Sea, the white marl hillocks round Jordan's course, the drab-coloured mountains, with shadows blue and black, are, however, the features which rise to the memory in recalling an autumn day on Nebo.

And now, having detailed the features of the landscape visible from Neba or from Siâghah, it remains to compare them with the Old Testament account of the scene visible to Moses, or to Balaam when he would have cursed Israel had he dared.

When we turn to the account of the death of Moses (Deut. xxxiv. 1—3), we find a description which answers well to that above given, with only two exceptions. The land of Naphtali (extending to Tabor) can be seen, and the mountains of Gilead, the land of Ephraim and of Manasseh, of Judah, with the Negeb (the dry or south country), are seen for more than a hundred miles. Jericho, the city of palm-trees, and its plain, is at our feet unto Zoar, which lies at the foot of the Moab chain. If we make the simple change of reading 'towards' instead of 'unto' in the cases of Dan and 'the western sea'—a change not forbidden by the meaning of the Hebrew particle—the whole account reads as correctly as that of an eye-witness; but it is certain that Dan (if the site near Bâniâs be intended), and the utmost, or 'hinder,' or most western sea, cannot be visible from Nebo to any mortal eye. It is a physical impossibility to see either, because the Palestine watershed hides the Mediterranean, and the ridge of Mount Gilead bars out the view of Hermon. The reader, then, must choose either to accept the very small modification of translation here suggested, or to attribute to Moses a superhuman power of vision.

Scarcely less interesting are the indications to be derived from the poetic vision of Balaam; but these may be better considered in connection with Baal Peor—for, in strict accordance with the Biblical account, we find that Israel, only partly visible from Nebo, would be better seen from Bamoth Baal and Peor.

We have not, however, yet finished with the subject of Pisgah and the Field of Zophim, for close beside the knoll of Neba we found, to our great delight, an ancient monument which seems to have escaped the attention of other explorers, namely, a dolmen, standing perfect and unshaken. Subsequent research proved that others are to be found on the southern slopes of the mountain, a little below the Field of Zophim, and another specimen, which has been overturned, occurred to the west of the cairn of Nebo. A great rude-stone circle was also found on the southern slope, and the extensive dolmen centre of the Maslûbîyeh is only just the other side of the gorge. Clearly we are in the presence of an old centre either of burial or of worship, and in another chapter will be given in detail the reasons for supposing that these monuments are altars rather than tombs. How strikingly, then, not only at Nebo, but also at Bamoth Baal and Peor, do these words recur to our minds, 'Build me here seven altars, and prepare me here seven oxen and seven rams' (Numbers xxiii. 1).

I will spare the reader my own reflections on these subjects. The facts are before him, and they are strong enough to speak for themselves. There are few episodes in the Old Testament so pathetic as is the story of the death of Moses, who had steered his fellows through so many dangers and through such woes safe to the border of the Land of Promise, and died when his work was done, leaving the fruits for others to gather. There are few incidents more dramatic than the tale of the wild seer of Pethor, restrained from cursing and compelled to bless, standing amid the smoke of the sacrifices, and gazing on the black camp in the white gorge below while the rude dolmen tables ran red with the blood of oxen and rams, and the words of his chant came without thought of his to the lips. Any paraphrase of mine would but dilute the beauty and the power of the ancient words, and each must draw his own reflections from the stories so variously appealing to various minds.

The base line having been measured, the Survey spread east to the limit of the 'Adwân country—a line drawn from Sàmik to the east of Medeba. Heshbon, Elealah, Medeba, Beth Meon were included, with the gorge of Callirhoe as the extreme southern boundary, but we were compelled to leave unvisited the palace of Chosroes at Mashita, and the mound of Dibon, far south of the 'Adwân limits. A word or two about the above places and concerning Zara, Samego, Shophan, and other sites, may here find a place; but our main attention must be given in conclusion of the present chapter to Baal Peor,

Bamoth Baal, the route of the Israelites, the grave of Moses, Callirhoe, and the plains of Moab.

The ruins at Hesbân, on the edge of the plateau high above the spring, are those of a large Roman town, but present nothing of special interest. The great dolmen centre on the ridge west of Sihon's city will be described later. The steep path from the valley leads through a sort of cutting which may once have been closed by a gate. This cutting stands out conspicuous on the sky-line as seen from the stream, and recalls the words, 'Thine eyes—pools in Heshbon, by the gate of Bath Rabbim' (Cant. vii. 4). 'The gate of the daughter of great ones' might perhaps have here led to the fishpools, which occur all along the stream.

Elealah, further north, is similar to Heshbon, with a great central mound. Of its ruins, as of all others in the district, detailed notes were collected. Medeba, in the middle of the plateau, was probably the largest town in the district, and remains of a fine church exist west of its citadel mound. Two pillars with an architrave block above stood before the west door, and are called 'the gallows of Abu Rôk,' after a powerful chief of old times, who is said here to have done justice. A colony of Christians, under the leadership of a Latin missionary, has recently been here established. We found the priest dwelling, like an ancient father of the Church, in a cavern, and the picturesque mixture of Arab costumes with those of the Roman Catholic ecclesiastics seemed to transport one back, in the dusky light of this smoky cave, to the days when Jerome was translating the Scriptures in his cell at Bethlehem. The congregation has been won from the Greek Church at Kerak, an ancient Christian community, no doubt tracing back to the times when the Franks built that great castle. The good Padre Paolo found them sunk in woeful ignorance, and believing that the Saviour was an ancestor of Mujelli, Sheikh of Kerak.

Beth Meon, a fourth ancient site to the south, commands, from its great citadel mound, an extensive view. On the north, Jebel Osh'a in Gilead appears behind Heshbon; on the east, the whole Belka, stretching to the low blue hills of the 'Anazeh and to the Syrian desert, is seen. On the south, Dibon, the famous town of the Moabite stone, is visible, with the gorge of Arnon and the low flat summit of Shihân, which preserves the name of Sihon. Kerak cannot be seen, and on the west the ground rises to the lip or edge of the plateau and entirely shuts out the view. This, then, cannot be, as some have thought, the site of Bamoth Baal. A more desolate scene than that of the Hameideh country, south of the great Zerka M'ain valley, as seen from Beth Meon, could hardly be conceived. The land is not so flat as it is to the north, and the grey or drab-coloured hills, the deep ravines, the shapeless stone-heaps, present a monotonous and dreary waste, like that of the Judean desert, a land well called Belka, or 'empty,' treeless and untilled as it now is.

More than one new discovery was, however, made during our survey of the plateau. In Sâmik we may recognise the Samego of Josephus. In Beit Zer'ah his Zara, and, perhaps, the Jazer of the Old Testament. In Medeineh, Madmen of Moab. In Sufa, the Shophan of Reuben. In Jemail, perhaps Beth Gamul of Moab. In the Tal'at el Heith, south of Nebo, Jeremiah's 'Ascent of Luhith.' In Minyeh, not impossibly Minnith, famous for its wheat (for there are plough-lands here even now). In Aleiyan, perhaps Holon of Moab. In Makhsiyeh, the long lost Jahaz. But yet more interesting is the investigation of the course pursued by Israel on the journey from Arnon to the plains of Abel Shittim, of which a few words may here be said.

The earliest and most detailed account of the advance of Israel (Numbers xxi. 13—20) mentions six stations, namely, Arnon, Beer, Mattanah, Nahaliel, Bamoth Baal, and Pisgah. Each of these camps would, on an average, be about four miles from the next, and each, no doubt, was pitched near one of the springs or streams of the country, except at Beer, where a well was dug (v. 18). From another passage (xxxiii. 45) it appears that Beer was probably close to Dibon. We may thus easily recognise Mattanah as the great Wâdy Wâleh, with its rude stone monuments and brook. Nahaliel, 'the valley of God,' is the gorge of Callirhoe, above which, on the north, stands another great group of both menhirs and dolmens, and thus Bamoth Baal falls into place as the ridge south of the stream of Wâdy Jideid, now called el Maslûbiyeh, or the 'Crucified One,' which presents a group of more than a hundred rude-stone monuments. The Israelite journey was thus in a straight line to Pisgah, and their camps were at distances equal to those which the Bedawîn accomplish on an average in their moves. Each great brook is mentioned, and the line is that which a large body of men must, of necessity, take, on account of the absence of water on the flat plateau further east.

The strange gorge of the Zerka M'ain, where the springs of Callirhoe still exist, was then the ancient Nahaliel, or 'valley of God.' It is not impossibly to this valley that allusion is intended where we read that God buried Moses 'in a valley in the land of Moab, over against Beth Peor,' for, as will be seen immediately, there is reason to suppose that Beth Peor stood on the ridge immediately north of the great ravine of Callirhoe.

The high places to which Balaam was brought by

the King of Moab, that he might thence see and curse Israel, were three in number, each sacred to a Moabite deity, each commanding a more or less extensive view over the Jordan valley. The first (Numbers xxii. 41) was that same Bamoth Baal, already shown to have lain south of Nebo, whence only a peep could be obtained, and which was 'a bare hill-top.' The second was that Field of Zophim of which we have already spoken. The third was the 'Cliff of Peor that looketh towards Jeshimon,' and whence apparently the whole host of Israel was visible in the plains of Abel Shittim. The first, then, was the hill of Baal the Sun-god, the second that of Nebo, or Mercury, the third of Peor the Priapus of Moab, who resembled the Egyptian Khem. At each site seven altars were raised, one to each of the seven planetary gods, the Cabiri of Phœnicia, whose aid was invoked against the God of Israel.

Whether we consider the Jeshimon waste west of the Dead Sea, or Beth Jeshimoth, close to the north-east corner of the same lake, to be the place mentioned in connection with Peor, it seems clear that this third ridge cannot have been far from the other two stations; and if the view was more extensive, we must search for a point projecting further west than the other two. Such a ridge we find immediately south of that of Bamoth Baal, in the narrow spur which runs out to Minyeh. The very name at once suggests a connection with Peor, for it means 'luck,' or 'desire,' and is intimately connected with that of Meni or Venus—the proper wife of Peor; while a legend of a magic well springing from the spear of 'Aly attaches to the spot. It was, therefore, a most interesting discovery to find, on the very edge of the cliff at Minyeh, a line of seven monuments of large stones, concerning which nothing could be learned from the Arabs save that they were very ancient. In each case a circle has existed, with a central cubical stone, such as the ancient Arabs used to consecrate to their chief female divinity, and each had originally a little court or enclosure on the east, where the worshipper may have stood with his face to the rosy west, the proper quarter of Hathor or Venus in Egypt—the home of the evening aurora seen behind the mountains of Judah.

The view from this 'Cliff of Peor,' which is over against Jeshimon, is more extensive than that from either Bamoth Baal or Nebo. It does not materially differ from the scene described already in connection with Pisgah or Nebo, save in this respect, that it commands a more complete view of the plains of Shittim from Beth Jeshimoth to Nimrim, while on the south-west the watershed, sinking from Hebron towards the Beersheba desert, is more distinctly seen.

Here, then, we may picture Balaam standing on the lofty knoll just south of the seven circles, setting his face to the wilderness of Judah beyond the Salt Sea (Numbers xxiv.). Hence he saw the twelve black camps of Israel abiding according to his tribes spread out like the black groves which fringe the Jordan's tributary streams. Hence Moab, Edom, and David's city could alike be seen. Here the rocky nest of the Kenite, never to be wasted till Assyria carried him captive, appeared as a peak on the south-western horizon, at the ruin of Yekîn, where later monks showed men the grave of Cain. Here was pronounced the doom of those children of Sheth who adored, in Peor and Nebo, but other forms of the 'pillar' Set, so sacred to Hittites and to early Egyptians also.

Of the extraordinary monuments of el Mareighât, further east on this ridge of Peor, above the springs and oleanders of the 'valley of God,' an account will be given in a subsequent chapter, and from the high place of Balaam's prophecy we may descend into the deep chasm of Callirhoe itself—the lower part of the same Zerka M'aîn, or Nahaliel ravine, to visit the springs where the diseased body of the Edomite tyrant (Herod the Great) was vainly bathed before his horrible death at Jericho. On the 30th of September we rode south from Minyeh through white desert slopes, growing only sage and the retem broom, and caught glimpses from time to time of the calm blue waters of the Salt Sea reflecting the western precipices. At length we reached the brink of the gorge—here some 1700 feet deep—the stream being, near the springs, still 1600 feet above the Dead Sea. Tawny cliffs of limestone capped with chalk rise on the north, and are seamed with gulleys, where the marl has been washed down like snow-streaks left in summer, beneath the cliffs. On the south, is a steep brown precipice with an undercliff of marl, and a plateau stretching thence to another and yet another ridge ; beyond and above this plateau (on which are the stone heaps of Machærus), appeared the shining waters of the lake and its western cliffs, fading away into a blue mist on the south. But the central feature of this ghastly scene of utterly barren wilderness was the great black bastion projecting from the southern cliff, and almost blocking the gorge—an outbreak of basalt which shows like a dark river in the valley of Callirhoe, as seen from the west side of the Dead Sea. It resembles the high spoil-heaps of an English coal-mine, and bears witness to the volcanic action which has made the springs in this gorge of boiling heat, and which no doubt accompanied the sudden depression of the enormous fault now known as the Jordan valley.

It took a full hour to reach the bottom of the gorge, and the scene beneath was wonderful beyond description. On the south, black basalt, brown limestone, gleaming marl. On the north, sandstone cliffs of all colours, from pale yellow to pinkish purple. In the valley itself the brilliant green of palm clumps, rejoicing in the heat and in the sandy soil. The streams, bursting from the cliffs, poured down in rivulets between banks of crusted orange sulphur deposits. The black grackle soared above, with gold-tipped wings, his mellow note being the one sound re-echoed by the great red cliffs in this utter solitude. The brooks (which run from ten springs in all) vary from 110° to 140° F. in temperature, and fall in little cascades amid luxuriant foliage, to join the main course of the stream, which is far colder and fresher, flowing from the shingly springs higher up the valley, and forming pools beneath white rocks of chalk, which we found full of fish, and hidden in a luxuriant brake of tamarisk and cane. The weather being very hot, the thermal streams were not smoking, but a strong smell of sulphur was very perceptible at times. Crossing three rivulets, from each of which our horses, apparently aware of the heat of the water, shrank back in fear, we reached the principal hot-spring, which has formed a ledge of breccia-like deposit in the valley, just north of the basalt cliff. Here the chasm is narrowest, and the main stream below could be seen winding among black boulders, which impede its course, with the dark precipice frowning as though about to fall, like Sinai in the ' Pilgrim's Progress.' The stream has bored through the sulphurous breccia, and runs in a tunnel of its own making, issuing from this hot shaft about 100 feet lower, in the gorge itself. Here our Arab friends stripped, and steamed themselves, sitting on a frail platform of retem boughs, over the boiling spring, which is surrounded with incrustations, white, yellow, or orange, of pure sulphur. Here we heard again the legend of Solomon's black demon slave, who discovered this healing bath for his master, and we observed remains of a channel, leading possibly to the baths, now buried beneath the incrustations from the stream. And of all scenes in Syria, even after standing on Hermon, or among the groves of Banias, or at Engedi, or among the crags of the Anti-Lebanon, there is none which so dwells on my memory as does this awful gorge, ' the valley of God ' by Beth Peor, where, perhaps, the body of Moses was hid—the fair flowing stream which Herod sought below the gloomy prison of John the Baptist at Machærus—the dread chasm where the Bedawin still offer sacrifices to the desert spirits, and still bathe with full faith in the healing powers of the spring.

From Callirhoe we returned by the plateau under Minyeh, where the grave of an English lady is still carefully respected by the 'Adwân chiefs, and from this plateau, which extends to the top of cliffs above the Dead Sea shore, the road leads north to the wide basin of the Ghor es Sâfieh, or Seisebân plain, the old Abel Shittim into which Israel descended from Nebo.

This plain extends to Nimrim on the north, and is the property of Goblân towards the south, and of 'Aly Diab. Near Nimrim it is partly cultivated with maize, but much of its soil lies fallow, with scattered groves of the sidr or lotus. Here grow the tall 'oshír shrubs, with their dusty apples of Sodom, and here are mounds which mark the sites of Beth Haran, Beth Jeshimoth, Kefrein, Beth Nimrah, and in all probability of Zoar. The white tombs of Arab chiefs stand on these mounds, or beside the streams which run to meet the Jordan; and looking east, one sees the three ridges of Nebo, Bamoth Baal, and Peor, running each further into the plain. The hummock at Siâghah, the peak at Minyeh, are each distinct against the sky-line at Kefrein, and we thus look back from Israel's point of view at the enchanter by the dolmen shrines, or at the venerable leader of Israel, taking his last look with undimmed eye at the western land before he sank to rest in the 'valley of God.'

The whole extent of low spurs at the foot of the Moab mountains between the Wâdy Hesbân on the south and Kefrein on the north is thickly sown with dolmens, and menhirs, and rude circles. Here, then, again we find these monuments, as before on Nebo, or its companion heights, still existing at a spot once consecrated to the worship of a Moabite deity. It was among the groves of Shittim that the daughters of Moab seduced the Israelites to worship Baal Peor. It was not on the 'Cliff of Peor,' a day's journey distant, but at some shrine in the valley of Shittim that these sacrifices seem to have been offered, and the occurrence of rude stone monuments, in each case, at spots which are identified, on independent considerations, as Moabite sanctuaries, cannot but be considered a very striking circumstance in connection with the history of dolmens and menhirs.

There is one more question which demands attention in concluding this sketch of the land of Sihon, for it is in this plain of the Seisebân that students have of late looked to find traces of the 'Cities of the Ciccar,' which were overthrown when Lot escaped to Zoar. It is probable that every important name has now been collected in the plains of Shittim, yet although Zoar may perhaps be considered as fixed, no traces of Sodom or Gomorrah were discovered by the surveyors. The cities were destroyed, blotted out, so that their names never appear again in the Bible topography, and Josephus believed—as some still do in England, in spite of geological evidence—that they lay beneath the salt waters of the Dead Sea.

Zoar, 'the little' city, might in Arabic be recognised as Saghîr, 'the little,' and as first pointed out, I believe, by the Rev. W. F. Birch, there is a ruined mound, called Shaghûr in the Shittim plain, near the foot of the Moab range. The name is perhaps as nearly equivalent to the Hebrew as would be likely, and the site is certainly appropriate. Zoar formed the limit of Moab (Jer. xlviii. 34), and of the Jordan plain (Deut. xxxiv. 3). It was not in the mountains, but in the lowland (Gen. xix. 19), and the site of Tell Shaghûr answers all these requirements. It is a whitish mound, about forty feet high, and one hundred and seventy paces north and south, by fifty-five paces east and west, stony, and quarried on the east. A little spring rises on the north, and on the east a larger spring is surrounded with grass and rushes. There was once a little hamlet about three hundred yards to the west, and the site appears thus appropriate for such an insignificant village as Zoar is described to have been. It is here, perhaps, that we may picture the trembling Lot looking on at the destruction of the Cities of the Plain, and from hence he fled to the cave in the mountains above, ' for he feared to dwell in Zoar.'

CHAPTER V.

THE LAND OF AMMON.

LEAVING on the south the valley of Heshbon, we enter a district at a somewhat higher elevation, draining north towards the source of the river Jabbok, which has its head-springs at 'Ammân (Rabbath Ammon), whence its course is at first in a northerly direction. We here enter the territory of Gad, which extended from the vicinity of Heshbon (Joshua xiii. 26), and from Jazer (probably Beit Zer'ah) to Ramath Mizpeh and Betonim (on the north), and from Mahanaim unto the border of Debir. This lot of Gad included the cities of Gilead and half the land of the children of Ammon, with cities in the Jordan valley, namely, Beth Aram (Râmeh), Beth Nimrah (Nimrîn), Succoth (possibly Tell Deir 'Alla), and Zaphon (or 'Amâteh). In the present chapter the southern half of this district will be considered, including Rabbath Ammon and the important ruins of Tyrus.

The children of Ammon no doubt originally owned

the country westwards to Jordan, but became subject to Sihon and his Amorites, or 'highlanders.' Israel took from them the western or more fertile half of their land, driving them into the desert east of their capital; but in David's time we find them again fortifying Rabbah (2 Samuel xii. 26), and at this period there would seem to have been a lower city beside the stream, and a fortress which was reserved for the final attack in David's presence. The cruel sacrifices of the defeated which are recorded to have followed the capture of the city are sometimes thought to have been intended, like those of Carthage or of Rome, as a thanksgiving for victory.

The site of Rabbath Ammon is one of the most weird and suggestive in Eastern Palestine. The traveller from the south finds his way from the bare plateau down into a silent valley, with a clear stream, running over a pebbly bed and flanked here and there with oleanders, while the cows and camels are cropping green turf in the flat meadow between hills utterly bare of tree or shrub. A great apse at the spring-head, with a modern Arab graveyard, first appear, and then a little Roman bridge with scattered sarcophagi on the right. Gradually the Roman city of Philadelphia comes in view in a gorge between hills some 300 feet high. In the foreground a fine tomb of Corinthian style, and behind this the ruins of a church and of the Roman baths. On the south a steep brown cliff, on the north-east the hill of the citadel, and close to the church or cathedral an early mosque with a short minaret. The ruins of the Roman houses and tombs cover the slopes, and the miserable wattle huts of a Circassian colony, here planted by the Turkish Government, are now perched above the ruins of the city built by the Antonines. Some of these poor exiles have seized on the theatre, living where wild beasts were once caged, or where gladiators awaited their fate. At this site, close to the mosque, we pitched our camp for a fortnight, and again in 1882 I revisited the spot.

'Ammân has so frequently been described, that little seemed likely to be new in our investigations. It is one of the finest Roman towns in Syria, with baths, a theatre, and an odeum, as well as several large private masonry tombs built in the valley, probably in the second century. The fortress on the hill, once surrounding a considerable temple, is also probably of this same date. The church, with two chapels further north, and perhaps some of the tombs, must belong to a later age, perhaps the fourth century. The fine mosque and the fine Moslem building on the citadel hill cannot be earlier than the seventh, and are perhaps as late as the eleventh century, and we have thus relics of every building epoch excepting the Crusading, of which there appears to be no indication.

There is not much to be learned from a study of the Roman town, but it is very striking to find how large and rich a population must clearly have inhabited this district in the second, and probably as late as the sixth, century. At Nueijis on the north, at el Kahf, es Sûk, and other sites on the south, splendid monuments still exist, which appear to have been tombs of noble families. When we connect these with the ruins of Heshbon, Medeba and Meon, and Dibon on the one side, and with the great city of Jerâsh on the other, with the innumerable early Christian towns of the Hauran (miscalled Giant Cities of Bashan), the endless Greek inscriptions of all Peræa, and the relics of churches found even as far south as Dibon, we perceive that, in spite of apparent barrenness, the richness of Bashan, Gilead, and Moab had been discovered by the Romans; and that, in spite of the Nabathean and other nomadic tribes on the east and south, a large settled population, represented even in the time of Christ by the Greek settlers of Gadara and its allied cities of Decapolis, spread over the plateau, even as far south as the Arnon, and converting, in the second century, the Beni Ghassan tribes from Yemen to a Christianity represented by the present Melchite church, held its own, no doubt, until the great wave of Arab conquest, under Omar, reduced Peræa to its present condition of ruin.

More interesting, however, than any ruins of past Christian times, were the early Jewish and prehistoric monuments, which we were apparently the first to discover at Ammân. West of the citadel, on the slope of a hill, we lit upon a very fine group of dolmens, like those of Nebo or Heshbon. On the south-west a single specimen of 'demi-dolmen,' perhaps the largest of those east of Jordan, was also found standing quite alone, and on the hills to the west and to the north of Ammân we found several magnificent menhirs, which seemed possibly to mark ancient boundaries of the city lands.

In one of those curious archæological notes, of which several are found in the Book of Deuteronomy, there is mention made of the bedstead of Og; 'his bedstead' (*arish*) 'was a bedstead of iron; is it not in Rabbath of the children of Ammon? nine cubits was the length thereof, and four cubits the breadth' (Deut. iii. 11). This passage has exercised the ingenuity of many commentators, and is generally supposed to refer to a basalt sarcophagus; but there is no basalt at Rabbath, while all we know of early tribes would render it very doubtful if Og was likely to be buried in a sarcophagus. The word may, however, mean a hut (as in Arabic), or, more probably, a throne, while it is not impossible that the word rendered 'iron' may mean (as in Talmudic use) 'strong' or 'princely.' The monument, in such case, would be Og's throne rather than his bedstead.

A memory of Irish dolmens suggested to me a possible connection between Og's throne and some rude-stone monument which tradition might have indicated as a giant's seat, just as in Ireland dolmens are the 'beds of Grain and Diarmed,' and connected with legends of giants. It was, therefore, very striking to find a single enormous dolmen standing alone in a conspicuous position near Rabbath Ammon, and yet more striking that the top stone measured 13 feet (or very nearly nine cubits of 16 inches) in length. The extreme breadth was 11 feet. It seemed to me possible that it is to this solitary monument that the name 'Og's Throne' might be attached, and I here give the suggestion for what it is worth.

In the valley west of the city, and again on the hill to the north, we found many specimens of the oldest form of tomb, such as was used by Jews and Phœnicians, namely, chambers with *kokim*, or tunnels for corpses, in the side walls. Immediately north of the citadel we found also a great underground reservoir, having at its mouth a concealed passage, which might perhaps have once led to the interior of the fortress. This passage may be that of which

Polybius speaks as being used by the defenders of the citadel during the siege by Antiochus the Great in 218 B.C. The secret was betrayed by a prisoner, which led to the surrender of the garrison.

The principal Roman cemetery lay south of the town, the earlier Jewish, Ammonite or Amorite graves are to the north and west; but we could not discover any traces of pre-Roman ruins at 'Ammân, with exception of the early tombs, although the citadel hill was no doubt fortified in some manner in David's time, sufficiently, at least, to make the assault no easy matter.

The beautiful little Moslem building on the citadel hill is one of the most interesting monuments of the town. It appears to be an erection all of one period, although the south wall has been injured, and perhaps partly rebuilt. The building measures $85\frac{1}{2}$ feet north and south, by $80\frac{1}{2}$ feet east and west. It has a central court 33 feet square, and an arched chamber leads back from each side of the court, measuring about 18 feet either way. There are four other chambers in the four corners, and on the north-west was a staircase to the roof. The total height is 27 feet, and it did not appear to me that there was any evidence that the central court had ever been roofed in. It is incorrect to describe the building as cruciform in any sense.

The interest of this building consists in the architectural style of its details. Each alcove, or chamber, opening into the court has a fine arch of peculiar shape, being very nearly semi-circular, but having that same slightly elliptical form at the top which can be recognised in the arches of the Dome of the Rock at Jerusalem, which would, I believe, if they could be measured carefully, be found not to be truly semi-circular.

On each side of the arch is a panel decorated with bas-reliefs in stone. These represent arches supported on slender coupled pillars. The arch in this case is represented of horse-shoe form, and decorated with a dog-tooth moulding. It stands on a sort of cornice, supported by three small sculptured arches, each with dwarf twin-pillars. Above the large arch is a second order of these arches also on dwarf twin-pillars. The spaces under all these arches, between the pillars, are elaborately ornamented with geometric designs, which have a somewhat Byzantine appearance.

The main features of this wall and arch are so closely similar to those of the Sassanian palace at Ctesiphon, and so unlike anything else in Palestine, excepting the Dome of the Rock at Jerusalem, that one cannot but suppose the 'Ammân building to be of Sassanian or of very early Moslem origin.

The Ctesiphon example dates from 550 A.D., but the panels at 'Ammân have been compared by Professor Hayter Lewis with details of Greek churches of the eleventh and thirteenth centuries, at Athens and elsewhere. The dog-tooth moulding is also found in Crusading work of the twelfth century, and in Arab work of the fourteenth, although not quite of the same character as that at 'Ammân. As regards the arches, the larger structural ones are, as already said, very slightly elliptical; the sculptured ones are in some cases horse-shoes, and sometimes round. They are not very carefully executed, and those which ought to correspond are not always quite of the same shape. Each of the smaller arches is cut on a single stone, and none are structural.

In 1882 it was discovered that a second building like that just described had once stood on the north, close to the outer wall of the fortress, but presenting no new indications of style. The question thus raised is one of considerable importance in connection with the history of Arab architecture, and with that of the building of the Dome of the Rock at Jerusalem. The existence of a mosque, in the valley with round arches, seems to show that the Moslems already were building here in or before the ninth century, when they first began to use the pointed arch; and as there is no distinctly pointed arch in the building under consideration, we should in the first instance be inclined to ascribe its erection to the same period.

Ibn Khaldun, the historian, tells us that the Arabs of the centuries immediately succeeding the Hejirah employed Persian architects to build their mosques, and Greek builders were also employed, as, for instance, at Damascus, by Welid, the Ommiyah Khalif, successor of Abd el Melek (705—715 A.D.). The Byzantine style will, perhaps, be finally found to owe as much as does the architecture of the early Arab period to the Sassanian style in Persia, and for these reasons it may perhaps be suggested that the Greek churches above-mentioned owe their peculiarities to Persian influence, rather than that they were the models which Moslem architects copied.

The outer wall of the Dome of the Rock appears most probably to be a structure of the ninth century of our era, its gates bearing the date 831 A.D., and the beams in its roof 913 A.D. The arches are round, and the same peculiarity of a large arched panel with a smaller arcade above, supported by twin dwarf pillars, is here to be observed, as at 'Ammân or at Ctesiphon. It is an indication, perhaps, of Sassanian influence among the Arab architects of the time of el Mamûn and his successor, and a valuable comparison may thus be obtained in Syria itself between the Jerusalem dome and the 'Ammân building.

The indications of date which are thus to be traced seem, then, to be as follows. An example in Persia of the sixth century and one at Jerusalem of the ninth, or early in the tenth. Details in Greece which are variously dated from the sixth to the thirteenth centuries, the later date being more probably the true one. An Arab mosque of the ninth century, or earlier, existing at 'Ammân, and a Sassanian palace of the seventh century at Mashita. The general impression obtained from such considerations seems to me to be that in the mosque and the two buildings on the hill at 'Ammân we have remains of the most prosperous Arab period—the ninth and tenth centuries, A.D.— when the great Abbasiyeh Khalifs were ruling at Baghdad; when science and art were being so eagerly learned by the Arab from the conquered Persian and Greek; when peace was established and trade flourished by sea and land—a period including the 'golden prime' of Harun er Rashid, the ally of Charlemagne, and the days when Baghdad, 'the City of Peace,' was the seat of learned societies of literature, law, theology, and poetry; when Arab grammar was invented, and ancient books translated; the age in which Islam was really great, and the Arab race really civilized.

To this age we owe much of our architecture, our poetry, our mathematical and astronomical science; and while Charlemagne was struggling with heathen and barbarians, it was the Arab who tended the lamp of knowledge, who spread the light through Africa and Spain, and who treasured for future generations the great discoveries of the Chaldean, the Persian, and the Greek, at a time when Aryan races were plunged in darkness, and when all that man had already learned seemed in danger of being forgotten.

The Circassian colony at 'Ammân is one of several planted by the Sultan in Peræa. These unhappy people, chased from their homes by the Russians, and again driven from their new settlements in European Turkey by the late war, are now scattered in the wilderness, where land has been assigned them to cultivate. They have, however, the listless and dispirited look of exiles who find it impossible to take root in the uninviting district to which they have been sent. Hated by the Arab and the Fellah, despoiled of money and possessions, and having seen many of their bravest fall or die of starvation, they seem to have no more courage left, and will probably die out by degrees, or become scattered among the indigenous population. Our appearance at 'Ammân at once aroused their apprehensions. They believed us to be the pioneers of a Power which was about to seize the country, and anxiously inquired whether they would be allowed to remain where they were in case of an English or French occupation. It was in vain that I protested that our work had no connection with politics. The Emîr begged hard to be made the confidant of a secret which, he insisted, we knew, and I was at length obliged, in order to get rid of him, to express the opinion, that whether French or English took Syria, there was no reason to suppose his settlement would be disturbed, or that he would (as he seemed chiefly to fear) be given up to the tender mercies of Russia.

It is from such incidents, not less than from the faces of the dead looking skyward on the field of battle, that a man may judge of the sorrow which is brought upon the weak and poor by the restless ambition of conquering races.

Leaving 'Ammân on the 20th of October, we crossed the bare brown plateau to the south-west, and descended into the deep valley called Wâdy es Sîr. The scenery in this, and in the other gorges near it, presents a striking contrast to that of the plateau. Clear brooks are running between lawns of turf, or breaking in falls over high precipices, hung with brambles, and green with fern: thick oak woods of most English character climb the slopes, and here and there crown a white chalk-cliff. Lower down are yellow, red, and purple sandstones, the peaks and narrow ridges of the marl just over the Jordan plains, broad wolds, dotted with trees and with dark Arab encampments, and the deep ravines, each with a narrow bed, in which the murmur of the stream is heard, but its course is concealed by the tall canes, or by the dusky oleander bushes, blushing with ruddy blossom.

It was to this valley of Sîr that the priest Hyrcanus retired from Judæa. He was the grandson of the daughter of the celebrated Simon the Just, the chief of the Sanhedrim in Alexander the Great's time. Joseph, his father, grandson of Simon the Juts, was a politician who had done great service to his country, but on his death Hyrcanus quarrelled with his brothers, and finding his faction too weak to oppose their forces, he retired to Tyrus beyond Jordan (12 Ant. iv. 11). Here he made war against the Arabs, and erected a strong castle surrounded by a lake, and having on its walls representations of 'animals of a prodigious magnitude.' He also made, in 'the rock that was over against him,' caves several furlongs in length; banquet halls and living-rooms are specified by Josephus, and the caves appear to have been supplied with water. These retreats were intended as fortifications against the assaults of the Arabs, and there were large gardens and courts near them. The name Tyre, given to the site by Hyrcanus, probably meant 'rock' or 'stronghold,' and indicates the cliff in which his caves were excavated. Here he ruled for seven years, while Seleucus was reigning at Antioch; but on the accession of Antiochus Epiphanes (or in 176 B.C.), seized with fear lest his cruelty to the Arabs should recoil on his head, he slew himself with his own hand, and his wealth was confiscated by the King of Antioch.

This account agrees in a most exact manner with

the character of the ruins still existing in Wâdy es Sîr, at the site known as 'Arâk el Emîr, or 'the Prince's Cliff.' The name Sîr, and that of the neighbouring ruin of Sûr, no doubt preserve a memory of the ancient Tyrus. A cliff here exists on the north side of the valley, with a gallery, about a third of a mile long, cut in its face, and a double row of caves, the upper, 46 feet above the ground, opening on to the gallery, the lower on to the ground. A sloping way appears once to have led up to the gallery, and the entrances to the various chambers are narrow, just as Josephus decribes them, while several cisterns are hewn beneath the level of the gallery floor. In the upper tier is a rock-hewn stable, with rock mangers for a hundred horses, and over the door of another chamber is an Aramaic inscription in large bold letters, which still remains a puzzle to the archæologist.

It may, perhaps, be suggested, with regard to this inscription, that the best reading would be '*Adniah*, which is quite borne out by comparison with Aramaic texts of about the same age, although the second and third letters might be otherwise rendered. Adniah would come from Adnah, 'pleasure' or 'delight,' and is connected with the Hebrew Eden. The inscription might be compared to the 'Salve' on Roman thresholds, and would be appropriate to a banquet-hall, such as Josephus makes Hyrcanus to have hewn in this cliff. It is a suggestive relic of the short-lived reign of luxury and pleasure which the renegade priest here enjoyed during his tyrannical lifetime.

At the west end of the cliff a single boulder is carved out, with niches placed in rows, such as are sometimes found in the façades of Jewish tombs. These, no doubt, once held lamps, illuminating the façade of the cliff in times of festivity. Looking down from the gallery, one perceives a terrace partly natural—a bank in the valley formed originally by the stream—partly artificial, and levelled as a garden or the site of a village. This platform is an irregular triangle in shape, the base towards the cliff on the north, and near the apex are the ruins of a hamlet.

On the south, about six hundred yards from the west end of the cliff, and at a level considerably lower than that of the platform or terrace just mentioned, are remains of a castle or palace, standing in an enclosure, which is at a somewhat lower level than the mound on which the building is erected, and which has on the south and east a kind of dam with a retaining wall. On the east are remains of a gate, and traces of an aqueduct occur to the north. A raised mound leads from the vicinity of the gateway to the knoll on which the palace stands. It seems clear, therefore, that the palace was intended to be surrounded by water, and part of its surrounding sunk-terrace or ditch is even now often wet from the collection of surface drainage. The south wall of the enclosure measures about 320 yards, and is 100 yards south of the palace. The latter measures 125 feet north and south, by $62\frac{1}{2}$ feet east and west. The east wall is standing at its corners apparently to the full original height of one course above the cornice, and the three courses have a total height of 21 feet. Two huge headless lions, facing north, follow each other at the north-east angle, and measure about 9 feet in length by 6 feet in height. Two other lions, also headless, and facing south, occupy the two corresponding blocks of the third course in the east wall, above the simple cornice. The palace had a gate on the north, another on the south, and at least seven entrances on the east. Traces of interior walls are visible. The great stones are drafted, like those of the Jerusalem Haram, and some of the blocks are 20 feet long and 10 feet high. In the east wall are remains of two loopholes, at different levels, and a stairway seems to have led to the roof. The details of the pillar capitals, cornices, and bases, present a rude approximation, in some cases, to Ionic forms, in others almost to the Egyptian. It seems, however, not improbable that the building was never quite completed.

A curious feature of the ruin is the occurrence of pairs of stone cippi, placed at intervals of about twenty yards, each pair three or four feet apart. The stones are about four feet high, each with a hole seven inches in diameter near the top. The holes are countersunk on one side, nine inches in width through half the thickness. These pairs of stones were traced all along the mound leading to the palace, and northwards for some two hundred paces, and there were at least seventeen pairs. Near one pair lay a stone 25 feet long, 8 feet high, and 2 feet 3 inches thick, and this seemed to suggest the original use of the cippi. They were no doubt intended to aid in the removal of the huge stones from the cliff or caves where they were quarried to the palace standing in the lower ground. The holes may have served as rude pulleys through which ropes were passed, and the stone, placed on rollers, would be hauled towards the pair of cippi in front of it. The stones being only a little over two feet in thickness, would, when raised on end, pass between the pairs of cippi, and the distance of twenty yards, though perhaps too long to allow of tree-stems being fitted in a sort of staging between the cippi, is not too long for a rope. The purchase obtained by passing the rope through such a pulley would, when the hole was greased, be considerable, and the stone fallen beside this line of posts, seems at once to indicate the use which they served, and also the unfinished condition of the palace when deserted by its builders.

This palace is called Kasr el 'Abd, or the 'Black Slave's Tower,' by the Arabs, and a legend attaches to it which will be mentioned later. It has been called by De Saulcy an Ammonite temple, and supposed to have been only in part the work of Hyrcanus. For this conjecture there appears to me to be no foundation whatever. The building is quite unlike any known temple of Syria, Assyria, or Egypt, in form. It was clearly a defensive structure, with interior rooms, like a palace. It answers exactly to the description of Josephus, and his account is the only one we possess. The style of the architecture approaches that of the tombs near Jerusalem, which are referred to the second century B.C., and there is certainly nothing in the Bible or elsewhere which would lead us to suppose that the rude sons of Lot, Ammonite or Moabite, or the Amorites the Zuzim and the Zamzummin who preceded them, ever erected temples of such unusual form and of such classic style. The archæologist in Syria is always tempted to give a greater, rather than a lesser antiquity to any important ruin than it can be shown historically to possess, and the Ammonite temple of Tyrus must in my opinion be classed with the 'pure Phœnician' work of Athlit, of Banias, or of any other Crusading site, as a product of archæological imagination which ignores the evidence of history.

It was a well-chosen spot that Hyrcanus here

adorned. The view to the south is extensive, Nebo and Pisgah, and even Peor, being visible above the nearer ridges, which are dotted with trees. The stream breaks rapidly down, forming dark cool pools under the shadow of the great oleanders, which have grown almost to the size of forest trees, reminding one of the groves of Daphne, and of the dawn-nymph changed into this dusky tree, with its blossom yet blushing red with Apollo's kiss. Surely it was the *dafleh* or oleander, rather than the poisonous laurel, which the Greek mythologists connected with the name of Daphne (the older Dahana, or dawn), and there is no flower in the East whose delicate tint approaches nearer to the flush of the aurora than does the great blossom of the dafleh or oleander.

Here, then, the luxurious son of Joseph lived in enjoyment of freedom and fair scenery. Here, from his caverns, he looked on at the Arab slaves dragging great blocks to the palace rising on its island in the artificial lake. Here, perhaps, he stored wine of Helbon in his rocky cellars, and beautiful horses snatched from Nabathean nomads were stabled in the cavern above. Here, finally, he fell by his own hand, and the silence of the wilderness descended on the scene of his cruelty and pride.

More than one interesting indication is afforded by the study of the ruins of Tyrus. Here we find drafted masonry, nearly double the dimensions of the stones which Heród carved, and capitals which bear evidence of Greek and Phœnician or Egyptian influence. We see that megalithic masonry is not of necessity to be considered of immense antiquity, but rather indicates a period when man had attained the ambition of executing great works, but had not learned the art of easily constructing them by aid of such cement as the Romans used. The invention of mortar enabled the architect to produce great results with much diminished effort, and buildings like the Theban temples, the Jerusalem Haram, the Parthenon, the Tyrus palace, point rather to human power still in its infancy, and to a rude civilization intermediate between that of the illiterate dolmen builder and that of the true engineering genius of Rome.

The inscription on the face of the cliff is equally instructive. It is in a character akin to that of the Hasmonean coins, and presents affinities to that of the long text over the tomb of the Bene Hazir, near Jerusalem, popularly called the Tomb of St. James, in the Kedron valley. The Palmyrene inscriptions of the second century after Christ present us with specimens of a later development. The Moabite stone and the Siloam inscription show us the Phœnician-like character of an earlier age. Thus we see gradually developing from the 'broken' character originally common to Moabite, Phœnician, and Israelite, that later 'upright' or square character which is now known as Hebrew. The uncial Greek, the Samaritan, the square Hebrew, are each and all descendants of the original Semitic alphabet, which we trace monumentally to the ninth century B.C. Square Hebrew is scarcely older than Jerome's time as a distinct alphabet, and the Hebrew points have an equally insignificant antiquity ; but the mystery of the origin of the Aramaic alphabet is still a question to be solved, although the researches of Dr. Isaac Taylor, and the discoveries of Halevy, and of others, have of late done so much to clear up the history of the alphabet. The Bene Hazir and Kefr Bir'im alphabets, in Palestine, trace back for us the origin of the square types to the second and first centuries A.D., and perhaps even earlier, confirming the Talmudic accounts of the parallelism of this alphabet with the older Phœnician forms. Scarcely less interesting are the discoveries respecting Nabathean, Himyar, Sabean, Pali, and Æthiopic forms of the same age, in the study of which the four Nabathean inscriptions found at Medeba, and copied by us in Jerusalem, may perhaps prove of importance.

CHAPTER VI.

MOUNT GILEAD.

THE previous chapters on Moab and Ammon refer to the district surveyed in 1881. The country north of 'Ammân, as far as Jerâsh, I was enabled to explore in April, 1882, through the kindness of their Royal Highnesses Prince Albert Victor and Prince George of Wales, when I had the honour of attending them on the first visit paid since the twelfth century by any royal personages to the country beyond Jordan.

In the present chapter it is proposed to examine certain Biblical questions concerning the sites of Penuel, Succoth, Ramoth Gilead, and Mahanaim, and to say a few words concerning the famous ruins of Jerâsh, thus concluding the geographical part of the present volume, from which we may turn to consider rude-stone monuments, Arab customs, Syrian superstitions, and Bedawîn folklore.

The tentative suggestions of a great authority

have a tendency to become established opinions among his disciples. It is thus that Gibeah of Saul and Megiddo have been popularly fixed at sites suggested by Dr. Robinson, but never shown to be appropriate. East of Jordan the important town of Ramoth Gilead has, in the same manner, become popularly identified with es Sâlt, in consequence of a mere conjecture of Gesenius, due to an equally indefinite suggestion of Eusebius, which is not followed by his translator, Jerome. As with many other cities once famous, the incidental notices in the Old Testament leave the situation of this town very vaguely indicated. Those for whom the Books of Joshua and Kings were first written knew so well where the more important sites of their country lay, that it would naturally not occur to a Hebrew writer specially to define their positions. All that we can gather as regards Ramoth is that it was a strong city in Mount Gilead, and apparently not far from the northern border of that mountain district, for it became the prey of the Kings of Damascus, and the Bashan district was ruled in Solomon's time by a governor whose seat was at Ramoth Gilead (1 Kings iv. 14).

Another indication of some importance is also to be found in the fact that chariots were employed in a battle near this city (1 Kings xxii. 31—35) by an army which came down the valley of Jezreel to encounter another army, apparently advancing from Damascus. Chariots could never have been driven over the rugged ridges of the Jebel 'Ajlûn, but in the plains of Bashan, in the plateau near Jerâsh, and further east, it would be possible to employ them. To reach es Sâlt, where Ramoth Gilead is generally shown, in a chariot, would have been a feat which no ancient charioteer is likely to have attempted, and still less any general commanding a force of chariots.

Ramath Mizpeh (Joshua xiii. 26) has been thought to be possibly identical with Ramoth Gilead, and also with the Mizpeh of Gilead where Jacob erected a cairn; but these names are both so common in Syria and in the Old Testament topography, that we can feel little certainty in the matter. Ramath Mizpeh was on the north boundary of Gad, and is mentioned with Betonim—a name which may survive in that of the district of el Butein, south-east of the Sea of Galilee.

The most probable site of Ramath Mizpeh seems perhaps to be Remtheh, west of Bozrah, in a situation which agrees with the Talmudic boundary of the Holy Land, which passed a Mizpeh supposed by the Rabbinical writers to be that where Jacob and Laban met; but although this district is one in which chariots might be used, it does not seem to be sufficiently within the limits of Gilead to be the proper situation for Ramoth Gilead. A more probable site for this latter may perhaps be that suggested by Ewald, namely, the village of Reimûn, west of Jerâsh and north of the Jabbok. There is open ground on the east, in the vicinity of Jerâsh, which might be reached from the Jordan valley by chariots following the course of the Jabbok; and the place is evidently an old site, for there are rock-cut tombs on the west. It should also be noted that the later Jews connect Ramoth Gilead with Jerâsh, and although this may not be a strong argument, it is certainly not one to be altogether overlooked.

The Mizpeh in Gilead where Jacob and Laban met (Genesis xxxi. 49), and the Mizpeh where Jephthah had his house (Judges xi. 34), presumably in the Land of Tob (Judges x. 17, xi. 3), may perhaps be the same. The land of Tob was, according to the Talmud, the district south-east of the Sea of Galilee, and its old title survives in the modern name Taiyibeh, which applies to a village in this direction, and which is radically the same with the Hebrew signifying 'goodly,' or fruitful. The most appropriate site for Mizpeh would in this case be the present Sûf, a village north-west of Jerâsh, and only some 3 miles from Reimûn; and it is very remarkable that a fine group of rude-stone monuments exists near Sûf, showing in all probability that there was once a sacred centre here. It is indeed curious to note how closely connected are the dolmen centres of Eastern Palestine with the early history of Israel. We have seen this to be the case at Nebo, Bamoth Baal, and Peor, as also in the plains of Shittim; Gilgal and Bethel seem clearly to have been places where menhirs once stood, and the group opposite es Sâlt may perhaps be connected with the great altar Ed, if, as Josephus clearly states to have been the case, this altar was erected east of Jordan. At Dan, where Jeroboam's calf temple was erected, dolmens are still found, and if Sûf be indeed the Mizpeh of Gilead we find a rude-stone centre also remaining at the Galeed of Jacob.

Another place of importance still unsettled is Mahanaim, where, according to the Septuagint, Israel 'saw the camp of God encamped:' to which David fled from Absalom, and where the sacred dance was celebrated which is mentioned in the Song of Songs. Dr. Grove believes that it should be sought south of the Jabbok rather than at the northern site of Maneh, where later travellers have placed it; and there is another indication which points in the same direction, namely, the identification of Succoth north of the Jabbok. Jacob went from Mizpeh to Mahanaim apparently on his way to Edom (Genesis xxxii.), but fearing the approach of Esau, he 'passed over' Penuel and over the Jabbok. It is not quite clear whether Penuel was reached before or after Jacob himself crossed the ford, but from the expression 'sent them over the brook' (verse 23), it would seem that the patriarch at Penuel was alone on the side of the stream opposite to that on which his wives, children and property were awaiting him.

Now the later name of Succoth, according to the Talmud, was Terala, and Mr. Selah Merrill has pointed out the survival of the latter name in the present Tell Deir 'Alla in the Jordan valley north of the Jabbok. If we accept this position for Succoth (and no better suggestion has been made by any writer on the subject), it would appear that the crossing of the Jabbok was from south to north, not from north to south, and that the intention of Jacob was to place a natural barrier between himself and the brother whom he feared. In this case Penuel must be sought south of the Jabbok, which may perhaps be considered to agree with the mention of the same place in the account of Gideon's pursuit of the Midianites, for Gideon passes from Succoth to Penuel (Judges viii. 6—8), and thence to Jogbehah, which has been identified in a perfectly satisfactory manner at the large ruin of Jubeihah, on the plateau between es Sâlt and Ammân.

Penuel signifies the 'face,' or 'appearing,' of God, and may be compared to the Phœnician term, Pene Baal, which was an appellation of the Carthaginian goddess, Tanith or Artemis. The pagan idea was the same as that found in India, where every male deity has his Sakti, or 'power,' a goddess who is the manifestation of her lord, and without whom he cannot act. The Hebrew name, Penuel, was, however, derived from the manifestation of the angel, or messenger, of God, with whom Jacob strove. We have seen that in Phœnicia the name 'Face of God' was applied to a magnificent promontory on the Mountain of Light. The Biblical Penuel would seem also to have been a ridge of some kind, since Jacob 'passed over' it as the sun rose. The place which seems indicated by such considerations is the high summit of Jebel Osh'a, north of es Sâlt, and although the name Penuel has not been certainly recovered, it may perhaps prove finally to exist. A valley called Fânch is shown on Murray's map, running down from Jebel Osh'a to the Jabbok, and this name would be exactly the most probable form in which the Hebrew Penuel might survive. I failed, it is true, to obtain any confirmation, in 1882, from the 'Adwân guide, who seemed, nevertheless, to know the district well, but further inquiry may yet establish the correctness of the title. Even if the name be lost, the identifications of Succoth and Jogbehah seem to point to some position like that of Jebel Osh'a as representing the ridge of Penuel, 'the appearance of God.'

The site of Mahanaim should apparently be sought further east. Jacob was on his way to Edom, no doubt along the old pilgrim road from the north; and in the account of the boundaries of Gad, we find Mahanaim specified as opposite the border of Debir, or 'the edge of the ridge' (Joshua xiii. 26). It would seem that these terms give the east and west boundaries of the tribe, the other places mentioned in the same passage defining the north and south limits, and the Jordan valley being enumerated separately. In this case Debir may be understood to be a general term rather than the name of any town, a suggestion which applies equally to that Debir or ridge (Joshua xv. 7) above the valley of Achor, which marked the border of Judah.

From another passage we learn that Mahanaim was near some plain which lay between it and the wood of Ephraim, where Absalom was killed (2 Samuel xviii. 6 and 23). The wood was east of Jordan, according to Josephus, and may have been one of those fine oak woods which clothe the slopes of Mount Gilead, and from which the Saltus Hieraticus of the fifth century was named, whence the modern town of es Sâlt takes its present title.

East of es Sâlt is the extraordinary crater called el Bej'a by the Arabs, 'the plain,' or sunken plateau, surrounded by sandstone and limestone ridges, and possessing a fine extent of arable land. Perhaps somewhere east of this plain Mahanaim may yet be identified, and over this plateau the messenger of evil tidings may have run to tell David of Absalom's death. The word rendered plain is *ciccar*, or 'circuit,' commonly applied to the Jordan valley, but also to the vicinity of Jerusalem. It would apply with much propriety to the round basin of the Bej'a, if we are correct in supposing the Wood of Ephraim to have been east of Jordan. The dance of Mahanaim (Cant. vi. 13) has been thought to have been a religious ceremony, and Dr. Grove suggests that this city was consecrated as the meeting-place of Israel with the angels; the translation of the verse quoted is, however, uncertain, and our English version reads instead, 'the company of two armies.' That Mahanaim was not near Ramoth Gilead we may judge from the fact that it was in Solomon's time the capital of another province, namely, that of Gilead (1 Kings iv. 14).

The brink or cliff of Jebel Osh'a commands one of the finest views east of Jordan. Here may be seen the whole western watershed from Jericho to Tabor, and far below are the sandstones of the lower spurs which run out into the Jordan valley, beneath an almost precipitous slope. Seen in the shifting lights of an April day, this wide view of mountain and valley which opens as the traveller reaches the edge of the cliff is wonderfully picturesque and suggestive. The distant ranges, faint and blue in the afternoon shade, the strange peaks of the marl at Sartaba and near Jericho, the dark line of Jordan, the green corn in its valley, the warm hues of the sandstone, the wild-broom and cytizus, the thyme and rock-roses, the thorny bell'an and bushes of arbutus and laurestinus, which form the foreground on this breezy height, combine to produce a picture in some respects not unlike one in the highlands of Scotland, and remarkably unsuggestive of the burning East. On the south the Dead Sea is hidden by a projecting ridge, but the plateau of Neby Musa, the plains of Jericho, Olivet, Neby Samwil, and Baal Hazor, are all distinguishable: over the valleys of Phasaelis and Far'ah are seen the Samaritan ridges, Ebal, Gerizim, Neby Belan, Sheikh Beiyazid, the Sartaba, Jebel Hazkin, with the isolated tops near Tammûn and Tubâs. From the Râs el Akr'a the Gilboa chain commences, and Tabor, Neby Duhy, and the site of Bethshean are all prominent objects. The Damieh ford (the ancient Adam) is distinguishable on the road from Sâlt to Shechem. The grey barren ridges of 'Ajlûn, whence Gilead obtains its name of 'rocky land,' run out on the north, concealing Hermon, and here on the sky-line stands the Crusading castle of er Rubud, one of the strongest of their chain of strongholds.

Close to this summit in a hollow stands the little shrine of Neby Osh'a, with a large tree beside it. Several other fine forest trees, oak and terebinth, are scattered over the range, and stunted firs are also frequent, but the forests are at a lower level covering the slopes above the streams, which dip down to the Jordan valley both north and south of this summit, but especially in the region north of 'Arâk el Emîr where is a great wood of oak and terebinth and other trees, possibly part of the ancient Wood of Ephraim where Absalom was slain.

The Samaritans state that the prophet who gives his name to Jebel Osh'a was Hosea, not Joshua (Hoshea); but whatever be the true origin of the present title, the fact remains that this is one out of the very few sacred domes east of Jordan. In Moab not a single ancient shrine appears to exist, save perhaps the grave of Abdallah near Nebo. To the north, where villages are found, shrines are more frequent, and near Jerâsh we have Neby Hûd and Bekr Elîyeh, but Osh'a is the most conspicuous and famous of the Trans-Jordanic shrines, and thus the hill is still a sacred place. The reasons which seem to indicate Jebel Osh'a as a possible site for Penuel have been already given, and it may perhaps be thought that the name 'God the Saviour' (Hosea) has some connection with the older title Penuel, 'the manifestation of God.'

In the valley to the south is the town of es Sâlt, dominated by a small Crusading fort, rebuilt of late years by the Turks, but still showing traces in its rock-cut fosse, and foundations with drafted masonry, of its mediæval origin. Sâlt appears also to have been a Christian town at an earlier period than the twelfth century, for there is a rock sepulchre in the valley to the south-east, which was converted at one time into a Byzantine chapel with frescoed walls, while some of the tombs here appear to belong to the same period—the fifth or sixth century. It is only within the last fifteen years that the Turkish Government has succeeded in gaining a firm footing in this district, which was previously independent, and paid no taxes. Once gained, the Turkish influence is not likely to be very soon lost, for a castle and a garrison and a Kurdish Governor keep the village beneath them in awe. Under the wing of the Government, missionary enterprise has extended even to this remote mountain district, and a Protestant school has been established some ten years since. The town stands above vineyards and pomegranate gardens. The flat roofs are dominated by the low minaret of the mosque, and a Greek convent is one of the most conspicuous buildings. There is a fine spring, called 'Ain Jeidûr, with a stream running down the ravine, called Wâdy Jeidûr, and in this name we may perhaps recognise the original title of the site, a Gedor or Gederah, named from the 'sheep-cotes' of Gad before the present Latin appellation had been given to the district. The Saltus Hieraticus, mentioned among episcopal towns in the fifth century, appears, as Dr. Grove points out, to be probably es Sâlt. In the twelfth century Sâlt was a stronghold of Saladin, and its fortress, destroyed by the Mongols, was rebuilt in the thirteenth century by the famous Bibars. It is now a town of some 2,000 inhabitants, including about 400 Greek Christians.

Passing north-east from Sâlt through the crater of the Bej'a, which is full of ruined sites, and over stony hills commanding a fine view of the grey chain of 'Ajlûn, dotted with dark oaks, the traveller reaches the great gorge of the Zerka, or Jabbok, where, between sandstone hills in a fertile vale, the rapid stream runs in an eddying course, fringed by tall canes and rushes. Hence on the north-east expands a plateau, green with corn, on the slopes of 'Ajlûn ; and, crossing oak-dotted hills, the visitor approaches this remote fertile basin, hidden in the bosom of Gilead, and sees before him, amid the corn, by the side of a stream falling in cascades

DOLMEN NEAR HE-SHBON

into an oleander-crowded gorge, the great streets of pillars, the triumphal arch, the temples, theatres, and baths of Roman Gerasa. More than 200 columns are still standing on this site, and the ruins of the city wall show the extent of the town, which seems to have risen suddenly, as though by magic, at the command of the emperor. It is strange that in this great city we find one of the noblest ruins of Syria almost without a history, for the rise and fall of Gerasa seem to be confined to a period of some four centuries at most. A town existed here in the time of Alexander Jannæus (85 B.C.), and its name is mentioned as that of a bishop's see in the fifth century, but there are no traces of Crusaders or Saracens, any more than of earlier Eastern races, although Baldwin II. attacked the place in the twelfth century. All is Roman, either pagan or Christian. The two temples, the two theatres, the hippodrome, and baths, belong to the second century of our era, and bear inscriptions including the names of the Antonines; there are also other Greek inscriptions, with crosses, occurring in a building which seems to have been a fine church. To the student of classic art this site, so unspoilt by the additions and mutilations of any subsequent inhabitants, presents an almost unique example of a great Roman city, yet to an Orientalist it has but a faint interest on account of the comparatively recent date of its monuments.

At Jerâsh we have a good example of the curious circumstance that the historic sites of Syria are very rarely connected with its most important monuments, or even with its most remarkable natural features. At Shechem, at Kadesh, at Bethel, or at Nazareth, no magnificent remains of early date exist. Baalbek, Kedes, Jerâsh, or even 'Ammân, are towns beautified by some of the finest Roman monuments of the Levant, yet their history is almost unknown, and their connection with Jewish or Israelite chronicles is of the slightest. It is in the rock tomb, the dolmen, the rude ledge where the libation was poured, that we see existing evidences of the old condition of the land in Hebrew times, and the cold magnificence of cities built to order by the Roman conquerors awakens no memory of the familiar stories of Hebrew prophets or rulers.

Travelling westwards from Gerasa we traverse a region whose rocks are bored with Roman sepulchres, and, passing by Reimûn, the possible site of Ramoth Gilead, and by Sâkib, on its cliff down which a stream falls in a long cascade, we gain the beautiful glens which run down from the rugged 'Ajlûn to the green valley of Jordan.

With exception of the woods of Tabor (now

sadly thinned), the copses of Carmel, the oaks of Harosheth, and the groves of Banias, there is nothing in western Palestine which can at all compare with the beauty of the ravines of Gilead between Wâdy Hesbân on the south and the Hieromax on the north. Beside clear mountain brooks the horseman wanders through glades of oak and terebinth, with dark pines above. The valleys green with corn, the streams fringed with oleander, the magnificent screens of yellow, green, and russet foliage, which cover the steep slopes, present a scene of quiet beauty, of chequered light and shade, of un-Eastern aspect which makes of Mount Gilead a veritable Land of Promise.

Sycamore, beech, ilex, wild fig, are said to be among the species of its forest trees, and the carpet of wild flowers in spring is more luxuriant than elsewhere. Clover and ragged-robin, the red and white cistus, clematis, crow's-foot, purple lupins, squills, the pink phlox (commonly called Rose of Sharon), the anemone, cyclamen, corn-flower, salvia, asphodel (both yellow and white), with vetches and wild mustard, marigolds, borage, moon-daisies, pheasant's-eye and cytizus, also orchids and broom, star of Bethlehem and poppies, tulips and buttercups, are among the familiar plants on these hills. The mock-orange (styrax), the may, honeysuckle, and antirrhinum are found in the woods; and the oleaster, or wild olive, is not unfrequent. The lentisk, which is so common a shrub (with arbutus and laurestinus) is akin (at least according to some) to the balm of Gilead; but whatever be the real plant or shrub of the balsam, the traveller who has wandered over the Moabite deserts, or the scorching plains of Bashan, will not fail to find that there is 'balm in Gilead.' In its glades he may hear the blackbird's note, the nightingale, and the twitter of many familiar song-birds. Here the tomtit, the hoopoe, the beautiful jay, the roller, and the bee-eater, rejoice in the shade of the woods by the clear streams; here the roe and the fallow-deer still find a covert. The visitor cannot wonder that Gilead should be indicated to the persecuted Jews as a refuge and home, and, perhaps, had Israel known what lay before them in the dark mountains of the west, it would not have been only Reuben, Gad, and Manasseh who chose for their lot the eastern hills.

But Gilead still remains a prey to the wandering Arab and the Turk. The Romans built cities, and made roads marked yet by milestones in these rugged ranges; but with the fall of Italian power the country has reverted to the primeval nomad, who seems destined to outlive each conquering race which for a time makes Syria its own. Without roads, and far remote from centres of commerce, a peaceful population like that of a Jewish colony would find but little opportunity for the development of the national industrious and trading spirit. The colonies would be exposed to constant apprehension of Arab attacks, and would live a life like that of the priestly Hyrcanus. If ever Palestine is to be re-peopled by the Jews, it will be from such a centre as Haifa or Jaffa that the colonies will most probably begin to spread, in districts where the population is peaceful and settled, where communication with the west is easy, and where commerce rather than agriculture may be developed with security.

CHAPTER VII.

RUDE-STONE MONUMENTS.

THE exploration of rude-stone monuments in Palestine is perhaps one of the most interesting features of the Survey expeditions, and it has resulted in discoveries and observations which may prove materially to assist the study of this obscure but fascinating subject. Not that it was a new addition to our knowledge that such monuments should be found to exist in Syria, for they had been already mentioned and described by Irby and Mangles, by Finn, Stanley, and Tristram, as well as by earlier writers on Phœnicia, by Palgrave in Arabia, and by Lieutenant Welstead in the neighbourhood of the Red Sea : while the explorers of the Sinaitic peninsula reported the existence of circles, which they believed to belong to pre-historic times. No traveller had, however, the opportunities enjoyed by the Survey parties, of studying at leisure a very large number of examples of these relics of the past, and nothing apparently has as yet been written concerning their relations to the rude-stone monuments of other countries, or respecting their affinities with the Arab stone erections of ancient and modern periods.*

The distribution of the centres where these monuments occur in Syria is also a matter of no little importance, concerning which the completion of the Survey of Western Palestine and the exploration of the greater part of the country east of the river now permit us to express a definite opinion. No dolmens, menhirs, or ancient circles have been discovered in Judea, and only one doubtful circle in Samaria. In Lower Galilee a single dolmen has been found; in Upper Galilee four of moderate dimensions are known. West of Tiberias is a circle, and between Tyre and Sidon an enclosure of menhirs. At Tell el Kady, one of the Jordan sources, a centre of basalt dolmens exists, and at Kefr Wâl, north of Sûf, near Jerâsh in Gilead, there is another large centre. At 'Ammân several fine dolmens and large menhirs are known to exist, and east of the Damich ford beside

* The principal authorities consulted in writing the present chapter were: Fergusson's 'Rude Stone Monuments' (1872), Sir John Lubbock's 'Pre-historic Times' (1869), Forlong's 'Rivers of Life' (1882), the 'Journal of the Anthropological Society' (1881, 1882), 'Indian Antiquary' (1881), Du Chaillu's 'Land of the Midnight Sun' (1881), Borlase's 'Antiquities of Cornwall' (1769), Le Normant's 'Lettres Assyriologiques,' 'Transactions of the Institute of British Architects' (1878).

the road to es Sâlt there is another considerable group. It is doubtful, however, if all these examples added together would equal the great fields of rude-stone monuments to be found in Moab, for it is calculated that 700 examples were found by the Surveyors in 1881, and of these over 200 were measured, sketched, and described in detail in a regular register of dimensions, while photographs were taken of the most important examples of both menhirs and dolmens.

The relation borne to these ancient structures by the rude-stone monuments of the modern Arabs serves also to throw light on the subject, and several interesting details of construction in the Moabite examples may also be noticed as not having been previously described in European examples. Canon Tristram was fully aware of the great numbers of the dolmens, but his journeys have been too hasty to allow of careful study of the various groups. He believed that cairns, circles and dolmens were peculiar to distinct districts, and that they were the erections of distinct tribes, whereas the Surveyors found cairns, circles, dolmens, and menhirs, all existing together in one district, and were able to point out distinct centres where the monuments occurred in immense numbers, while between these centres the country was almost entirely destitute of even single examples.

Before detailing the results obtained from an examination of the Syrian rude-stone monuments, it will, perhaps, be well briefly to review the general question as at present understood. Borlase, who wrote on Cornish antiquities in 1769, and Stukeley, and Sir R. Colt Hoare, are old-fashioned authorities enough, and many modern archæologists appear to have accepted the conclusions of Mr. Fergusson, whose dissent from the earlier writers is vigorously expressed in his magnificent volume on rude-stone monuments, published in 1872, wherein the Palestine Exploration Society is reproached with having found no dolmens in Palestine, although one example, at least, had then been discovered by the Survey party. Mr. Fergusson believes nearly all dolmens to be sepulchral, all menhir alignments to be rude representations of victorious armies, arrayed in order of battle. He dates Stonehenge as belonging to the post-Roman period, and will not allow any of these structures to be of pre-historic origin. The weakness of these conclusions may, however, perhaps, be recognised when we reflect that no single instance of sepulture in a 'free standing' dolmen (or under a stone table not covered by any mound or cairn) has as yet been proved, while so careful and scientific an authority as Sir John Lubbock has not hesitated to acknowledge Stonehenge and Avebury as pre-historic temples of the bronze age. The observations of members of the Anthropological Society respecting isolated menhirs outside stone circles have also cast much light on the question of the use of such circles, and the study of Indian examples among the Khonds, the Khassia, and other pre-Aryan tribes of India, is equally instructive. It is thus by no means a settled matter that all such monuments are to be regarded as sepulchral, and the remarks which are about to be hazarded will be seen to be founded, not on the obsolete ideas of the earlier antiquaries, but on some of the latest and most valuable observations of our own times.

Rude-stone monuments have been found in India chiefly on the west coast and in the central provinces, but also in the Khassia hills north-east of the Ganges. They are also known in the vicinity of Peshawur, and in Afghanistan. They have been described in Persia and in the centre of Arabia. They are numerous in the country of Moab and Gilead, and along the eastern shores of the Black Sea, in the Crimea, and on the mainland to the north. They have not been described in Asia Minor, but may very possibly still be found there, as they are also known in Greece and in the Morea. As we advance west, the number of known specimens increases enormously, the shores of Tripoli already giving several examples, while the Algerine dolmens are, perhaps, the most numerous in the world. In southern Spain they are known in the province of Grenada, and all along the north coast, as well as in Portugal. In Italy they occur only in Tuscany, so far as is yet known, although the rude Abruzzi mountains may perhaps yet remain to be explored. In the southern part of Corsica, on the north border of Lombardy, and round the Lake of Geneva, other examples occur, while a somewhat similar class of structure is recognised in Malta and in the Balearic Islands.

France is, however, of all European countries, perhaps the most fertile in known examples, but this is in some measure due to the attention which has been given to the subject in that country. Along the southern shores of the North Sea and Baltic similar monuments occur, in Hanover, Mecklenburg, and along the Elbe; they are numerous in Denmark and Sweden, and are found also in Prussia and east of the Baltic. In our own islands they are met with from north to south, but principally on the east coast of Ireland and in Wales and Cornwall, while in Scotland they are found both in the lowlands and highlands, in the Orkneys, and western islands; in Anglesea also, and in the north-west of Ireland, as well as in the Isle of Man and in the Channel Islands, examples occur. No doubt other countries not as yet known to possess such remains will be found in course of time to present new examples, as has been the case in Norway and Sweden, where Du Chaillu has recently described newly found dolmens; but even with such knowledge as we possess it appears clear that the dolmen-building races most probably belonged to some ancient Asiatic stock slowly spreading westwards into Europe—a course of migration which has been firmly established in the case of the Indo-European races through philological discovery. Rude-stone monuments have not been described among negro races, and the antiquities of America are of quite a distinct character: but, on the other hand, the existence of such monuments among Semitic tribes is a question of immediate interest in connection with the present inquiry; and it may perhaps appear probable, from considerations about to be put forward, that in the dolmens and menhirs of Asia and Europe we find the remaining works of an ancient stock preceding both Aryan and Semitic races, and belonging to the illiterate and consequently prehistoric ages of the use of bronze and of flint.

There are, indeed, two branches to the present inquiry. First, regarding the age of the monuments in various countries, and their relation to the history or traditions of the lands where they occur; and secondly, respecting the meaning and use of the various structures under consideration. These may be divided into seven classes:—

1. Menhirs, and alignments and avenues.
2. Circles, both of stone and of earth.

3. Dolmens, or stone tables, free or covered.
4. Cairns of all sizes.
5. Mounds, including cists or solid.
6. Barrows and sepulchral structures.
7. Disc stones, which have been found in Moab.

Each of these classes requires some preliminary description before the Syrian examples are specially considered.

The menhir, or 'long stone,' is the simplest, and perhaps the oldest, of human monuments. It is the ancestor of the obelisk, and no doubt the earliest method of marking a locality famous, whether as a sacred spot, or as the burial-place of a chieftain, or again because of some historic or traditional event there occurring. We should, however, be but half recognising the character of such erect stones if we failed to see in the menhir something more than a memorial. Students of Indian archæology will be aware that the stone lingam symbolizes something beyond a mere cippus, or monolith. It is an object of adoration, and even a personification of deity; and the living stone, which is inhabited by a divine soul, meets us wherever we turn in studying the Asiatic mythologies. It may be necessary to give a few instances of this original significance of cippi in various countries, but the student of the Bible, or of heathen antiquities, will alike acknowledge a period when ' all our fathers worshipped stocks and stones.'

Arnobius in the fourth century acknowledged that before becoming a Christian, 'whenever he espied an anointed stone, or one bedaubed with oil, he worshipped it as though some person dwelt in it, he addressed himself to it, and begged blessings from a senseless stock.' At the present time the inhabitants of Tahiti believe that even stones have souls, which return to the deity when the stone is broken. In Brittany the great menhirs are intimately connected with peasant superstitions and with marriage ceremonies. Some of the great groups of standing stones are traditionally supposed to be wedding-parties turned by enchantment into stone, and it is very remarkable, as Mr. Fergusson has pointed out, that the same legend attaches both to a group of menhirs near Peshawur in India and to another in Somersetshire. Dances are still executed round the menhir in the Orkneys by moonlight, on New Year's Day, and round the menhir of Croisie, in France. Other menhirs erected near water in Brittany are said to have been prayed to in times of drought as able to grant rain. Holy stones were worshipped in parts of Ireland as late as the ninth century. Maidens still lean against such stones in remote rural districts, expecting to see their future husbands. On the Stone of St. Fillan the sick were laid as late as 1798, expecting to be healed, just as the great Hamathite inscribed blocks were (till removed by the Turks) considered capable of curing any person laid on them. Borlase has conjectured that the same practices were connected with Cornish dolmens, while among the subjects of Queen Victoria in India, many millions still worship the local lingam stones. In Feejee the sacred menhirs are marked with cups and circles approaching those which have been found on the rocks in Scotland or the north of England; and Mr. Fergusson has collected many interesting notes of the late survival of such superstitions.

In the seventh century the Council of Nantes decreed the removal and hiding of stones to which vows were made, and such worship was anathematized a century earlier by the Council of Tours, although it is even now not entirely stamped out in parts of France. A Council at Toledo subjects the worshippers of stones to various penalties in 681 A.D., and Charlemagne, in 789 A.D., condemned trees, stones and fountains alike as being objects of popular worship.

The menhir was also in many cases the conscious witness of a solemn oath. Thus the Woden Stone in the Orkneys has a hole through which men passed their hands, and thus holding them, swore faith to each other—a practice recognised by the law of the island down to a very recent period, for in 1781 the Elders were specially severe on a young man whose character was held in evil repute because he had 'broken the oath of Woden.' This stone is eight feet high, and stands outside the circle of Stennis. In the Isle of Man the laws are read annually by the stone of King Orry, to whom grass is offered, just as the sick on St. Fillan's Stone are covered with hay, and as the Indian kusa grass enters into the ceremonial of many Brahmin rites.

The Greystone on the banks of the Tweed could marry a couple. The holed stone of Apple Cross cured those who thrust their heads into it. The Irish still swear by the Stone of St. Patrick, in Cashel, and the Blarney Stone had its prototype among the ancient Kelts.

Among the tribes of the Khassia hills (the relics of pre-Aryan inhabitants of India) the erection of menhirs continues to our own days. These Khassias burn their dead, and the menhirs appear to have no direct connection with sepulchres. When the relatives of any pious stone-worshipper fall sick, he vows a stone in honour of some deity or ancestor to be erected if the sick recover. In cases when the prayer is supposed to have been heard, and the stone has consequently been erected, other members of the tribe will make similar vows, and a group of menhirs thus grows up on a certain spot, while in some cases a pair support a lintel, and thus form a trilithon or dolmen. These are often found beside the grave where the ashes of the ancestor invoked are buried; in some cases a sort of turban is formed by placing a broader stone on the top of the menhir, and we have here an approximation to the turbaned headstone of a Moslem grave. The erect stones are, however, not in themselves sepulchral, though occurring beside a tomb, for in the case of the famous Breton menhirs, and in many others, excavations have been made without any trace of interment having been found at the foot of the stone.

The preceding remarks show that the worship of menhirs, which may be said to be universal in India, where the original meaning of the emblem is perfectly well understood by the initiated, still survives in remote corners even in civilized countries of the West. In Spain, indeed, we have an example of a dolmen enclosed in a modern hermitage of St. Miguel, near Bilbao, in Biscay, and of a dolmen forming the crypt of a church in the Asturias, and we are thus reminded of the letter of Pope Gregory, preserved by Bede, which exhorts the missionaries of the Roman Church to reconsecrate to Christianity the ancient temples of the land where the common people were wont to resort.

We must not, however, conclude that such stone worship is of late origin, for it is certainly traceable to the most remote antiquity, and is found as early as we have any record of pagan rites. The cippus was erected as a memorial probably long before historic times, and men swore by sacred stones in Rome or Greece, or among the Assyrians and early Semitic tribes. The erection of rude-stone monuments no doubt denotes an advance in civilization from the helpless barbarism of aboriginal tribes, such as the cave men, the dwellers in lakes, or those whose kitchen middens are found in Denmark and Scotland; but the entire absence of inscription, and the primitive ornamentation of these monuments, seem evidently to indicate an illiterate age. We must not, indeed, suppose all rude-stone monuments to be of even approximately equal antiquity, for in our own times we see savage tribes erecting menhirs and dolmens; and the bronze age in northern Europe, when writing appears to have been entirely unknown, has been brought down by archæologists to a period considerably later than that of the early civilization of Egypt and Assyria. But in this case the rude-stone monuments of countries where the arts and literature were first known become of peculiar interest, because when they occur in great numbers in such countries, we may perhaps infer that they belong to a very early period, or are at least the productions of an earlier and ruder people, perhaps dwelling amongst the more civilized race which had learned to inscribe its monuments. For this reason the monuments of India and of Syria are of special interest and importance.

Menhirs do not only occur singly or in small groups. In France, in England, in Syria, and in India, great fields of standing stones are found. Amongst the monuments of Scandinavia, some of the most interesting are the menhir fields which mark the sites of battles. These appear, however, to be only headstones to graves belonging to the early historic iron age, as, for instance, the groups at Kongsbacker, where a battle was fought about 500 A.D., which may be compared with the gravestones of Greby in Bohuslän figured by Du Chaillu. In these cases the stones occur irregularly without alignment, the dead being buried where they fell. In other cases—as, for instance, at Braavalla Heath—circles surrounded the graves, and a cairn or a single menhir stands over them.

These headstones of a later age are, however, not of necessity illustrative of the older alignments; for, as we have seen, groups of 'votive' monuments occur in India, and no trace of interment has been detected in connection with the Breton alignments. Mr. Fergusson has suggested that the alignments represent bodies of troops drawn up for battle (see 'Rude Stone Monuments,' p. 55), and that dolmens, in like manner, are not ordinary graves, but sepulchral monuments on some ancient battlefield.

It must, however, be noted that there does not appear to be anything yet known in the habits of existing semi-savage races, or in the records of early history, which countenances the idea that such representations of battles were ever erected. The struggle for existence in an age of war, and of precarious subsistence on the products of the chase, would hardly allow of men devoting so much labour for so useless a result. A single stone would commemorate an event quite as well as the lines stretching for several miles which are found in France, while as regards the dolmens it would appear more probable that works of so great magnitude, and requiring so much effort, were slowly and successively erected, rather than constructed as graves on an occasion when many men were slain in one day. So far as history can guide us, the fate of those slain in battle has generally been, either a hasty interment on the spot where the body fell, or a consignment to some great general pit or mound. We shall, moreover, see later that dolmens cannot be considered to be always sepulchral monuments.

The most famous alignments in England are the lines near Merivale Bridge in Dartmoor, and the Sarsen stones at Ashdown. In the first case there are two parallel avenues, 200 yards and 300 yards long, running approximately east and west (286 degrees). The southern has a circle near its centre; the northern ends in a circle on the east. The Sarsen stones occupy an area of 500 yards north and south by 300 yards east and west, and occur in three groups. The two western groups are in rude lines in an east and west direction; the eastern stones are very irregular. All the stones are fallen, and they vary from 10 feet to 1 foot in height.

The Breton alignments are more remarkable than the English examples. The Erdeven lines run in a slightly serpentine course east and west for 1,500 yards, having a tumulus at the east and another at the west end. The great lines of Maenec and Kermario run south-west for no less than 2,200 yards, and end in an irregular enclosure on the south-west. The Kerlescant lines, north of the Kermario lines, are more irregular, and terminate on the west in an enclosure with a low tumulus.

These lines consist of from eight to thirteen rows of stones, some of the finest being the stones of Le Maenac, which are 11 to 13 feet high. The northeastern end of this, and of the other lines, consists of smaller stones, more irregularly placed, and only about 3 feet high. Another line at St. Barbe has stones about 20 feet high. Dolmens, tumuli, and menhirs are scattered over the whole district round these alignments; and the village of Carnac, the name of which is best known in connection with these monuments, is on the south-east of the longest alignment.

It would be rash to express a decided opinion on a question which has exercised the minds of such authorities as Lubbock, Fergusson, and many other famous antiquaries for so many years; but a few suggestions may perhaps be hazarded without presumption.

In the first place, these magnificent monoliths are intimately connected with superstitious practices, and with peasant legends, especially concerning marriage rites. Such traditions represent in France the survival of the old paganism of the Breton race, and there does not appear to be any legend connecting the French or English alignments with battles, whether historic or pre-historic.

In the second place, the direction of the lines is (as will appear later) a question concerning which careful local observations would be of value, because it has been clearly shown that the pointer stones of English circles have a connection with the solstitial rising of the sun.

In the third place, the lines lead to circles or mounds with which they are clearly connected, forming avenues of approach, like the great avenues which led to some of the sacred circles in England. The larger menhirs appear to have been regularly arranged, as though all erected at one time ; but the smaller scattered stones may perhaps be subsequent additions to elongate the line.

In Palestine we encounter a kind of monument, in common use at the present day, which singularly recalls the general idea of these alignments, and which may possibly serve to illustrate their meaning. The modern Arab, it is true, is far too indolent to attempt any such exertion as would be necessary for the raising of a granite block twenty feet high ; but his piety, on the other hand, compels him to leave some record of his presence at every sacred spot. Thus, along the main routes of the country stone monuments are erected by Moslem pilgrims at every point where a shrine first becomes visible. East of Jordan these monuments have reference generally to the mosque of Neby Mûsa, near Mar Sâba. On the west they may be seen, for instance, on the north road, where the Jerusalem Sanctuary first becomes visible ; and there is not a single shrine in Syria the appearance of which in the distance is not so indicated along all the roads surrounding it. Often and often I have seen the stone heaps suddenly appear, and lifting my eyes, have always distinguished the distant white dome, or the minaret of the mosque, built above some place of special sanctity. These monuments consist of little pillars of stones, built up from those lying everywhere on the ground. Sometimes there are six or seven stones, the smallest at the top, making a pillar two or three feet high—a miniature and degenerate representation of the ancient menhir. The appearance of a field of such pillars is very curious; they are naturally only frail structures, liable to be blown down in winter, and many are fallen, but it is considered impious to move them, and pious to add a stone or two to one half-fallen. They are called Meshâhed, or 'witnesses,' and each pile testifies the presence of the pilgrim who built it. When a great number of pilgrims pass a certain point a large group will suddenly arise. In some places where no stones can be found, groups of sticks in the ground appear to take their place. The stone piles are sometimes also found round the shrine, or in the courtyard of the mosque, and the Jews also erect such piles in sacred places, as, for instance, in the tombs of Zechariah and of Simon the Just.

Similar piles mark the boundaries of fields in some cases, but these are easily distinguished from the fields of pilgrim monuments, which appear to have no special arrangement, but are erected just where the pilgrim stands when first catching sight of the shrine.

This practice, taken in connection with the continual erection of memorial stones in India, may perhaps give some idea of the meaning of the menhir alignments. They also may have been memorials of visits to sacred shrines and circles, or votive stones before the graves of the famous dead. Many may have been erected at one time in regular rows, others added later by individual pilgrims; but however this may be, there is no doubt whatever that the menhir is the emblem of the man himself who erects it, and that such stones were of old considered to be themselves the habitations of divinities. The menhir-raising races were neither children playing at battles, nor mere utilitarians without religion, and their greatest efforts were called forth by their religious beliefs and by their faith in unseen powers.

It is easy, as we have seen, to find instances of the very late survival of superstitious practices connected with such monuments, but it is perhaps more important to call attention to earlier examples, and especially so in the case of Semitic races. Thus, for instance, in the Bible we find Jacob erecting a menhir at Bethel, and pouring oil upon it. He came by night to a 'place' or shrine—possibly that where Abraham's altar yet stood—and, as any other pious pilgrim of the time would have done, he left his memorial stone, or *Metzebah* (rendered 'pillar' in the English), at the spot, anointing it with oil—a custom common throughout Semitic countries, and also found among the modern Hindus.

The witness pillar of Mizpeh; the memorial pillar over Rachel's grave; Joshua's pillar under the oak at

Shechem, in memory of the oath taken to serve Jehovah; the stones of Bethshemesh, Ezel, and Ebenezer, are familiar instances of memorial menhirs among the Israelites. Saul and Absalom erected each a 'hand,' or memorial cippus, and Josiah found such pillars at Bethel. On the other hand, the 'pillars,' or cippi, erected by the Canaanites, and connected with the worship of Baal, were destroyed by the reforming kings Hezekiah and Josiah; and 'standing images,' 'images of stone,' are forbidden in the Levitical legislation (Lev. xxvi. 1). It is possible that such a cippus was erected by the Philistines at Geba, and again at Michmash, for the word rendered 'garrison' in the account of Jonathan's adventure is the same translated 'pillar' in other passages. To strike the sacred boundary-stone would indeed have been a bold action on the part of the subject Israelite youth (1 Samuel xiii. 3), and might well be the cause of an outbreak; but even if this be not the correct interpretation of the episode in question, the sacred character of the 'pillar' among Israelities and Canaanites alike is sufficiently illustrated by the other passages quoted.

The oiled stones worshipped by Arnobius have already been mentioned. At Tyre two stones called ambrosial were believed to exist under the sea: they are mentioned by Pausanias, and represented on Tyrian coins. Sanchoniathon, the Phœnician, speaks of the Bætuli, which were stones believed to be Bethels, or 'houses of God,' inhabited by a divine soul, and at Seleucia were the 'lapides qui divi dicuntur.' The famous black conical stone of Emesa was carried in procession by Elagabalus at Rome, as an emblem of the Sun-god; and the conical stone was sacred to Venus in Cyprus. At Pharæ, in Achaia, were thirty stones which represented Hermes, and among the Greeks long stones appear to have been sacred to this ancient Moon-god, and cubical stones to the mother Goddess, Cybele. Yet earlier at Uruk the seven black stones typified the seven chief gods—the mystic planetary Cabiri or 'great ones.'

Yet more important to our present inquiry is the stone-worship of the Arabs in the 'times of ignorance,' before the preaching of Islam. Thus, at Mecca we have the famous shrine which Muhammed only half abolished, leaving the holy stone, but removing the wooden dove and other images. The 'black stone' is about seven inches by four inches in measurement, and the surface is covered with depressions, said to be due to the kisses of the devout. A red stone, said to have been brought from the Belka (Moab), or even from Babylon, accompanied the black stone. The former appears to have been dedicated to Allât, the Venus or Mother Goddess of Arabia, and the red stone to Hobal, the male god of Fate. Moslem writers also state that (as at Uruk) seven stones surrounded the shrine, on which bloody sacrifices (apparently human) were offered, the stones being thus anointed with blood instead of with oil. Herodotus (iii. 8) speaks also of the seven stones by which the Arabs swore, and old Arab poems mention the practice of swearing by the blood on 'Aûd, and the sacred stones of S'air: the former name means 'the substitute' and the latter 'flame' or 'fire.' The Nabatheans at Petra worshipped a black stone about four feet high and two feet square, called Dhu Sher'a, or 'Lord of Desire.'

The chief Arab sanctuary at Taif contained a white cubical stone sacred to Allât, the Mother Goddess. On the hills of Safa and Merwah, near Mecca, stood the stones which represented the petrified lovers Asâf and Nâila,* and the stone Khalisah (or 'purity') was in the valley between them. In the valley of Mena (or 'desire'), in the same district, there were originally seven stones, of which three remain; and the pilgrims who return from Mount 'Arafat ('knowledge') still throw ten stones at each of these monu-

* Asâf appears to mean 'the cleaver'; he was son of Soheil or Canopus; he was also called Nahîk, 'the afflicted.' Nâila is translated 'she who embraces,' and she was the daughter of Dîk, 'the cock.' She is also called 'the nourisher of the bird.' These lovers are said to have desecrated the Kaaba (like Neptune and Medusa), and were consequently turned to stone. El Khâlisah appears to have been the Arab Venus. The Ansâb or Menhirs are specially condemned in the Kor'an (Sura, v. 92).

ments, in memory of the defeat of Iblis by Abraham, when he was tempted to offer Ishmael as a sacrifice. St. Porphyry writing in the fifth century tells us that the Arabs of Dumah used annually to sacrifice a child, and bury it at the foot of a sacred cippus. We see, therefore, that among the early Arabs, as among Assyrians and Phœnicians, the menhir was a sacred emblem, supposed to be the habitation of a deity, who was appeased by libations of oil or of blood poured or smeared upon the stone.

From menhirs we naturally pass to the consideration of circles composed of standing stones, and of bilithons, trilithons, and menhirs enclosed in circles; but before so doing there is one peculiarity connected with menhirs and dolmens which is worthy of notice, namely, their connection with water. Du Chaillu has remarked on the occurrence of rude-stone monuments beside rivers in Sweden; and among the Celtic races menhirs occur near springs, wells, ponds and swamps, and were prayed to for rain. The Tyre stones were under the sea, and east of Jordan the centres appear invariably to be connected with fine spring heads: where there are no streams no menhirs are found. Many explanations might be offered of this circumstance, for rude tribes would not have wandered far from water, and whether as habitations, tombs, or sacred places, the connection is not unnatural between their monuments and the water supply, but it must also not be forgotten that living water is extremely sacred in the eyes of all Asiatics, and that the genii of the springs had their shrines down to the very latest pagan times. Further observations on this connection, and also concerning the shapes of the mountains, and the distant views at centres where dolmens and menhirs are found, might probably lead to interesting results.

The great earthen circular mounds, from 100 to 300 feet in diameter, found at Stonehenge, Avebury, Penrith, Arbor Lowe, and other places, are said by Mr. Fergusson to be almost peculiar to England, although there is one at Brogar, in the Orkneys. They sometimes (as at Stonehenge) enclose rude-stone circles, and there is no doubt that in some cases they were meeting-places for the dealing of Justice, Motes or Things, like the circle of Fiddes Hill, which has a sort of raised daïs on one side, and where a court was held as late as 1349. In Ireland a stone mound 300 feet in diameter surrounds graves which contained unburned bones; but no remains have been found within the great circles of Avebury or Stonehenge, although the latter is surrounded with barrows of the bronze age, while outside the circle of Hakpen Hill many rows of skeletons were discovered, lying with their feet towards the circle. At Crichie, in Scotland, sepulchral deposits existed within a circle, at the foot of each stone composing it. The Stonehenge barrows appear to have been shown to be of later date than the great monument itself, and at Arbor Lowe tumuli of the bronze period also occur outside the sacred circle.

Such instances seem to show that in our own islands some circular enclosures] are sepulchral, and that others are centres round which extensive and ancient cemeteries have gathered, and which may thus fairly be thought to have been once venerated sanctuaries, near which the Celtic barrow-burying tribes interred their dead; just as the Jew, the Moslem, the Christian, or the Hindu desires to be entombed close beside some sacred temple of his faith. There is, however, another feature of the Celtic circles which has of late attracted the attention of antiquaries, and promises to lead to important conclusions. In the case of many British circles a single menhir has been found standing outside the circle, on the north-east, or at angle five degrees east of north-east, the bearing being taken from the centre of the circle. This direction approximately agrees with that of the rising of the sun at midsummer, as seen from the middle of the circle. It has been proved by repeated actual observation that any person sitting in the middle of the altar-stone in Stonehenge circle will see the sun on midsummer-day rising behind the 'Friar's Heel,' a stone on the outer ditch, towards the north-east. At Avebury, the

Ring-stone, on the other hand, appears to have a similar relation to the southern circle, but points to the rising of the sun at the midwinter solstice, while the Kennet avenue has the same relation to the great outer circle at the same site. Such pointer-stones occur in many other instances, as, for example, at Rollrich, where the King-stone stands outside, on the north-east, as does the Hautville's Quoit-stone at Stanton Drew; and the stone on Stapeley Hill has the same relation to the circle of Michell's Fold, in Shropshire. There are instances in which a menhir also occupies the centre of the circle, and at Arbor Lowe there is a central dolmen. At Brogar the dolmen is on or near the circumference, and the same arrangement is found at Stanton Drew. The position of the Watch-stone in the Stennis circle answers to that of Hautville's Quoit above noticed. Long Meg, at Penrith, is a menhir twelve feet high, outside the circle of her sixty-eight daughters; but on Stanton Moor the King-stone is westwards of the circle of the Nine Ladies. There are, however, several circles in this vicinity. The circle of the Grey Yawds, near Cumrew and Penrith, consisting of eighty-eight stones, has an outer menhir answering to Long Meg.

The subject of the relations of circles and solitary stones has perhaps as yet not been sufficiently studied, and the position of circumferential dolmens is also (as we shall see later) a matter of great interest; but the investigations of members of the Anthropological Society during the years 1881-82 seem to leave little doubt as to the fact that in many cases the pointer-stone indicates the direction of sunrise at either the winter or the summer solstice, while in other cases the sunset is also marked in the same manner.

The builders of rude-stone monuments were, as we have before noticed, not mere savages, but early migrants of the later stone and bronze ages. It is well known how much attention was paid by the Aryan pastoral tribes, no less than by the nomads of Semitic stock entering Chaldea from the south, to the phenomena connected with the sun's path throughout the year. The Rita, or Asha, probably also the Egyptian Ma, were originally but the unerring course of the great luminary in winter and summer, by day and night. The Persians (following probably the earlier Accadian and Sumerian sunworshippers) believe that the boundary mountain, Alborz, had a hundred and eighty apertures, through each of which the sun rose successively; and this idea is borrowed in the later Book of Enoch. It can be traced back to a time when the Aryans were dwelling no further south than 49° 20′ north latitude, or north of the Caspian, and no doubt roughly corresponds with an amplitude of 90°, the sun rising in the north-east in summer, and the south-east in winter. It is evident that the solstitial rather than the equinoctial rising would be the first to be observed by rude tribes, for the sun could at these times be seen to retrace his course on the horizon, as noted in connection with any definite point—tree, stone, or cairn.

The return northwards heralded the commencement of a more favourable season, the escape from cold and famine, the approach of spring with its gifts of herbage, and new-born increase of the herd and flock. Little need we wonder, then, that in days when calendars were unknown, when the certainty of revolving seasons even was not yet a matter beyond dispute, and when time was measured only by days and nights, the shepherds and primitive agriculturists looked anxiously for the time when the wintry sun should begin to retrace his course, or marked with apprehension his return southwards on the horizon—little need we marvel that they erected monuments which could serve as rude means of measuring the movement of the sacred orb, and specially indicated the furthest points north and south of the true east, which the sun was observed annually to reach in the new latitude of the immigrants' new home.

Thus far, we have considered the sepulchral and astronomical relations of British circles only, as well as their connection with the administration of justice. The same conclusions will be found to present themselves in glancing at the sacred enclosures of other lands. It is, however, interesting to note that in the examples already quoted, the external pointer bears generally a male name, while the circle is female—a group of ladies or daughters, with a king beside them.

The Khonds in Eastern India, remnants of the Dravidians or pre-Aryan populations, are a people whose rites are said still to include human sacrifice, and who worship in groves or on hill-tops, by streams and springs. They have been found to use circles in connection with the worship of the rising sun, the tallest member of the circle being towards the east. The worshipper perambulates the circle with the sun, and sprinkles the stones with the blood of a cock (as I am informed by Mr. W. Morrison), and we shall find later a somewhat parallel case among the modern Arabs of Moab. In Western India circles also occur, with a graduation of size from a central stone, and this central stone is the local lingam, or male deity, to whom a cock is sacrificed, as mentioned by Mr. Fergusson.

Sepulchral circles also occur in India, as, for instance, at Amravati, and in the Nilgiri hills. In these cases the circle is the enclosure which hallows the tomb, and not the tomb itself, which is a cist or trench inside, just as will be described among the Arabs. In the dark ages we must remember the magic circle protected the enchanter—whether of Semitic or Aryan race—from the power of external demons. At Shahpoor, Colonel Meadows Taylor found circles connected by alignments running east and west, and the tumuli of Algeria have similar connecting lines of stones.

Mr. Fergusson believes the rude-stone monuments of Moytura to mark the sepulchral sites of ancient battlefields, but his evidence tells curiously in favour of a connection with early solar mythology. As the battles were supposed to occur 1,900 years before Christ, and as the authorities quoted (the 'Annals of the Four Masters') belong to the seventeenth century of our era, the evidence of the historical occurrence of the battles cannot be said to be contemporary. When, moreover, we note that the battle was fought on midsummer-day, and that a king with a silver hand took his share in the fight, we at once recognise the mythical element. In India we have the gold-handed Savitar, and Hobal at Mecca had an arm of gold. The gold or silver hand is a well-known emblem of the sun—the great workman of heaven; and the battles of Moytura, like those of Arthur, are probably but Celtic versions of the ceaseless conflict of Indra with his enemies. Enclosures containing menhirs and dolmens may in some cases be sepulchral, but in others they are certainly not so, and such an enclosure as that at Luneberg appears to bear a close resemblance to the Dravidian circles of India with their sacred lingam stones.

It is quite possible that the Tara circle in Ireland may date as late as the fifth century, but it should not be forgotten that we have much earlier notices of stone circles in Asia, as, for instance, at Gilgal or under Sinai, and in these cases the enclosures are not connected with sepulture. Moses is related in Exodus (xxiv. 4) to have built an altar under the hill, and to have erected twelve menhirs, or pillars. The altar was sprinkled with blood, as was the congregation of worshippers. The name Gilgal appears to imply a circle, and applied to several sites, all apparently sacred centres. At one Gilgal were 'pitched' the twelve stones from Jordan (Joshua iv. 20), which were emblems of the twelve tribes, and as late as Samuel's time Gilgal was a place where justice was dealt by the judge, while some translators have even suggested that when Samuel is represented as going 'in circuit' to Bethel, Gilgal, and Mizpeh (1 Samuel vii. 16), the real meaning is that he perambulated or walked in procession round the sacred enclosures at these three shrines.

From the consideration of the menhirs, whether

alone or in alignments, circles and other groupings, we must now pass to that of monuments consisting of more than single stones. We have seen that the Khassia tribes in the north-east of India erect trilithons as well as menhirs as votive offerings to gods and ancestors. In the talyots of the Balearic Islands we have an even simpler erection, a T-shaped monument, or bilithon, made by placing a large flat stone on a single erect one; but generally speaking, wherever the menhir is found the trilithon also occurs, and the Stonehenge example finds an almost exact parallel in the great trilithons discovered by Palgrave near Eyûn, in Arabia.

The term 'cromlech,' or 'round stone,' is sometimes applied to this class of monument, though perhaps more correctly to circles of menhirs. The word 'dolmen,' usually rendered 'table-stone,' should, according to Max Müller, be translated 'holed stone,' implying either a gateway, such as is formed by the trilithon, or else applying to menhirs and dolmens pierced with a hole, as in the cases of the Ring-stone, the Odin-stone, and in a peculiar class of holed dolmens.

It is evident that an erection of two or more stones, with a flat stone roof or table above, may have had several uses. It might be an altar, a tomb, or a dwelling-house; and chambers of great size are formed under mounds by parallel rows of great stones, roofed with flat flags. The earliest architectural efforts of mankind are represented by this piling-up of drystone monuments, consisting of blocks sometimes quite unshaped, but in other cases rudely hewn, and even ornamented with rough sculpture. In the case of dolmens, we have to consider not only trilithons and stone boxes of four, five, and six stones, but also galleries, like those called 'Grottes des Fées' on the banks of the Loire, built of perhaps a dozen stones in all, together with the great chambered tumuli of the bronze and late stone age, the kune-beds of Scandinavia, the giant beds of Ireland or of Ammon, the demi-dolmens of France and Moab; while the cists in the tumuli of the iron age, and the Arab trilithon altars of our own times, are but degenerate representatives of the older dolmens. It is clear that no hasty generalization is possible in such a case, and that dolmens are structures of primitive architecture, which may include more than one class, and may have been built for more than one purpose.

One very clear distinction may in the first instance be drawn—namely, between the free-standing dolmen and the dolmen covered by a mound or cairn. In studying the Moabitic groups, it became quite clear that most (and probably all) of them could never have been covered by any mound at all. Mr.

Fergusson, who may be considered the champion of the sepulchral theory, points out very clearly that it is an error to suppose that all dolmens were once hidden beneath mounds. Instances occur in France and Algiers where a dolmen stands free on the top of a mound; and even if in such cases a grave were found beneath (of which as yet there appears to be no known instance), the free-standing dolmen would not be itself a sepulchre.

As regards buried dolmens, the evidence appears to be strongly in favour of their having been sepulchral chambers. Thus, for instance, we find in Scandinavia the dolmen of Axevalla, which contained nineteen cists, and was reached by a passage like that leading to the chamber at Uby. Du Chaillu mentions a similar chamber at Karleby, where, in 1874, were found more than sixty skeletons, with flint implements and a bronze spear-point. This great tumulus had three chambers, and near it were several other graves with passages, the general rule which was observed being apparently that the passage, which was closed only by a stone door, was on the south or east, and never on the north.

In Brittany we have a magnificent example of this class of monuments in the passage and chamber of Gavr Innis; and in Ireland at New Grange, near Drogheda, is a similar structure under a tumulus; but in the latter case there seems some evidence of the re-use of stones not originally destined for their present purpose. In India we find instances of burials in dolmen-like structures down to the present day, as, for example, in North Arcot, where Colonel Branfill found structures $8\frac{1}{2}$ feet high and $16\frac{1}{2}$ feet long, built of slabs of schist, and surrounded with circles of menhirs, some of which were 10 feet to 15 feet high. Bones, beads, and pottery, with human skulls, were found within, and some examples had a hole in the eastern end-stone. Some of the pottery had Tamil inscriptions of the fourteenth and sixteenth centuries; the holes varied from three inches to two feet in size. Colonel Meadows Taylor gives instances of similar stone boxes also with holes in the end-stones, and containing bones and human ashes; but he also gives instances of monuments not closed: and Mr. Fergusson mentions a singular practice among the Mala Arryians, who make a miniature dolmen box, in which is enclosed a small stone, supposed to be the habitation of the soul of the dead man, to which offerings of sweetmeats and arrack are made. In this case, the dolmen seems to be connected with the idea of arks, such as are found among some of the Indian hill-tribes, or like the *tebah* of the Egyptians.

But while we must admit that buried dolmens are but a large variety of the chamber, or cist, found in later tumuli of the iron age, and that stone boxes, even when not so covered, are sometimes ancient sepulchres, it does not by any means follow that all trilithons, or other structures presenting a flat surface or table-stone, are to be regarded as tombs. Nor does the fact of their use to the present time in India, or in Arabia, contradict the fact that such monuments were erected in pre-historic times. Mr. Fergusson has cited examples where rude stone crosses occur in India in connection with dolmens and caves, as though proving a late and Christian origin for Indian examples; but he can hardly fail to have discovered that the cross in India is found as a sacred emblem among Buddhists and Brahmins alike from a very early period. Nothing could be, *primâ facie*, more improbable than the erection of rude-stone monuments by Christians in India.

Dolmens with holes of various sizes in the endstone are not uncommon in France, while holed menhirs, as we have seen, have special importance. In buried dolmens, or tomb-chambers, such holes, or rather large openings in the end-stone, are often found, and Irby and Mangles give an account of dolmens west of es Sâlt which seem to have similar entrances. In cases where a gallery on the east or south is found, we have perhaps a development of the same idea. Holed dolmens occur in Circassia, but not a single specimen was found in Moab. There appears to have been a superstition in early ages that the dead could not rest in peace in tombs without an inlet for air, and this would perhaps account for the larger openings in chambers and free-standing dolmens; but it will not explain the holes in the Woden-stone, the Ring-stone, the Stone of Applecross, which would seem to be connected with some ancient rite.

In connection with this subject, it should be noted that some free dolmens, or trilithons—as, for example, in some cases near Carnac, in the Lanyon Stones, or the Scandinavian dolmen of Oroust— have a 'sentinel stone,' or menhir, so placed that its shadow falls within the opening of the trilithon doorway at certain seasons of the year.

No dolmens are known to bear any inscription, and we may therefore fairly suppose that they belong to an illiterate age. There are, however, well-known instances of sculptured monuments of this class, and many cases in which the stones have been hewn. The lintel stones of Stonehenge have sockets on the under side. The hewing might, however, be, as Sir John Lubbock has proved, accomplished with a flint tool, even in the case of granite, and the sculpture is of that rude character which is not uncommon among half-savage tribes. The famous example at Confolens, where the table rests on four pillars, of a character not earlier than the eleventh century, is not conclusive, as the side-stones may have been sculptured later than the time of the original erection. The Nilgiri dolmens bear representations of Hindu gods, but we know that rude-stone monuments are erected down to our own time in India. The markings on the dolmen of Herrestrup are also probably later than the dolmen itself. The Dol ar Marchant in Brittany; the rude spirals at Gavr Innis; the fern patterns and concentric circles at Loch Crew, and at Douth and New Grange, appear to represent the highest ideas of art in the dolmen-building age. Similar 'cup and ring' marks are found on stones at Inverary, and on rocks in Scotland and the North of England, and they recall (as do the fern and palm-leaf patterns) in a remarkable manner the rude attempts at ornamentation scrawled on the walls of sacred places in Palestine by an utterly illiterate peasantry. The spiral, the palm-leaf, the badly-drawn concentric circle, will be found smeared with henna inside almost any *kubbeh* or saint's-tomb in Syria, and it seems scarcely necessary to suppose any deep significance to attach to such primitive attempts at ornamentation. It is perhaps more remarkable that the *Swastica*—a form of cross common among Buddhists and others in India—should have been discovered on the rocks of Rumbold's Mow; but this sign is evidently of great antiquity, and reappears among the mediæval masons' marks, while in India it is a caste-mark among Vishnaivas. It is indeed only a variation of the Tau wherewith Ezekiel is commanded to mark the faithful, and was probably brought by immigrants from Asia, for it has been found on Assyrian bas-reliefs, and at Troy, as well as in Cyprus, Attica, China, and Japan.

No ornamentation of any kind has been found on Syrian dolmens, excepting the tribe-marks of modern Arabs, which are evidently quite recent. Such sculpture as is above mentioned might well belong to the illiterate bronze age, of which period no inscriptions have been found; but so far as the evidence of comparative date afforded by such markings gives any indication, the Syrian dolmens would appear to be of great antiquity.

A far more important indication is afforded by the existence of certain hollows observed in the table-stones of dolmens. Du Chaillu speaks of these in describing the free-standing dolmen near Fasmorup, in Skane, and although he is a firm believer in the fashionable sepulchral theory, he yet considers it probable that 'sacrifices to the dead were prevalent.' There are eight holes shown in his sketch, and he gives their diameter as about two inches. Fergusson describes a somewhat similar feature in the passage at Gavr Innis, where three hollows are sunk in an upright stone: 'Not only,' he says, 'are the three holes joined, but a ledge or trough is sunk below them, which might hold oil or holy water, and must, it appears to me, have been intended for some such purpose.'

Such hollows had been observed by Borlase, in Cornwall, a century earlier, in rocks, near cairns and dolmens; and also at the Giant's Castle in the Scilly Islands. He observed them near the 'Cairn of Burning,' with grooves or channels communicating between them. Near the Tree Cairn and the Rock of Burnings a dolmen is said to exist with small basins scooped in the table-stone, and channels leading to two of larger size; and several rocking-stones have such hollows in their tops, while, according to Borlase, they occur in connection with all cairns in Cornwall. Such hollows are commonly found on the table-stone of Moabite dolmens, as will be seen later, and two facts were perfectly clear respecting them: first, that they were artificial, and not natural, and secondly, that they were intended to hold some liquid. We have seen that stones used to be smeared with blood and anointed with oil in ancient times, and the most natural conclusion appears to be that reached by the various authorities above mentioned, namely, that in these hollows we find evidence of sacrifices or libations of blood shed on the table-stone, or of oil or water poured on it. To this question we must, however, return later, in speaking of the inclination of the table-stones.

Hollows in flat rock-surfaces are common in Palestine. In some cases they appear to be little mills for grinding corn or for making gunpowder; but in others they are too small for such purposes. It has long been a question what could be the use of these smaller hollows; but in 1882 I found that the sacred rock on Gerizim had a well-marked hollow of the kind, near the centre. It was evidently artificial, and the Samaritans informed me that it marked the site where the brazen laver stood in the court of the temple which they believe Joshua to have here erected. The Sacred Rock is a flat surface, dipping down westwards, on which side a cave or trench has been scooped beneath its surface. In all probability sacrifices were once offered on this rock (as Gideon also offered sacrifice on a rocky floor), and the blood flowed into the cave, while that required for sprinkling the congregation would be preserved in the hollow. The hole in the Sacred Rock at Jerusalem may, in like manner, have been originally intended to allow of blood being drained into the cave beneath. In Moab the hollows are sometimes found, not on the dolmen itself, but on a flat rock beside it; and it is possible that in Judea dolmens may once have stood where now the rock, with its hollow cup, alone remains.

It may, however, be argued that evidence of sacrifice on a dolmen is no evidence that the monument was not sepulchral. We know that human sacrifices were offered to the manes on tombs in primitive ages, and we know that hollows occur on Moslem graves, which might be survivals of the dolmen hollows. We know that the Jews offer burnt-offerings at Joseph's tomb on the pillars with cup-shaped tops which stand at either end of the grave; and that shawls and silks are burned in Galilee, at the tomb of Simeon bar Iochai. The menhirs round the grave-dolmens in Arcot have hollows in the top, perhaps intended for a similar purpose; and such hollows have been found in the tops of menhirs in Moab. Further evidence is, then, required to prove that dolmens are, when 'free-standing,' not of necessity sepulchral.

It will be conceded that a trilithon is hardly what would be expected as the form for a tomb. In the early stone age men were buried in a sitting posture. In the bronze age most tribes seem to have burned their dead, though burying and burning sects then lived side by side, as they still do in India. In some cases the chief personage seems to have been buried, and his slaves or wife burned—perhaps alive, unless, indeed, these instances can be proved to show in all cases a secondary interment. The practice of burying in an extended position seems to be very late in Europe, and the cists in covered dolmens, or the bench round the chamber, generally exhibit skeletons crouching on their hams. This would, of course, be a possible position for a body beneath an ordinary trilithon, or in any free-standing dolmen; but in the Moabite examples it was often certain that, if ever a body was buried beneath the table-stone, it must have been placed above the natural surface of the ground, for the majority of the dolmens there stand on naked, untouched rock. There are other instances in which the table-stone is supported, not on upright blocks, but on several horizontal slabs; and in some of these cases, at least, it is quite clear that this was the original construction, and not the result of oversetting. In these examples—and, indeed, in all those dolmens which have tables only some foot or two feet above the surface—it is impossible to suppose that they ever covered a crouching corpse; and in many instances there is no room for any corpse at all beneath the table.

The examination of the free-standing dolmens of Moab does not, therefore, favour the sepulchral theory, and we have already seen instances in which the trilithon appears to have had other uses. Such are the dolmens placed like gates on the circumference of circles, or as altars within the circle. Such are the rocking-stones of Brittany and Cornwall, with their curious names and traditions. Such are the demi-dolmens, one of which, in France, has been consecrated by a wooden cross; and these demi-dolmens occur in great numbers in Moab, sometimes of diminutive size, sometimes merely formed by prizing up a stratum of sloping rock, and supporting it on the down-hill side by a stone. The object in such cases is to obtain a flat table, and not the construction of any box or coffin of stone. We must, also, not forget the sacred dolmen forming the crypt of a Spanish church; and we shall see later how miniature trilithons are used as altars by the Arabs. The traditions connected with dolmens are also of importance. In Ireland they are the beds of giants, and there is a curious superstition connected with crawling through dolmens, which must be compared with the ideas concerning passing between trees or pillars, or through holes in rocks, and under door-sills, etc., which are found among Celts and Hindus, Arabs and Turks, alike in East and West. Thus, for instance, such practices are found at Kerlescant, in Brittany, at Rollrich, in Oxfordshire, at Ardmore, in Waterford, and at Craig Mady, in Stirlingshire—a resort of the newly wedded. The dolmen in these cases is the sacred gate leading to Paradise, and to pass through it is to attain new life, or immortality—an idea not directly connected with sepulture. We shall find in Moab one ancient and many modern examples of such altar-gates.

It may, however, be said that the existence of so many dolmens at one site precludes the idea that they were only altars; but we must remember that Balak erected no less than twenty-one altars at one time in Moab, on three sites, and that Hosea might be thought to have a dolmen centre in his mind's eye when he says, 'Their altars are as heaps in the furrows of the field' (xii. 11). The dolmen as an altar is not indeed mentioned in the Old Testament, unless Jacob found one at Bethel, 'The Gate of Heaven' (Genesis xxviii. 17); but Saul used a great stone for sacrificing (1 Samuel xiv. 33), and Isaiah condemns the practice of preparing a 'table for Gad' (lxv. 11). New altars were built apparently whenever an important sacrifice was to be offered, and sacred centres would thus in time become crowded with such structures, 'like heaps in the furrows of the field.'

In concluding an inquiry into the general subject of early monuments, which has, perhaps, already rather exceeded the proper limits, we must say a few words as to cairns and mounds.

Cairns are often sepulchral, are sometimes beacons, and often memorials. The most interesting question in connection with such stone piles is that of their gradual accumulation round a menhir. Thus, in India (as Dubois tells us), stones are thrown at the village lingam stones, not from any disrespect, but as a sacred ceremony. The lingam in such instances becomes the nucleus of a memorial cairn. The Arabs throw stones at the menhirs in the Mena valley in just the same way, and Greek ceremonies often terminated by lithoboloi, or stone-throwings, commemorating the ballot-stones thrown at Hermes (the menhir deity) by the gods who purified him after the murder of Argus. We find traces of such practices mentioned in the Bible: for instance, in Proverbs (xxvi. 8), 'As he who throws a stone on a heap, so is he that giveth honour to a fool.' Jerome renders it, 'As he who throws a stone on the back of Mercury:' and the practice of throwing stones in honour of Marculim, or Mercury, is mentioned in the Talmud and by Maimonides. When Jacob erected a menhir at Mizpeh, his followers made a heap of stones—apparently round it (Genesis xxxi. 46); and the Highland proverb mentioned by Sir John Lubbock, 'I will add a stone to your cairn,' throws some light on the meaning of this rite. The small stone thrown on a cairn was an even simpler witness of the presence of any individual than the pillar or menhir. The greater the number of pilgrims, worshippers, or mourners, the larger the cairn, and the greater the honour done to the deity or the deceased. Mr. W. Morrison tells me that cairns are still so erected in the Highlands, each mourner adding his contribution, and hence the saying above quoted is equivalent to the expression of regard for the person addressed.

Cairns over the dead are common among Arabs, but in cases where no interment has occurred, the cairn has probably some such origin as above stated. Near Jerusalem there are great cairns which do not appear to be either sepulchres or beacons, but which may, perhaps, be sacred piles of the same kind as those above noticed.

The use of mounds is very similar to that of cairns. In all countries the dead are covered with tumuli, but other great mounds are also found in all lands which are not sepulchral. Such are the dagobas or 'blind topes' found in India and in Afghanistan, which in some cases have a menhir standing upon them, while near Carnac, at Rollrich, and in many other cases, single menhirs stand on mounds and knolls, which are but miniature sacred mounts. The Tells of the Jordan valley have been excavated by Sir Charles Warren, and found to be solid, without any chamber or cist. In the Hittite country, both in Asia Minor and Northern Syria, the plains are covered with these great mounds or Tells, which, in some cases, appear to have been faced with stones, inscribed in Hamathite characters, or covered with bas-reliefs. The Tells, like the dolmens, always appear to occur close to water, and are not generally in defensive positions, but in open plains. It may, perhaps, finally be found that most of these mounds were sacred places, and, indeed, in many cases they are so still. The great mound near the sources of the Jordan, called Tell el 'Ajjûl, or the 'Hill of Calves,' suggests a connection with Jeroboam's calf-worship, and the white dome of a Makâm may often be found to crown the summit of these great hillocks of clay or sun-dried brick.

Here for a moment we must pause, for the disc stones of Moab may be left for the next chapter. We have seen how the original idea of the menhir is that of a memorial stone, often considered to contain a divine soul. We have seen how the sacred circle, though sometimes consecrating tombs, is originally an enclosure connected with the worship of the sun, and how the avenues and alignments have, at least in some cases, an astronomical origin. We have distinguished between the dolmens which are sepulchral chambers, and those which appear to be sacrificial tables or symbolic structures, and between memorial cairns and those which are sepulchral, as also between tumuli and sacred mounds. The religion of the ancient races is intimately connected with all rude-stone monuments, and temple and tomb are as closely united as they still are in a cathedral, with its famous dead, in our own land. Famous stones have names which seem to give them a human individuality. Such are the King-stone, Long Meg, or the stones of King Orris, Woden, St. Patrick, St. Declare, or St. Fillan in the British

Isles. In France we have Pierre Martine and others, and the names given to stones by the Khassia tribes, such as 'stone of the oath,' 'of grass,' 'of salt,' are equally instructive. The student who neglects the indications afforded by tradition, and endeavours to make the monuments tell a new tale without crediting that related by the descendants of those who erected the menhir or dolmen: who leaves out of account the beliefs and hopes and sorrows of those childlike ages, and thinks that man in savage times was but the utilitarian which civilization has made him, is not likely really to penetrate into the mystery of these earliest of human monumental structures, and fails to sympathize with the ideas of builders whose conceptions of rugged grandeur, and of the moral effect of huge masses and of number, still excite the admiration of men in times when art and skill have so far surpassed the first efforts of the illiterate and pre-historic period.

CHAPTER VIII.

SYRIAN DOLMENS.

THE previous chapter has, to a certain extent, cleared the ground, and indicated the important questions to be considered in connection with the rude-stone monuments of Syria. We have to inquire first as to the observations which seem to indicate the origin and use of these monuments, the names and traditions connected with them, their situation and relative positions, their method of structure, and their more important details or peculiarities; and secondly, we may study their distribution in the country, with a view of discovering, if possible, the approximate date to be assigned to them, and the race which may be supposed to have probably erected them.

South of Sarafend or Zarepta, between Tyre and Sidon, and about a mile south of the ruin of 'Adlûn, Consul Finn has described a rude-stone monument in Phœnicia. It was a quadrangle originally, consisting of sixteen stones, six on each longer side.

Of these ten remain standing, and there are two outlying stones on one of the longer sides. The stones are from four to six feet high, and two or three yards apart. They have been hewn, but not squared. Traditionally, they are said to have been wicked men turned to stone by a prophet while reaping, and the name of the prophet seems to be Zer, or possibly Zîr (of whom more hereafter). A depression in the ground was remarked in the centre of the enclosure, and the place is called Sûk Sairi, from the neighbouring village of Seirîyeh. It is possible that the prophet should be called Seir from this village, as in other cases.

The next nearest dolmen-centre is that discovered west of Tell el Kâdy in 1882. We here found dolmens made of basalt, at a ruin called Dhahr es Saghir. These dolmens are smaller than those of Moab, evidently because of the great weight of the basalt as compared with limestone. They occupy the southern side of a low spur between the Nahr Leddân on the east, and another affluent on the west. The spur is all of black basalt, with one or two small thorn-trees. It commands a magnificent view of Hermon and of the Crusading Castle at Banias, with the poplar groves below, while close by, on the east, is Tell el Kâdy, 'the Judge's Mound,' with its magnificent terebinths and its fine springs in the cane-brake. On the north is Lebanon, on the west the Galilean ridge, and on the south the broad plain of Jordan reaches to the Waters of Merom, which shine in the distance. It is nearly always at such sites, near clear streams, at a spot commanding a fine distant view, that Syrian dolmens have as yet been found in great numbers.* The most perfect example in the present instance is towards the west, where a table-stone 5 feet long and 3 feet broad, is supported on smaller blocks, the upper surface being 2 feet above the ground. It is carefully adjusted by two small pebbles inserted on each side, and there is a flat hollow or cup in the stone near one end.

A second example further east appears to have been either partly destroyed, or more probably is a demi-dolmen. A stone 5 feet long is supported at one end by a cubical block $2\frac{1}{2}$ feet high, and rests at the other end on the ground. On the south-east was found another structure, evidently artificial, a great block of basalt, of about the same length as in other examples, being supported on smaller stones laid flat beneath it. Thus an inclined table is obtained, the highest point of the surface being four feet above the ground. In this case also a small pebble is inserted to steady the top-stone, and there

---

* Detailed accounts of the dolmens and other monuments explored in Moab and Gilead, with measured plans, sketches, and photographs, will be given in the Memoir of the Survey.

are remains of a rude circle of smaller stones surrounding the principal block. The fourth example, a little further east, is a dolmen like many in Moab, a great flat stone supported on others also laid flat. There are numerous remains of other dolmens on the sides of the knoll, some apparently overthrown on purpose, others presenting heaps which are not easily distinguishable from the natural basalt blocks of the vicinity; but the four examples above mentioned are clearly artificial structures, and it is very curious that they should not previously have attracted the attention of the many visitors who must have passed close by them in going to Tell el Kady.

In Upper Galilee a few examples of the same kind were found by the Survey party in 1877. Four of these, near Meirûn, are mentioned in the Memoirs and shown on the Survey; they stand on flat ground east of the summit of Jebel Jermûk, the highest mountain in Galilee. One is called Hajr Muneik'a, 'the stone of the little cup or mortar.' The covering stones in these specimens measure about 11 feet by 7 feet, and are $1\frac{1}{2}$ feet thick; these tables are raised only a few feet above the ground.

South of Meirûn, separated from it by a valley, is a ridge on which stands a stone called 'Hajr el Hubleh,' or 'the Pregnant Stone,' near the ruin of Shem'a. North of the Sea of Galilee there is another dolmen on the ridge of 'Alieh, and this is called Hajr ed Dumm, 'the Stone of Blood.' In 1882 I visited the so-called Hajâret en Nasâra, west of Tiberias, at the top of the open valley which is called Wâdy Abu 'Amîs, and which permits the traveller from the west to obtain his first view of the lake beneath. This is the modern site of the miracle of feeding the five thousand, which in the Gospels is mentioned as occurring on the east side of the lake. It is a rude circle, ten paces in diameter, of basalt blocks unhewn; the largest is now called 'the Table of Christ,' and chips of the stone, believed to have miraculous power, are taken from it by the Russian pilgrims. It is possible that this site may represent a prehistoric Gilgal, or circle, above the lake.

In Lower Galilee a single rude-stone monument was found in 1872, on Mount Gilboa, near Deir Ghuzâleh. It is described in the Memoirs, and appears to be the first dolmen ever observed west of Jordan in Palestine. A stone nearly 7 feet long here rests on supports about $3\frac{1}{2}$ feet above the ground at the upper surface. Other stones, beside this sort of door, form a rectangle of about 14 feet side, and within this is a single upright stone 6 inches thick, 2 feet broad, and 3 feet high, placed opposite the centre of the doorway. The bearing of this monument is 30° east of north, on the line from the single stone towards the centre of the door. The place commands a view west over the plain of Esdraelon, but there is no water near the ruin.

Crossing over Jordan, we must next mention the dolmens of Sûf, which have been described by Consul Finn, and by several subsequent travellers. These specimens appear to be of chert, or that brown, flinty stone which runs in bands through the chalk. The covering-stones in some instances measure 11 feet by 6 feet, and an end-stone, as well as two side-stones, is found. The table is generally about 4 feet from the ground. Mr. L. Oliphant speaks of similar monuments, apparently further north, near Mahneh, where some believe Mahanaim to have stood. Mr. Fergusson speaks probably of the latter group as not far from Tibneh, at a place called Kefr el Wâl, whence they extend for three or four miles towards Sûf. There are evidently, therefore, dolmen-fields in Ajlûn which may still be found to rival in extent those already explored in Moab.

Advancing southwards, we find another important group south of the Jabbok, on the road leading from the Dâmieh ford to es Sâlt. It was discovered by Irby and Mangles, in 1817, near the foot of the hills; and in their hurried glance at the spot they recognised twenty-seven dolmens. Their account is remarkable, for they speak of the end-stones as if pierced for a door, and they distinctly state that this was not the case in groups further south. The size of the dolmens in this group appears to be about the same as in the Sûf and Tibneh fields. The Arabs do not know of any other group in the valley between that at the Jabbok and those east of the Seisebân plain.

At Rabbath Ammon both dolmens and menhirs were found by the Survey party in 1881. South-west of the town is a single example of great size of the demi-dolmen class. The top-stone measures 13 feet by 11 feet, and is inclined at a flat slope eastwards. On the west it is supported by a stone 6 feet high and 5 feet wide, and there is a side-stone on the north. In the middle of the table is a hollow about 2 feet across and a few inches deep, and a regular network of channels leads to this from the higher or western end of the table. There are two other large hollows, and nine smaller ones, in different parts of the stone, several having little channels leading to them. There is also a pair of such hollows on the flat rock, just east of the stone. The monument stands on bare rock on the west slope of a hill near the top. It commands no particular view, nor is it near water. The stone is a limestone, and the blocks, which are from $1\frac{1}{2}$ to 2 feet thick, do not seem to have been hewn at all.

North-west of 'Ammân is a group of dolmens made of flint or chert. They seem to have formed a rude circle, but this may be merely accidental. There are two standing and two fallen, one being a trilithon, the other having an end-stone, as had also the two fallen ones. The top-stones are from 8 to 12 feet long. There is another very small one near them, a stone 6 feet by 4 feet being supported at one end by a stone only about a foot high. One of the larger examples has a hollow $2\frac{1}{2}$ feet by 1 foot by 6 inches deep in the cap-stone. This group is on the south-west slope of a hill in a very hidden situation. There is no water near, nor any view; but due west, on a hill divided by a deep valley, there is a menhir $4\frac{1}{2}$ feet high and 4 feet wide by $1\frac{1}{2}$ feet thick. This is still standing, and in its top surface there is a well-shaped hollow, 6 inches in diameter and 4 inches deep.

South-east of Ammân are possible remains of two other small monuments, and on the hill north-east of the citadel in the ruins of Haddâdeh is a fallen menhir 12 feet long and $6\frac{1}{2}$ feet wide by 2 feet thick, having a hollow in its side 9 inches deep. It seems to have stood on a sort of stone socket still remaining near it. Further north-east we found another dolmen or demi-dolmen with a cap-stone 8 feet long, and near it two smaller examples, with table-stones laid almost flat on the natural surface, but just propped by a small stone at one end, so as to give them an inclination from the horizontal. These stones were 5 feet and 9 feet long respectively, and west of this group is a great block or menhir 8 feet high and 9 feet broad at the bottom, still standing in its proper position.

South of the Ammân monuments we find not a single example until the vicinity of Heshbon is reached, and here, in Wâdy Hesbân, the dolmens occur in great numbers. A spur called el Kurmîyeh runs out west from Heshbon, and from it there is a view down the valley with its clear stream and over to the Neby Mûsa downs west of Jordan, above Jericho. There is a knoll at the end of the spur, and on this is a ruined cairn about 15 feet in diameter, of small stones. It appears to have had a circle of stones about 2 feet high round it, and the diameter of this circle would have been about 15 paces. The flat rocks are here pitted by many round holes 1 to 2 feet in diameter, and 6 inches to a foot in depth. There are traces of a sort of double circular enclosure lower down the slope on the west. The two rows are about 8 feet apart, and the stones, many of which are curiously pointed, are 2 feet high. The diameter of this circle would be about 200 feet. The slopes beneath are sown with dolmens, some being the finest we found in all Moab. The first discovered, on the north-east of the central cairn, was a trilithon, with a cap-stone 6 feet long, supported on side-stones to a clear height of $5\frac{1}{2}$ feet beneath the table. A small stone placed on one side allows any person mounting on it to reach the upper surface of the table with his hands. Lower down on the north slope is a group of five dolmens, one of which is a magnificent example of stones which seem to have been rudely squared. The cap-stone is 9 feet long, and there is a clear height of $5\frac{1}{4}$ feet beneath it. Of this example Lieutenant Mantell obtained an excellent photograph. Twenty-six dolmens in all were examined on the slopes of this hill, varying in size from the specimens mentioned to little structures of a single stone 5 feet long, supported at one end by a block only $1\frac{1}{2}$ feet high. Many examples were fallen, others (as at Tell el Kády) consisted of a table with other flat stones beneath it, a sort of pile which could not have been intended to form a cist or box. In one case a stratum of rock had been prized up, and supported at one end by a stone. A menhir 5 feet high was also found, and there is a rock-cut wine-press on the hill. These monuments stand on hard rock, and have no floor-stone, nor any excavation beneath them. There is no orientation, and they seem to have been built just where the stones were found lying on the hillside. None are at the top of the hill, and the builders do not seem to have been able to carry the great blocks very far or to any great height. Lieutenant Mantell observed that the sidestones were almost invariably parallel to the contour of the slope, so that the cap-stone might evidently have been slid down hill and brought over the uphill and flattest stone, to rest on the taller or downhill block. These observations apply to the groups mentioned later, as well as to the Kurmîyeh dolmens. In some instances hollows were found in the topstone, in others they occurred in the rock beside the monument.

We subsequently found other dolmens near Sûmieh, further down the valley, and a group of about twenty more on the north side of the stream, near the same site. These present no new peculiarities, but one fallen example had five cup-hollows in the cap-stone more regularly formed than is usual, and varying from 2 inches to 10 inches in diameter. All these specimens were drawn and measured. Some curious excavations in large boulders or in cliffs occur, here and elsewhere, in connection with the dolmens. They are possibly tombs, but if so, the body must have been buried in a cramped position, for the chamber—often carefully cut out—is generally from 3 feet to 5 feet long, and about 3 feet wide and high.

Proceeding south, we reach Mount Nebo, and here a well-defined dolmen was found north-west of the flat ruined cairn which marks the summit of the ridge. The cap-stone was very thick, and its top is some 5 feet from the ground. The side-stones were rudely piled, and none of the blocks were cut or shaped. A photograph was taken, and a fallen example with a cap-stone 6 feet by 8 feet was found further west. In subsequent visits, it was ascertained that on the south slope of the mountain there is a circle about 250 feet in diameter, with a wall 12 feet thick, consisting of small stones piled up in a sort of vallum. At least one other dolmen is still standing on this side of the mountain.

The great valley immediately south of Nebo is called Wâdy Jideid, and the spring of Jideid rises in it. East of the spring is the hill called Kuweijiyeh, and south of it is the ridge of el Maslubîyeh. Above the spring in the upper part of the valley is the great circle called Hadânieh, or 'Sepulture,' in which we camped. It is an oval, 250 feet in major diameter, with walls some 40 feet thick, formed by stones about 2 feet in diameter, quite undressed and heaped up into a vallum. The interior is divided into two unequal portions by a similar stone-heap wall, 6 feet thick; and on the south-east, outside the circle, is a modern Arab sacred circle with a grave. This is 19 feet in diameter, and has on the north-west a little trilithon, formed by two stones a foot high supporting a table 2 feet long. This little altar was covered with offerings, including small copper coins, a knife-blade, and some pieces of blue pottery. This is a good example of the grave circles which the Arabs erect round the tombs of celebrated chiefs or holy men, and it is from the existence of the smaller circle probably that the place comes to be named Hadânieh.

The district round this circle presents a greater number of dolmens than any other yet visited. They extend from the plateau east of Kuweijîyeh, and all along the north slopes of the Maslubîyeh hill, and some of the specimens are magnificent. No less than 150 were here sketched and measured, and in some instances there are rows of large trilithons almost touching each other. In one case a floor-stone was found inside the dolmen-chamber, with a cup-hollow in it. It was clear from this great group that these dolmens could never have been covered with cairns or tumuli, and that they conceal nothing beneath, for they stand mainly on hard rock, and even the floor-stones were apparently found not to cover any cavity. It was remarkable that though there are over a hundred on the south side of Wâdy Jideid, only one was found to the north; but the reason was clearly that the dip of the strata is such as to present a slope strewn with loose blocks on the south, while only low cliffs without fallen stones are found on the north, where the marl also occurs in considerable thickness.

In the Jordan valley the dolmens reach from Wâdy Hesbân to the hill east of Kefrein, occurring in great numbers, but of small size, on the low spurs just at the foot of the mountains. The number, explored chiefly by Lieutenant Mantell, in this district, was supposed to be some three hundred in all, in a distance of two miles. Several of these dolmens were found on the top of a hillock which is a natural feature, arranged apparently in a rough circle, and with them a fallen menhir 11 feet long, with a recess in the side. There were remains of circular enclosures round the menhir and dolmens, and the mound itself, which is called 'the ring-hill,' seems to have had some kind of vallum round its sides.

The next important centre is at Minyeh, on the crest or shelf which looks down on the plateau above the Dead Sea cliffs. The monuments here found are of a distinct character, although one somewhat similar was remarked by Lieutenant Mantell in the Jordan valley at the site just mentioned. There are seven distinct monuments at Minyeh, most of which are in so ruinous a condition as to be almost indistinguishable. The best preserved, of which a photograph was taken, presents a cubical stone in a circle of large stones rudely piled. The central stone is $3\frac{1}{2}$ feet by $2\frac{1}{2}$ feet, and $3\frac{1}{2}$ feet high. The diameter of the circle is about 8 feet inside, and the walls are 4 feet thick, and consisted originally of two courses of undressed blocks piled up without mortar. On the east a little courtyard, 30 feet across, is formed by a single ring of stones. The Arabs have no tradition concerning these monuments, though a legend of the miraculous creation of the spring ('Ain Minyeh) by the spear of Aly exists, as will be detailed in another chapter. There is a flat rock just outside one of the monuments in which a trough has been cut, 18 inches by a foot in dimension, and 3 inches deep.

On the north bank of the Zerka M'aîn, just above the springs which form the head-waters of the stream in this 'Valley of God,' is a yet more remarkable site. It is three miles east of Minyeh, but on the same ridge, and it was visited, but only partly explored, by Irby and Mangles. Here on a flat plateau stands a single menhir called Hajr el Mansûb, a name identical radically with the Hebrew word rendered 'pillar' in the English version of the Bible, and applying to the Canaanite menhirs. The same word is also used of the stones erected and worshipped by the early Arabs before Muhammed.

The Hajr el Mansûb is 8 feet high, $4\frac{1}{2}$ feet broad, and 2 feet thick. It has evidently been hewn, for the top is rounded like an ordinary headstone to an English grave, while a groove 6 inches wide and $1\frac{1}{2}$ inches deep is cut right across on one side of the monument 4 feet from the ground.

The 'Adwân, Beni Sakhr and 'Anazeh tribe-marks are scored on the stone, but it is otherwise without inscription or ornament—a solitary and silent monument of an unknown past. It is not a milestone, for we know what Roman milestones are like in this country, and they are generally inscribed; nor is it an Arab monument, for they all acknowledge it as belonging to earlier times. The hills north, west, and south-west of the Hajr Mansûb are sown with dolmens, some being very perfect specimens. There is a large wine-press on the slope east of the menhir.

Travelling south-west from the Hajr Mansûb for about three-quarters of a mile, we find a flat piece of ground in which rises a low knoll, while a kind of theatre of low hills surrounds it on north, west, and east, a steep slope leading down on the south to the springs in the great valley beneath. This place contains one of the most remarkable monuments of Moab, namely, a large group of menhirs surrounded by dolmens. The summit of the low knoll is occupied by three very conspicuous stones standing erect, the longest being 6 feet high. There seems to have been a circle of smaller stones 15 paces in diameter round them; and another circle, perhaps 300 yards in diameter, round the knoll, is formed entirely of small menhirs from 3 feet to 6 feet high. East of this are alignments of similar stones, three rows north and south being distinguishable. There appears to have been a square enclosure defining the limits of this site. The remains of a row of menhirs, running east and west for thirty yards, are visible at the southern edge of the plateau, above the steep descent, and there is also a line running north and south from this at the east end of the little plateau. The enclosure thus defined would be about a quarter of a mile either way, and it is sown with small menhirs erected without order on the south and east of the circle round the knoll. There is a single dolmen just adjoining the circle on the west, and the hills to the north and east are covered with dolmens, extending towards the Hajr el Mansûb. There must be at least 150 dolmens at this site, and the number of the menhirs is even greater. The place is known as Umm Zuweitîneh, 'Mother of the little olive trees,' although no such trees exist here. The Arabs say it was once an oil manufactory, and point to the wine-press already noticed as an oil-press. Those acquainted with the stone presses west of Jordan will, however, be well aware that a wine-press with shallow chambers can never have been used in the manufacture of oil. The menhir group is called el Mareighât, 'the things smeared' (with oil or other thick liquids); but no tradition was collected as to the original meaning of the monuments.

In the next great valley south of the Zerka M'ain, known as Wâdy Wâleh, there appear to be other monuments of the same class which have not as yet been fully explored. Irby and Mangles here mention two menhirs, one 10 feet high, 4 feet wide, and a foot thick, south of the stream, a second of smaller size on the north bank. They were also visited by Herr Schick some years ago, and he speaks of the site as called Skander by the Arabs, apparently from some legend of Alexander the Great.

Another curious class of monuments are those called Serâbît by the Arabs. There are two groups of them on the spur called Mushukker, north of the 'Ayûn Mûsa; in one case there appear to be twelve pillars, $1\frac{1}{2}$ to 2 feet in diameter, and 3 feet to 8 feet high, each having a square block for a base, cut out of the same piece. In the eastern group there are twenty-four similar monoliths. They resemble Roman milestones, but there is no ancient road near the group, and they may be compared with the cippi over Phœnician graves at 'Amrît. A stone 8 feet long lies not far off, and is called Hajr el Mena, 'the Wishing Stone,' and considered by the Arabs to be capable of granting boons.

Three other ancient monuments must next be noticed, which resemble great millstones, but are too large ever to have been used for such a purpose. The one is at the village Kufeir Abu Bedd, a ruined site north of Nebo, at the edge of the plateau. It stands erect, and is $9\frac{1}{2}$ feet in diameter and $1\frac{1}{2}$ feet thick. It is sunk some three feet in the ground, and is not pierced with any central hole, as millstones usually are. The second, at the ruin of Kuweijîyeh, on the hill above the Hadânich circle, is also erect, and 6 feet in diameter; this likewise is not pierced as a millstone would be. The third is the so-called Mensef Abu Zeid, or 'Dish of Abu Zeid,' and is 10 feet in diameter, and $3\frac{1}{2}$ feet thick, pierced with a hole 2 feet in diameter. A tradition attaches to it which will be mentioned later; it lies flat in the plain beside a thorn tree, and it is difficult to imagine whence it was brought.

The great cairns and the modern stone monuments remain to be described. Canon Tristram speaks of cairns on the east of Kerak, and of circles some 100 yards in diameter, of which he found seven or eight south of the Zerka M'aîn, resembling apparently those larger examples already noticed at Hadânich and on Nebo. A ruined cairn is generally found on the hill-top where dolmens exist, as at el Mareighât, at Maslubîyeh, on Nebo, and at the Kurmîyeh. In cases where only the lower part of the cairn remained, it appeared that the heap had been erected on bare rock, and that it did not conceal any cist or dolmen. Some of the cairns, as at Sâmik and Meseiyik, are merely Arab burying-places, where bodies were placed on the ground and covered with stones. The older cairns may have had the same origin, or like Jacob's cairn at Galeed, may merely have been memorial piles. The largest we found was on a hill-top at Mekheiyit, and may be about 20 feet high.

The modern circles found in all parts of the Bedawîn country surround the tombs of celebrated or holy men : they are generally some 20 feet in diameter, with a grave in the centre, and a wall about 3 feet high, made by rudely piling up blocks of various dimensions. On the west there is a sort of little door or dolmen—a trilithon used by the Arabs as an altar, on which offerings to the dead are placed. This kind of altar is further noticed in another chapter.

The preceding pages are intended to give a connected account of all that is at present known concerning rude-stone monuments in Palestine, and beyond Jordan. The survival of Paganism among the Bedawîn is not less certain than among the Anseirîyeh in Syria, who have sacred stone altars at shrines in the midst of woods north of the Lebanon. It may now be interesting to summarize the important indications which are obtainable from a study of the Syrian dolmens and other rude-stone monuments.

As regards menhirs, by far the most important group is that of el Mareighât, discovered by the surveyors. Here we find a square enclosure, an inner circle, a central group on the top of the knoll, and alignments on the east. We find them called 'the smeared' stones, and we find the vicinity full of dolmens; and on the north side are three of those small chambers in the rock which have been already noticed near Sûmieh. At 'Ammân we find menhirs which may mark ancient boundaries, and which have hollows in the top or sides, as though for the receipt of libations or of small offerings. Taking these indications in connection with what we learn in the Bible concerning Jacob's stone at Bethel, and the stones raised by the Canaanites and overthrown by the reforming kings of Judah, we can have little hesitation in supposing the menhirs of Moab and Gilead to have been originally objects of Pagan worship, which were once anointed with oil, or smeared with blood. The alignments and scattered stones of el Mareighât may be supposed to be votive offerings of pilgrims to this shrine, standing above the head-springs of the 'Valley of God,' and on the ridge of Baal Peor—the deity of whom the menhir was the appropriate symbol.

With regard to the dolmens, we found in Moab no evidence which would in any way serve to connect them with sepulture. In many cases they were clearly inappropriate for such a use, and the main object of their erection seemed always to be the construction of a flat table, arranged with a slight tilt in the direction of its length. This tilt does not appear to be accidental, for in some cases where the monument is well preserved the supporting stones have evidently been arranged purposely so as to give an inclination to the cap-stone. We found the dolmens to occur in great numbers round certain centres, but without any particular order of individual position. The centres were generally near fine streams, and in places whence a good view was obtainable, but to these rules there are a few exceptions. Cup-hollows were found in the cap-stones, and in flat rocks beside the dolmens; and in one case the hollow was in the floor-stone of a well-built dolmen of five stones. Channels connected the cups in more than one instance, and the conclusion seems irresistible that they are evidence of some sort of libation on the dolmen. Circles surrounded the dolmens in many cases, and also surrounded the cubical stones of Minyeh, and the menhirs of el Mareighât. In the latter cases the circle had a dolmen on the west, and thus resembled the small Arab circles of the present day which consecrate graves. The dolmen in the modern instances is simply a table or altar for offerings.

In speaking of dolmens it should also be noted that at Hesbân, Sûmieh, Nebo, Mareighât, and elsewhere, large boulders or fallen crags were found near the dolmen groups, each pierced with a little chamber, generally about 3 feet square and 5 feet long. These are puzzling because of their small size. They seem to be tombs, but if so the body must have been placed in a cramped position, as in the 'stone age' tombs of Europe. It may perhaps be thought that in these excavations we find the real graves of the dolmen builders very rudely cut in rock at the sacred centre where their monuments were erected.

The large circles of Moab bear some resemblance to our English circular enclosures, allowing for the difference of the soil in the harder desert districts. They do not appear to have any outlying menhir, or any internal grave, and their object is not distinct. It should, however, be noted that in the case of the Hadânich circle, towards the direction of sunrise at the summer solstice, about three-quarters of a mile distant, the hill-top is crowned by a great cairn called Mekheiyit, or 'the Needle.' On the hill of Kuweijiyeh towards the south-west, half a mile away, is the great disc-stone elsewhere specially noticed. It is not impossible that these monuments may bear to the Hadânich oval a relation similar to that of outlying menhirs near British circles, as noted in the preceding chapter.

In addition to those previously described, Lieutenant Mantell discovered at Râs el Merkeb, east of 'Ammân, two other examples of stone circles, one close to a fine terebinth tree, the other about a quarter of a mile further east. They were not very large, being about 25 paces (or 60 feet) in diameter, of uncut stones, forming a vallum about 2 feet high. Close to each are remains of three or four smaller circles, which may be modern Arab graves, about 30 feet in diameter. A tradition of the 'kneeling-place of the Prophet's camel' attaches to this site, but was not apparently well known. Other examples of these large circles were found also at Kôm Yâjûz, Umm Huwatt, el Mâberah, and at el Mahder, a site with a name radically the same as the Hebrew Hazor. It is more than probable that all the old Hazors or 'enclosures' were named from such ancient circular monuments.

The cairns found in Moab may be either sepulchral or monumental. The Serabit must be classed with the menhirs. The disc-stones do not seem to have any parallel in Western Palestine or elsewhere (so far as I am able to learn), and their use and meaning must remain at present undecided. They may be solar emblems or they may have no religious meaning; but the only notices of such monuments of which we seem to have any trace refer to the Hammanim or 'sun images' (2 Chron. xxxiv. 4), which were destroyed by Josiah, while the name Diblathaim, or 'Two Discs,' applying to a town in Moab, as well as Diblath (Ezek. vi. 14), which I have proposed to recognise in the modern Dibl in Upper

Galilee, might be thought to have some connection. At 'Amrît, in northern Phœnicia, a similar stone disc, about 12 feet in diameter, stands on a block 15 feet square and 10 feet high, and is surmounted by a cone, giving a total height of 33 feet. This cippus stands above a tomb chamber.

The evidence, so far as it goes, seems to me to point very clearly to the use of dolmens in Moab as sacrificial altars. The cubical stones at Minyeh resemble those which were consecrated to Allât among the early Arabs; and the dolmen with its cup hollow is but a larger variety of the little dolmen-table of the modern Arabs. Still, it was not by Arabs that these monuments were erected, and so ancient do they seem to be, that only very vague traditions of their original meaning survive among the Bedawîn.

The distribution of the Syrian dolmens, and other monuments of the same class, may perhaps assist us in forming an opinion as to their origin. Not a single specimen was discovered in Judea during the course of the Survey, and only one very doubtful circle in Samaria. There does not seem to be any probability that groups of such monuments have been overlooked by the surveyors, who found them elsewhere, nor has a single specimen been discovered by any of the many careful explorers who have journeyed through the country. On the other hand, groups of fallen stones have been found more than once which seemed very probably to have once formed a dolmen, and cup-hollows have been observed in rocks at various places in Judea where dolmens might naturally be expected to occur.

In Galilee we find a few remaining dolmens, and at the site of Dan, where Jeroboam's calf-temple was erected, and which we know to have been long a sacred place, a large group has been discovered, most of the examples having, however, been overthrown, apparently on purpose.

In Phœnicia only one menhir enclosure is as yet known, but in Gilead and Moab there are probably more than a thousand dolmens, and many other rude-stone monuments. These occur at Nebo, Bamoth Baal, and Baal Peor, and probably also at Mizpeh—places where altars, cairns, and menhirs are mentioned as existing in the times of Jacob and of Moses. In addition to these indications, we have the fact that similar monuments are found in extraordinary numbers in the north of Africa, where the Phœnicians established extensive colonies, being there even more numerous than in Asia and Europe, where they may be attributed to old round-headed pre-historic tribes (akin to the Cushites, Accadians, Dravidians), the Esquimaux-like aborigines of Europe, preceding the Aryan migrants, to whom, nevertheless, the erection of later examples must be also attributed.

The conclusion which seems most natural is that dolmens and menhirs have been destroyed in Judea, but were commonly used by the Phœnicians, the Canaanite, Hittite, and Semitic tribes of Syria and beyond Jordan; and that the custom of their erection survived among the Nabatheans, Himyarites, and other early Arab tribes, and indeed still survives among their modern descendants, who unconsciously copy in miniature the older examples.

The rude-stone monuments of Syria have, so far as is yet known, neither ornamentation, nor rune, nor other mark of the engraver's tool: in comparatively few instances they are made of hewn stone, very rudely cut, but generally they are of rough blocks and slabs entirely unformed. Thus, if there be any scale of comparative antiquity on which we can rely, connected with the finish of the monument, the Syrian dolmens may claim to be considered among the oldest of their kind.

In the Book of Deuteronomy we find again and again repeated injunctions to 'overturn' the Canaanite altars, and to break, or 'smash,' their pillars. These exhortations we find carried into practice by Hezekiah and Josiah in Judea, and as the Book of Deuteronomy is held sacred by the Samaritans, we are justified in supposing that they also, at a somewhat later period, may have destroyed the stone monuments of Hivites and Amorites round Shechem. But Galilee was always a land of Goim, or 'pagans,' with a mixed population, over which the kings of Israel and Jerusalem had little control. Moab was the very centre of Baal worship in the days of Jeremiah, and the reforming zeal of Hezekiah did not affect the land where Chemosh and Ishtar, Baal Peor, Gad, Nebo, and Meni, yet continued to be worshipped. Thus, in Moab, the dolmens still remain, but in Judah they have been entirely destroyed. In Galilee only a few are left, and at Dan they lie fallen 'like heaps in the furrows of the field.'

At an earlier period, long before the Law of Moses existed, the fathers of the Hebrew race seem to have used the same stone monuments, which were subsequently condemned in consequence of the cruel and shameless rites with which they were connected in Canaanite paganism. Jacob anointed a menhir, Moses even marked the altar in his circle under Sinai with the blood of oxen. Joshua made a circle at Gilgal, and the sons of Jacob a cairn on Gilead. The dolmen is not distinctly mentioned in Hebrew Scripture, but the libation on a rock, the sacrifice on a great stone, the raising of 'hands' or cippi, is attributed to venerated heroes of the Hebrew race, to Gideon and Saul and Jacob, not less than to later worshippers of Peor and Chemosh. The names which still adhere to the Syrian monuments— 'smeared' stones, 'wishing' stones, stones of 'blood,' are valuable confirmations of what we gather from ancient authors concerning the unctions, libations and bloody rites connected with dolmens and menhirs.

The conclusions suggested in the preceding chapter, after a consideration of monuments other than those of Syria, seem thus to be confirmed by what we learn from the monuments of the Holy Land. The menhir is the emblem of an ancient deity, the circle is a sacred enclosure, without which the Arab still stands with his face to the rising sun. The dolmen, whether modern or prehistoric, is (when free-standing) an altar rather than a tomb. The cairn is not always sepulchral, being sometimes a memorial heap; the disc-stone is a distinct production, perhaps of a later age. Such evidence as we possess shows that the rude tribes beyond Jordan buried their dead in small chambers cut in the rock, or in tombs similar to those of the Phœnician and the Jew, and not beneath the table-stone of a free-standing trilithon; while the mounds of the Jordan valley and of the Hittite plains, whether citadels or sacred hills, have as yet never yielded sepulchral deposits.

To say that we still find the altars of Balak standing on Nebo may be premature. To point out the great dolmen at 'Amman as the throne of Og may be considered fanciful by some; but we may at least claim that we find structures which seem to resemble the early altars and pillars mentioned in Scripture still existing at places which, on entirely independent grounds, may be identified as representing the Mizpeh of Jacob, and the holy mountains of Nebo, Baal, and Peor; while in Judea not a single dolmen now remains standing, because in their zeal for the faith of Jehovah, the good kings, Hezekiah and Josiah, swept away for ever the 'tables of Gad.'

CHAPTER IX.

SYRIAN SUPERSTITIONS.

AMONG the original objects of research proposed in the prospectus of the Palestine Exploration Society was the study of manners and customs among the inhabitants of Syria. In 1878 I endeavoured to give a general sketch of this subject in 'Tent Work in Palestine,' and several papers of interest by various authors have since been published dealing with the subject. During my recent visit to the country I have, however, striven to collect information more especially concerning the local customs and beliefs which are connected with peasant superstitions, concerning which very little has as yet been written. The chapters of the present volume treating of Syrian superstition and Arab folk-lore will, it is hoped, form a novel contribution to the study of the native populations of Palestine.

The officers of the exploring parties have always been fully aware of the interest and importance attaching to this branch of research, and if the published Memoirs contain but few notes on the subject, it is not because it was forgotten or neglected. It was, however, always a matter of astonishment to me that so little could be extracted from the peasantry concerning their beliefs, even when they were least suspicious and best disposed. When we crossed over Jordan, we at once came among tribes who possessed tales and traditions which they were willing to repeat to us; but under precisely similar circumstances I found the Fellahîn still unable to do more than give a name or a very simple incident; and it is only gradually that it has been possible to form any conjecture on the subject of their beliefs. Throughout Syria we find shrines connected with the names of early patriarchs, such as Abraham, Noah, Cain and Abel; and legends which are more or less distorted versions of the episodes related in the Old Testament are repeated in connection with these shrines. With exception of these stories, and of certain beliefs which are survivals of the old Assyrian and Phœnician faiths, there does not appear to be any 'folk-lore' properly so-called among the Fellahîn, and the conclusions reached on the subject, as recorded in 'Tent Work in Palestine,' were fully confirmed by careful subsequent inquiry.

It is true that M. Clermont Ganneau, in his interesting paper on the Arabs (that is to say, the Fellahîn) in Palestine, gives one instance which would seem to contradict the supposition that but little can be expected from the search among the peasantry for folk-lore tales. He himself heard related at Sur'ah (or Zoreah), by Moslem peasants, various legends of Sheikh Samat, which appeared to be distorted reminiscences of the history of Samson. So much did this discovery interest me, that in 1881 I fixed a camp for several days at the village in order to investigate the question at leisure. As soon as we became familiar with the inhabitants we were told exactly the same story, but a circumstance entirely unexpected was brought to light. The village has for some years been the property of a Christian Sheikh named Kublân, from Beit Jâla, and on inquiring from the Fellahîn how they learned such tales of Neby Samat—suggesting that they had perhaps heard them from their fathers—we received at once the ready reply, 'Oh no! it was Kublân who told us;' and the fact that the legend was obtained from a Christian appeared in their eyes to increase its value, as the more educated Christians of the country are believed to know everything, like a Frank.

Here, then, was the explanation of the apparent anomaly, and the reason why legends of a kind not found in the more primitive districts were so glibly repeated in this instance. Kublân had for years been adulterating our sources of information by relating Scripture stories to his tenants, in whose dull brains they had remained half understood only, and thus came forth again in their strange guise, converted into exploits of a Moslem hero fighting the Christian infidels.

This instance alone is sufficient to show how careful the explorer must be to trace to its origin every tale he hears, and especially so in cases where the peasantry have come in contact with Europeans. The Latin monk, the Protestant missionary schoolmaster, have now for years been alike telling Bible stories to the peasantry round Jerusalem, and these tales are localized in the places commonly believed to be the actual sites of the Scriptural episodes. No doubt the monks and priests of the Middle Ages in like manner familiarized the Fellahîn of that period with traditions concerning the saints whose shrines were then rising in such numbers throughout the land, and this explains, perhaps, why it is that so many sites originally sanctified by Christian traditions have been adopted by the Moslems; as, for instance, the shrine of St. John near Castel Pelegrino (Athlît), the tomb of Moses near Mâr Sâba, St. Matthew south of Bethlehem, St. Paul and St. Gabriel in Philistia, St. George at Ascalon, at Blanche-Guarde, and at Darum, south of Gaza. In all these cases a purely Christian tradition is unconsciously taken over by a Moslem populace, but no legend appears to survive among them to tell how they first came to venerate the shrine, or what was the character of the saint they adore.

It is in the more remote corners of the country that information on such matters should be sought, not in the plains of Jaffa or the hills of Judea, where schools and chapels have been built, and where hundreds of pilgrims and tourists pass by every year. The pseudo-traditions which are being disseminated in the more civilized districts have no value in the study of the primitive condition of the peasantry, and where there is European influence no certainty can be attained concerning the genuine character of any story.

The Fellahin are not the only inhabitants of the country among whom curious customs and superstitions may be observed. The Oriental Jews are an eminently superstitious race. The Samaritans have legends peculiar to themselves. The Druzes, the Ism'aîleh, the Anseiriyeh, the Christian Maronites, have each and all peculiar superstitious ideas and sayings. The Arabs, or nomadic tribes of pure Arabian origin, have a religion and a folk-lore which must be treated as a distinct subject, and of all these, as well as of the superstitions of the Moslem peasantry, observations have been made during the course of our explorations.

The Jews, as the original people of the country,

claim notice in the first place, and it is well known that among Oriental Jews of the lower class (and even among European Jews, especially those of Poland and Russia), many superstitious practices occur which have certainly no connection with the Law of Moses. It is by no means easy for one not of their own nation to obtain any information on this subject, although the condemnation of such beliefs as that of the Tashlich may be found expressed in Jewish newspapers. The educated Jews of England, who belong to the nobler stock of the Spanish and Italian Sephardim, are fully aware of the degradation of their Oriental brethren; but any who take interest in the future of the nation, and in the Jewish projects for repeopling their native land, should bear in mind how wide is the distinction which must be made between the cultivated European Jew of the West and the ignorant and fanatical Jew of the East.

The Talmud itself contains much (especially in the Hagada) which is evidently derived from Persian sources. Its fables, its astrology, its legends, and its minute prescriptions, are often far less original than a Talmudist or a student not conversant with the history of other creeds would suppose. The Mishnah ought to be read side by side with the Zendavesta; the Hagada should be compared with the Parsee sacred books; the Æsop-like fables of the Gemara are certainly but adaptations of stories from an older

Aryan source. Take, for instance, the prescriptions for cutting the nails to which so great importance is attached. The Babylonian Talmud forbids that nail-parings should be left on the ground, lest women should tread on them and miscarry. The nails are to be cut on Fridays and in a certain order, and the parings to be burnt or hidden; they must not be cut on Thursday; and all these prescriptions are carefully observed by Oriental Jewesses, who hide the nail-parings in cracks in the house-walls.

The superstitions concerning nail-cutting which survive in England might be thought by those who believe our race to be of Semitic derivation (in defiance of philology and history) to have been taken from such Jewish ideas; but the student will find in the Pehlevi work called 'Shayast la Shayast' (and also in the older Vendidad), a Persian parallel which probably indicates the true origin of the Jewish practice. 'The rule is this,' says the Parsee legislator, 'that they should not leave a nail-paring unprayed over, for if it be not prayed over, it turns into the arms and equipments of demons.'

The Jew who desires to free his brethren from the grinding tyranny of Talmudic prescription cannot do them a greater service than by studying and comparing the Zendavesta with the Mishnaic texts.

I have on one occasion seen performed on a house-top in Jerusalem the ceremony called the 'Sanctification of the Moon,' which to an uninitiated person so closely resembles moon-worship, that I was hardly able at the time to credit my own eyes. This ceremony is, however, minutely prescribed in the Cabalistic writings. The worshipper, when the moon is in the first quarter, is to stand on one leg (an attitude common also to the Derwish sects and to Hindu hermits), and after glancing at the moon, repeats prayers, blessing her Former, her Creator, her Maker, her Possessor. In the Ma Yasht we perhaps find the real origin of this curious custom.

The Tashlich ceremony above noticed is supposed to be countenanced by a passage in Micah (vii. 19), and consists in laying the sins of any individual on running water, which is visited on New Year's Day. I have never detected it in Jerusalem, although the Jews visit the stream from the Bir Eyub when it begins to run in winter. They also believe firmly in the healing power of the intermittent spring called the Virgin's Fountain (possibly Bethesda), in which they stand waiting for the troubling of the water, as a cure for rheumatic and other complaints.

The 'hand of might' is another Jewish belief which may be supposed to have an Aryan origin. This hand (generally painted red) is drawn on the lintel or above the arch of the door. Sometimes it is carved in relief, and before one house in the Jews' Quarter, in Jerusalem, there is an elaborate specimen, carefully sculptured and coloured with vermilion. Small glass charms in the form of the hand are also worn, and the symbol is supposed to bring good luck. The Jewish and Arab masons paint the same mark on houses in course of construction; and next to the seven-branched candlestick, it is probably the commonest house-mark in Jerusalem. The hand is one of the oldest of pagan symbols. It appears on Roman standards and on the sceptre of Siva in India. The red hand in Ireland sculptured on crosses, the vermilion hand on temples in India, or in St. Sophia at Constantinople, the bloody hand of Mexico, are all no doubt examples of the same original conception. The Indian Sun-god Savitar is gold-handed, and Zoroaster had hands of gold and silver. So also had Hobal at Mecca; and King Madha, in Ireland, had a silver hand. It is not from a Semitic source, then, exclusively, that the symbol of the 'hand of might' can be thought to have been derived.

Jewish ceremonies connected with birth and sickness (as described by Chiarini) are equally instructive. The chamber where a birth is expected is inscribed with a charcoal line round the walls, and the names of Adam and Eve, and the words 'Avaunt Lilith,' for the Lilith, or female demon of the night, who assaulted Adam and lies ever in wait for his sons, is a succuba or lamia who is specially dangerous to new-born infants. She is often mentioned in the Talmud, and is even thought to be intended in Isaiah (xxxiv. 14), where the 'night monster' is rendered screech-owl in the English. The names of angels, Senoi, Sansenoi, and Samnangelaph, are also written on the walls, and when on the eighth day the circumcision takes place, an empty chair is placed for the invisible Elijah, whose presence is constantly supposed to accompany the devout on such occasions.

The sick are laid in bed, neatly dressed, and washed; the chamber is cleaned, and sweetmeats are placed round it, with fragments of choice food left to tempt the propitious spirits who may bring health to the patient. The Jew indeed in the East lives in daily dread of the *shedim*, or spirits, who are described in the Talmud as crowding every building or desert spot, who have claws like cocks, and may at times become visible. It is in all probability from Persia, with its hosts of genii and its endless struggle of guardian spirits and demons, that the demonology of the Jews is originally derived.

No less curious are the beliefs concerning death and the last judgment. The east side of the Kedron valley, east of the Temple, is covered thickly with Jewish tombs, and no doubt many pious souls are there laid by their own wish in sight of the loved and regretted sanctuary of their faith; but there is also no doubt that many are buried there in consequence of the belief that any Jew not having his sepulchre in the valley of judgment must, at the last day, perform a dangerous and painful underground journey to this valley—a pilgrimage beset with grievous obstruction from worms, serpents, darkness, and other obstacles. In Poland it is said that a kind of fork is buried with Jews to enable them to dig their way on this journey. In Russia, Jewish cemeteries are called 'Jehosaphat,' in order that they may become local substitutes in the day of judgment for the valley beside Jerusalem. Of the belief there can be no doubt, and it recalls strangely the old Egyptian idea of the subterranean pilgrimage of Osiris and his followers—the souls of the just—through the gloomy region of Amenti, with its demon serpents and other dangers.

The above are but a few examples of the innumerable superstitions which are noticed in the Talmud and credited by Oriental Jews. Such ideas as the bad luck of passing between two palms or two women, of black cats and witches at cross-roads, with many others mentioned in the Talmud, are clearly derived from some other source than the Hebrew Scriptures; and it appears to me very doubtful whether the Red Heifer Bridge, and some of the ceremonies therewith connected, as described in the Mishnah, should not rather be classed with the Persian myths of the 'Gatherer's Bridge,' and the cow which led souls across, than supposed to have any really historical origin.

The Samaritans have been constantly accused by the Jews of worshipping a dove on Gerizim, and, although they indignantly deny the imputation, it is curious that the Samaritan Book of Joshua contains an account of the messenger-dove which carried letters from Joshua to Nabih, king of the tribes beyond Jordan. The book in question contains many curious legends of the conquest which have no connection with the Bible narrative. Four long chapters are devoted to the history and death of Balaam: the conquest of Shechem is related, and the destruction of the Canaanites by flaming angels; the Kings of Greece, of Armenia, of Phœnicia and of Damascus gather to battle in the plain of Esdraelon; and at Keimûn beside Kishon Joshua and his followers are shut up between seven walls of iron. Summoned by the dove, King Nabih comes to his aid and transfixes the leader of the giants who have enchanted the Israelites with an arrow; a fountain springs up where the arrow falls, and the magic walls are destroyed suddenly.

These and other legends among the Samaritans have evidently a mythical origin. They exist only in a late literature, but appear to be copied from some earlier books. In the course of several conversations with two successive High-Priests, I have, however, found little that is not orthodox in their beliefs. Amram, the late High-Priest, knew, however, many things which his nephew and successor had forgotten. He knew the burial-places of all Jacob's sons, and such of these as his nephew remembered I collected in 1881, as may be found by those interested in the subject in the second volume of the 'Memoirs of the Survey of Western Palestine.'

The beliefs of the Druzes are no longer a secret to the Western world, since De Sacy and others have described their sacred books, found by the French in 1860 on Hermon. The whole system of their mystic faith is founded on the early Persian heresies, which resulted from the mixture of Moslem and Sassanian beliefs; and there is little which is of any peculiar interest or importance in their creed. It has been thought by some European inquirers that their highest grade of initiation leads to a knowledge of secrets which might be of importance and value; but those who know the Druzes best are of a contrary opinion. If we may judge from the facts that the Druzes are a prayerless people, and that they are allowed to deny or abjure their religion whenever they may think necessary, it would seem more probable that (as in the case of the earlier Ism'aileh) the highest initiation leads to a complete scepticism. The meetings in the Druze Khalwehs have a political far more than any religious importance; and the Druze, though brave and warlike, is untrustworthy, for this very reason that no oath can bind him and that nothing is really sacred in the eyes of his leaders. The brazen calf, which is known to be kept in the Khalwehs or solitary chapels on Hermon and elsewhere, is probably a surviving symbol of the early Paganism of the Hermon district. It is now considered an emblem of the folly of the heretical 'Akkal ed Derâzi, and raisins are derisively offered it to eat. Such cynical contempt of the very teacher whose name still clings to the sect, is just what should be expected of these sceptical mystics.

The Ism'aîleh, who take their name from the sixth Imâm, who died in 765 A.D., and was expected to reappear at the last day, represent a sect from which the Druzes have branched off. In Syria, a miserable remnant of this Persian schismatic sect of Moslems survives in the neighbourhood of Homs, in northern Syria. In the twelfth century they appear as the notable Assassins (that is, Hashshîshin, or Hemp-smokers), sworn to obey the old man (or Sheikh) of the mountain. The whole account of this Assassin sect gives clear evidence of its Persian origin, and Marco Polo describes a similar fanatical society with a similar earthly paradise much further east, in a later century. The Ism'aîleh have still grades of initiation, secret allegorical interpretations of the

Korân, a belief in the transmigration of the soul, and apparently a sacred drink like the Persian Homa. They are credited with yet more curious tenets by the Moslems and Christians of the Lebanon, showing a connection with the Indian lingam worship; but the study of such late and syncretic systems has little interest, because the various elements can be traced so much earlier in Asia, in the Mazdean and Brahminic systems, which survive in Syria mixed with Gnostic and Moslem beliefs in a meaningless and hopeless confusion.

The Anseirîyeh, who inhabit the range of Mount Casius, near Antioch, and extend southwards to the valley of the Eleutherus, are a similar sect. They were first studied by Walpole in 1851, and an account of their beliefs has been given by Mr. Laurence Oliphant which is derived from an Arab source. The Druzes consider them to be schismatics, who separated from them on the question of the divinity of Aly. In the Korân, the name 'Ansar' is applied to those converts to Islam who joined Muhammed in Medina after the Hegira; but the Anseirîyeh claim to take their name from a certain Nuseir, who came in 891 A.D. from Persia, and disseminated new doctrines in Syria. They have a ceremony of initiation with a libation of wine. They never allow women to become initiated, and the females of these tribes are, perhaps, more miserably degraded than any in Syria. They have a custom of eating bread over a new grave, which recalls the ancient funeral feasts; and the lingam worship certainly survives in their secret meetings. The name of Christ is venerated by them with those of many other prophets, and their mystic ceremony of wine-drinking is in their catechism connected with the Christian Eucharist; but they are at the same time sun and star worshippers, and are separated into four smaller sects, who adore the moon, the stars, the air, and the dawn respectively.

Professor Palmer* gives other details concerning this sect, including their deification of Selmân el Farsi, and their triad, which combines his name with those of Muhammed and Aly, contrasted with an evil triad of the first three Khalifs. Their third degree of initiation teaches that only the powers of nature are really divine, and discards all historical dogma. Their great feast of the 'Consecration of the Fragrant Herb,' which recalls the ceremonies of the Druids recorded by Pliny, is apparently a survival of the Homa-worship of Persia; but this does not invalidate Professor Palmer's comparison with the Assyrian rite noticed by Ezekiel (viii. 17).

From M. Blanche, the learned and devout French Consul at Tripoli, I gathered a few further particulars. He believed the Anseirîyeh to be a race distinct from

---

* See Besant and Palmer's 'Jerusalem,' p. 424.

others in the mountains, being, like the Druzes, tall and fair-haired, with blue eyes. Their sacred places are rude altars in groves of oak, the altar built of four stones, and supporting little lamps. The Anseirîyeh, he said, swear by these altars, and a murder was discovered to his own knowledge by the fact that the perpetrators refused to perjure themselves by swearing innocence on one of their altars. One of these sacred places is called Martmûra, and is in the hills above 'Arka, north of Tripoli.

From such indications it is clear that the Paganism of Syria and the Mazdean faith of Persia are not yet dead. The miserable relics of mystic sects which survive in the north, together with the Druzes and the Metâwileh (who are Shi'ah or Persian Moslems) further south, are the surviving results of the great struggle which commenced in the second century and continued till the tenth. They are the pools left on the shore by the great waves of opinion which resulted from the struggle of Christianity and of Islam against the ancient and fast-rooted systems of Semitic and Persian Paganism. From the syncretic spirit sprang the innumerable Gnostic sects and the Moslem heresies, the Ism'aileh, the Shi'ah, the Druzes, the Metâwileh; and however curious may be the products of these various mixtures of heathen, Moslem, and Christian doctrines, there can be no reason to suppose that the initiated possess any new

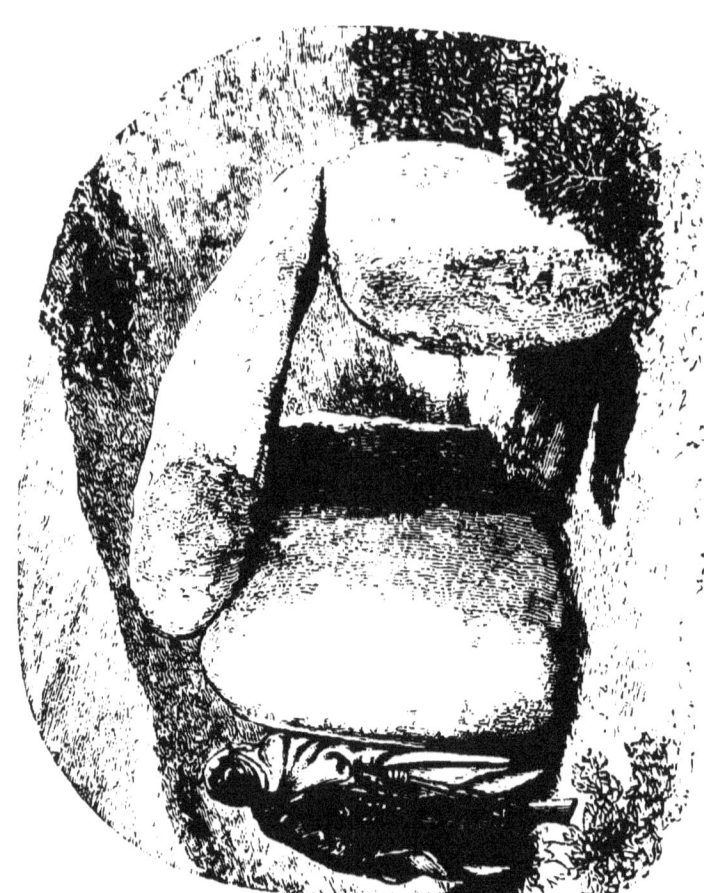

DOLMEN NEAR HESHBON.

secret which is worth the knowing for the educated student of the West.

The Christians of Syria are not less superstitious than their Moslem fellow-countrymen, and those liberal-minded Englishmen who have wished to promote unity between Western and Eastern Churches are apparently not aware of the utter degradation of the Oriental ecclesiastical body, whether Greek, Armenian, or Maronite. The ignorance and venality of the clergy is only equalled by the superstitious fanaticism of their flocks; and the verdict which will be found general amongst those who have longest known the Oriental Christians will prove to be invariably unfavourable to their morality and intelligence alike.

Among the Maronites several curious ceremonies survive, which seem to bear a relation to the old Paganism of the Phœnicians. The bride, conveyed to her new home, is pelted with corn and raisins, and on arriving she flings a pomegranate amid the party, which is greedily seized and divided by the bridegroom's companions. She then takes from her bosom a piece of dough and sticks it on the door-post, while the bridegroom, standing on the flat roof of the house over the door, holds a sword above her head. It is unnecessary to point out the pagan origin of these customs, or their relation to marriage practices still extant also in Europe.

The Maronites divide the month into lucky and unlucky days. The first five lucky, the next five unfortunate ; then four good days and four bad, three propitious, three unlucky ; and lastly two good and two bad, making a lunar month of twenty-eight days in all. The same kind of division will be found on the Accadian tablets translated by George Smith. Both Christians and Moslems in Syria turn their silver money in their pockets at the new moon for luck ; and two persons meeting under the new moon will each take out a silver coin and embrace, saying, 'May you begin and end; and may it be a good month to us.'

The fear of sunstroke and moonstroke is said to be connected with the belief in the evil eye. This superstition, so common in Italy, is universal in Syria. The 'Ain Fârigh, or 'empty eye,' is specially dangerous to children, who are therefore left dirty and ragged, lest their beauty should cause them to be envied and stricken by some person having the evil eye. The houses are marked with signs in red paint for the same reason. Among Christians it is generally a cross; among Jews, the hand or the seven-branched candlestick; among Moslems, the sacred palm (which is carried before the coffin in every Moslem funeral procession), or the double triangle forming a six-pointed star. This last is also a caste-mark in India, and a common mediæval mason's mark. The bow and arrow is also a Moslem house sign, and in Tripoli good luck is ensured by any light-blue object. Eggs are there hung outside the houses with a blue glass bracelet round them. This last town is probably an old Kadesh, sacred to Venus, for the blue colour is generally sacred to goddesses, and red to male deities. In India, blue is the colour of the Neptune-like Vishnu. At Hebron, on the other hand, red is a female colour, as contrasted with green. Each patriarch's tomb has a green covering, while the embroidered cloths over the cenotaphs of their wives are red.

The evil eye, against which (and against all demons) such charms have power, is supposed in some cases to be so powerful that its possessor can slay with a single glance. In the Babylonian Talmud it is stated that ninety-nine persons die of the evil eye for one who dies naturally. The very poorest wear a leather amulet round their necks, as in Egypt, in Italy, or in India—the same charm which is called the scapular in Ireland. Some other very European ideas may also be found among native Christians, as, for instance, the practice of making April-fools on the day answering to the first of that month.

About the middle of September the Maronites light fires on the hillsides, and in 1881 our Maronite servants observed this custom on the Moab hills, as though at home. Such fires are common at midsummer in many lands. The belief in healing springs is another Lebanon superstition, and at Heitât, in the Greek Chapel of St. George, is a picture reputed to sweat oil, which is collected in a little cup below, and sold by the priest as a panacea. At es Sâlt we find the curious legend of a lintel-stone over the door of a ruined chapel which is said to drop blood at certain seasons in memory of Christian martyrs there slain. Above Râs Baalbek is a ruined convent in which a spring is said to rise, falling into a trough among the vaults : the water is believed to be capable of giving milk to women who are nursing, and the same belief exists with regard to the chips of limestone from the rock of the 'Milk Grotto' at Bethlehem, which are sold to be dissolved as a drink. In this last instance the white marl is held to have been originally coloured by a drop of milk from the breast of the Virgin Mother.

Maundrell, in 1697, noted as a curious fact that all the sacred sights in Palestine are shown in grottoes. The number of these holy caves has not decreased since his time. At Bethlehem the manger is in a cavern. At Jerusalem we have the cave-chapels of Adam, of the Cross, of the Prison, Peter's Cave on Sion, the Grotto of the Agony, and many cave-tombs under churches. At Nazareth the Holy House is a grotto ; on Olivet we have the caves of St. Pelagia and the Credo ; at 'Ain Karem are two grottoes sacred to St. John, each with a sacred stone ; on Carmel there is the cave-chapel of Elijah. The Moslems have their holy caves at Jerusalem and Hebron ; the Druzes have another on the top of Hermon ; with these are connected holy trees, sacred pillars, consecrated springs, holy footprints, objects of worship which are universally revered from England to India or China. When we read that the Bethlehem grotto was long used as a Mithræum, where the resurrection of Tammuz was celebrated (as Jerome tells us) down to the fourth century, and when we reflect on the holy fire which at Easter breaks forth from the Sepulchre at Jerusalem, we can hardly fail to recognise a connection between the monkish sacred grottoes and the old Accadian 'cavern of the dawn,' or that cave in Alburz which was the prototype of all Mithræa, and from which the sun went forth at morn.

Among the Moslem inhabitants the Derwish orders first claim our attention, but these are of Persian and Egyptian derivation, rather than indigenous to Palestine. Like the heretical sects already noticed, they are secret societies, with vows of obedience and grades of initiation, and have their prototypes in the Indian hermit orders, the secret Gnostic sects, the Templars or the Rosicrucians, of whose doctrines a survival appears to remain among European masons. There were twelve original orders of Derwishes, of whom the most influential is that of the Malawiyeh or dancing Derwishes, whose Persian founder was Hazret Moulana, buried in the mosque of Konieh in Lycaonia; they have monasteries at Aleppo and Tripoli, but their chief centre is at Konieh. In Egypt the followers of Seiyid el Bedawi are perhaps the most famous, and they also have their monastery at Tripoli. The Bektashi Derwishes, who are not one of the twelve great orders, belong to a society founded by Bektâsh of Bokharah, who lived in the fifteenth century and is buried in Asia Minor. They wear a vestment without sleeves, having twelve symbolic stripes; their rules include contemplation, retreat, and chastity. They have a sacred girdle (like the Persian Kosti) made of white wool with three knots. They have also a secret sign, like other orders, some of whom pass their hands over their beards in a particular manner; and the candidates are admitted in secret meetings, when they are said to stand naked on an altar with arms crossed and a rope round their neck, one foot resting on the other, as in the attitude of contemplation among the Malawiyeh, and among Buddhists in India. The altar is said to be twelve-sided, with a seat each side for the initiators, and a candle burning upon it. The candidate swears obedience, chastity, and other vows; prayers are offered on the door-sill, and a sheep is sacrificed, of whose wool the new girdle is made.

This sect blows a goat-horn, which is said to be symbolic of the god of love. Many of the details of initiation recall the practices of the Templars and of the early Gnostics, and there can be little doubt that absolute scepticism was general among the knights of the great order of the Temple.

The dance of the Malawîyeh Derwishes is evidently symbolic of the course of the planets; and the position of their arms—the left hand down, the right raised— probably typifies the female and male elements in nature, as in the Indian images of Hindu deities, where the arms are so placed. Their high conical cap resembles the Persian cidaris and the mitre of the Median magi. Among other orders, customs equally indicative of pagan origin exist. The Kadríyeh in Egypt adore the sacred shoe of the founder of the sect. The Ahmediyeh, who carry red banners, have a solemn annual ceremony of introducing an ass into their mosque, probably connected with the old Egyptian symbolism of Set or Osiris as an ass. The secrets learned in the higher grades of initiation are unknown to Christians, but there is good reason to think that among all Moslem secret societies, as among Buddhists, the highest teaching is a general scepticism; and that the lower grades who charm serpents, carry banners or nets, eat scorpions, or dance, or repeat the *zikr* (the name of God), are held in ignorance of the fact that these wonders are only intended by their chiefs to excite the admiration of the populace and add to the power and fame of the sect.

The mosque of el Bedawi, at Tripoli, contains in its court-yard a cistern, or pond, of sacred fish. These are believed to have disappeared during the Russo-Turkish war, and to have been transformed into Moslem warriors, who fought for the Sultan. After the war they resumed their fish-form, and returned to Tripoli, re-appearing in the tank. According to M. Blanche, the Beidawiyeh, as the mosque is called, takes its name from St. Antony of Padua, whose church once stood here. St. Antony, be it remembered, was the saint who preached to the fishes, and it is probable that the sacred fish-pond was found already existing by the Crusaders, and was then consecrated to the saint. Tripoli was once a sacred city of Venus, and stands on the stream of Kadesha, or Kadesh. To Venus the sacred fish were no doubt once holy, and at Ascalon and Accho, down even to the fifth century, the Syrian Venus had still her sacred ponds. It is interesting, therefore, to note that there yet remains at Accho (St. Jean d'Acre) another pond of sacred fish, and that a riot was caused in this town not many years ago by the imprudence of a monk who fished up and broiled for his own eating one of the supernatural fish of Accho.

Another very curious superstition relates to the passing through a hole, or between pillars, which is a sign of future happiness or a cure for disease. Among the Jews the reverse belief is found, for the Talmud states that it is unlucky to go between a wall and a palm, or between two palms (like passing under a ladder in England); two women, two dogs, two snakes, or two pigs must in like manner not be passed between. In Asia Minor, however, there is a sacred holed stone through which infants are passed to give them health and make them intelligent. In the Aksa mosque the pillars on either side of the Mihrab form two pairs, with a narrow passage between each pair, and it was till quite lately the practice of the pilgrims to squeeze between these pillars in order to secure a future entrance into Paradise. There is now an iron stanchion between each pair, placed by order of the enlightened Raûf Pasha to discountenance such superstitious practices; but the pillars may still be seen, worn thin by the constant repetition of the custom. A black slab which was let into the wall under the porch of the central north door (on the east side) has also been removed. It used to be the practice to walk from the porch to this wall with the eyes shut, and any pilgrim who so walking managed to touch the stone with his hand was secure of future bliss.

Superstitions connected with 'passing through'

are common all over the world. In Madras children are passed under the sills of doorways, and many sacred holes and clefts are crawled through in India. The same practice was connected with dolmens, and in England we have still survivals of such superstitions in the practice of 'threading the needle' in Ripon Cathedral, or in rustic superstitions concerning passing through willow hoops or trees, or between stones.

In the same connection may be mentioned the belief that it is unlucky to tread on a threshold. In all mosques a wooden bar at the door obliges those who enter to stride across the sill, and the same custom is observed in the rustic shrines. To step across spilt water annoys evil demons, according to Rashi, and is forbidden in consequence. In the Bible (Zephaniah i. 9) those who 'leap' (or hop across) 'thresholds' are condemned, and the priest of Dagon would not tread on the threshold where his idol fell (1 Samuel v. 5). The bride in Greece and Rome was also, be it remembered, not allowed to tread on the threshold.

Sacred foot-prints are common objects of worship in many parts of the world The feet of Vishnu and of Buddha in India, the foot-marks of Christian shrines in Italy, France, or Germany, are instances. Herodotus speaks of the foot-prints of Hercules in Scythia, and of the sandal of Perseus in Egypt.

Pythagoras measured such prints at Olympia and calculated *ex pede Herculem*. At Mecca are Abraham's foot-prints, and in Jerusalem we find Christians venerating the foot-print on the summit of Olivet, and Moslems adoring the Prophet's foot-print on the sacred rock, and the foot-print of Christ in the Aksa, which was shown as early as 600 A.D. The Prophet's foot-print was also supposed, in the twelfth century, to be that of Christ, and the prints on Olivet are mentioned by all the early pilgrims. At Hebron we have the print of Adam's foot in the Haram; beyond Jordan the Adwân reverence the print of the Turkomâniyeh, a prophetess who was on her way to Mecca, and made the mark on the roadside when mounting her camel. At Baalbek four giant foot-marks are shown on the margin of the tank, in the court of the ruined mosque, and are supposed to have been impressed by some patriarch or prophet. Dubois tells us that near Madura a large leather shoe is offered to a hunter deity, while the Kadriyeh Derwishes, as already mentioned, adore a holy shoe of gigantic size, an emblem of the sacred foot which once dwelt within. These practices are but variations of the adoration of foot-prints. The Latin monks have many sites where they show marks made by the body of Christ or of some saint, the rock having become as soft as wax for the time; and in the cave beneath the sacred rock, the mark of the Prophet's head is in the same way supposed to have been impressed on the rock before he flew to heaven through the hole in the roof of the cave, while Gabriel's finger-marks show how the rock was prevented from following, reminding us of Arthur's finger-marks on his Quoit near Barmouth.

Of sacred trees in Palestine it is not necessary to speak at length, since every great tree is sacred, and hung with rags (which each mark a prayer or a vow); for Syria is not the only land where trees are so consecrated, and the sacred tree of Egypt and of Assyria is traced back as far as history goes. No less certain is it that springs are believed by the peasants of Palestine to be inhabited by good spirits. The great cave at Gibeon is said to be sometimes aglow with a supernatural light, when the local prophet comes to brood above the water, and the greatest excitement was caused by the smoke of our magnesium torches, which was mistaken for a cloud in which the offended deity had descended. At the so-called 'Oven of Job,' near the Tâbghah springs, on the borders of the Sea of Galilee, I found blue beads and shells strung on thread, and hung on a stick between the joints of the masonry; pieces of barley bread had been thrown into the stream flowing from the well, and there can be no doubt that these were propitiatory offerings to the local deity, who is now called Job. This name is probably derived from the legend in the Korân, of the spring which rose when Job stamped his heel on the ground. The story is related of Ishmael also, as well as of Pegasus, from whose hoof rose the fountain Hippocrene.

The reader is referred to 'Tent Work in Palestine' for other details of the worship of local divinities, which is the real religion of the peasantry. The faith in ghouls, in the Jân, or Genii, who become visible as whirlwinds, in 'Efrits, or demons of hideous appearance, in Kerâd 'monkeys,' or goblins, is very strong and general, and the belief in ghosts (*Kheyâl*) is also common to Moslems and Christians, for at least two well-known instances of haunted houses are to be found in Jerusalem itself.

The offerings found in the peasant shrines are worthy of notice; pomegranates, pomegranate flowers, and little figs, with small coins, beads, blue pottery, and sticks, are the commonest. It should be noticed that the fig and the pomegranate are very ancient symbols of fertility in Asia.

The various indications thus enumerated seem clearly to show the survival of religious ideas quite distinct from those of sun-worshippers. It is the old tree and stone worship of the early Accadians and Canaanites which is still preserved; and the fact that mythical tales are absent is only natural among a people who have not yet emerged from the more primitive superstitions of a religion of fear, and of constant deprecation of evil and mischievous spirits—a kind of early belief which found expression in the magic tablets of the Accadians, long before the planetary cultus of the Assyrians had been systematized.

There are intelligent and cultivated men among the missionaries of Syria, who have spent their lives among the peasantry; and I have generally found them convinced that mythology, such as is preserved among Aryan races, has no existence in the traditions of the Fellahîn—a conclusion which is strengthened by the recent discovery of the folk-lore of the trans-Jordanic Arabs, who belong to an entirely distinct stock, and who readily repeat legends of great mythical interest.

The shrines of Noah and of other patriarchs have legends attached which are of considerable antiquity. The gigantic tomb of Noah is in the valley between Lebanon and Anti-Lebanon, but near Kadesh on Orontes a square enclosure of earth is pointed out as Noah's Ark, and not far off is the Tannûr, or 'Oven,' a name given to a spring whence the flood is said to have burst forth. South of Ramleh there is another Tannûr, with the same legend, at Gezer, and yet further south is the spring of Noah's daughter or wife. This legend of the Tannûr is found in the Korân, and the pious say there was more than one such mouth, and that all these cave springs assisted in swallowing up the water again when the deluge was over.

The legend of the dragon who swallows the water of the Virgin's Spring at Jerusalem when he is awake —which accounts for its sudden intermittent rise when he is asleep, is well known. It is curious that this spring is close to Zoheleth ('the serpent rock'), but the story may be compared with the Vedic myth of the struggle of Indra, the rain-god, with the dragon who keeps back the waters—who is generally supposed to have been a cloud.

Stories of Cain and Abel are told in Syria which are not Biblical. Abel was slain at Yekin, where Cain's grave is shown, south of Hebron; but the murderer was forced to carry the body on his back to Abila, north-west of Damascus, where Abel's tomb is shown on the mountain-top. Of Esau, also, the curious tale is told that his head was buried in the cave of Machpelah, but his body in the tomb at Si'aîr, north of Hebron—a story which can be traced to the Talmud. The legend of the gnat which penetrated into the brain of Titus, as related in the Talmud, is found also applied by the Arabs to Nimrod, and localized at Merd, north of Mâr Sâba.

Another personage of importance is Neby Shit, identified with Seth, but probably representing originally the Hittite and Egyptian deity, Set, who is perhaps ultimately connected with Thoth, the Hermes or Moon and pillar deity of Egypt and Phœnicia. Shem and Ham, Lot, Jonah, Caleb, Nun, and Joshua—Og even—have shrines in Syria, as well as the three patriarchs at Hebron, and most of their sons elsewhere; but perhaps the most generally venerated of prophets is el Khudr, 'the Green One,' who is confused with Elijah and with St. George; who is venerated by the Druzes in the Carmelite monastery, and at the springs of Jordan, as well as by Moslems in all parts of the country. There can be little doubt that the vivifying power of nature in the spring-time is personified in this green deity, who in the Korân is connected with Alexander of the two horns.

At Tyre we found in Neby Ma'shûk 'the prophet beloved of women,' a modern representative of the Tyrian Hercules. His shrine stands on the knoll, where probably the oldest temple on the mainland was pointed out to Alexander; and a legend is attached to the effect that a cave full of honey and of bees exists beneath, which if opened would cause the fall of the sacred monument. Here, as elsewhere in Moslem shrines, a palm grows; and the legend of the palm of St. Saba, the fruit of which is good for barren women, and which the saint planted and saw in a single night attain to full size and bear dates, will be remembered by visitors to the monastery.

A few stray legends attaching to other places may be worthy of notice. Thus on Ebal is the cave of Sitt Eslamiyeh, who is said to have flown from Egypt and torn open the rock, apparently to hide from her brother Selim. Others say her bones were carried through the air from Damascus; but, whatever be the right legend, the little lamp in the cave may be seen twinkling high up the mountain by night.

Neby Skander (or Alexander), whose shrine is on the volcanic peak west of the plain of Esdraelon, is reputed to have had two rams'-horns, like the Greek hero, who has become a mythical personage in Asia. He met Abraham at the foot of Tabor, and is thus connected with Melchizedek, King of Salem, who was believed in the Middle Ages to have encountered the patriarch at this same spot.

Still more curious is the legend of Neby Duhy ('the Leader'), whose tomb is on the conical hill south of Tabor. He is believed to have been killed near the Kishon, and his bones were carried by his dog to the hill-top and there interred. This story seems probably to have had a Persian origin, as the dog among the Parsees consecrates the corpse by placing its foot on it, while among the Semitic people the dog is an unclean animal. Near Banias lies buried a saint who is said himself to have been a dog, but I have not been able to gather any details concerning his career. Perhaps he may be considered to be a relation of the famous moon dog, Anubis, or of the Vedic prototype of Hermes.

The Jisr Mujâmi'a, or 'Bridge of Gathering,' in the Jordan valley suggests a connection with the Persian 'Bridge of the Gatherer,' which reappears as the bridge stretching from the Temple to Olivet, on which the red cow walked, and across which, according to the Moslems, the dead are to pass safely to Paradise, or else to fall from its sword-like edge into Gehennum beneath. The Jordan valley bridge is, however, said to be so-called because a gathering of poets here competed for the favour of a fair maiden.

In concluding this sketch of Syrian superstitions, it may be worth noticing how deeply impregnated with Paganism is the Moslem faith in all countries. Some writers appear to regard the religion of Islam as a pure monotheism of highly spiritual character. Yet even Muhammed himself was not so free from superstitious belief as to rise above the adoration of the black stone which he preserved at Mecca when he destroyed other idols.*

There is much in the Korân itself which is known to be derived from Talmudic sources. Such is the legend of Abraham's escape from the fiery furnace into which Nimrod cast him. Other beliefs are evi-

* See Appendix II.

dently of Persian derivation, as, for instance, the angels Munker and Nakîr, who sit on the two stones at head and foot of a Moslem grave, and question the soul—an idea also to be found in the Zendavesta. Muhammed retired to the cave in the Mountain of Light, as did Zoroaster to the cave in Alborz: and his ascent to heaven; his tempting by Iblis; his approach to the sacred tree of the limit, whose leaves fall to denote deaths; his wondrous steed Burak (or 'Lightning'), with a woman's breast, and wings; his escape, like Bruce, behind the spider's web, are all legends which have parallels in earlier mythology. The Korân also contains traditions concerning Christ, which are common to early heretical gospels, such as that of His birth under the bowing tree, and the phantom crucifixion of the Docetic Gnostics. Stone and tree worshippers were the Arabs of Muhammed's day, and such they still remain in rural districts, in spite of the higher teaching of Islam.

The eschatology of the Moslem faith has of late attracted special attention for political reasons, but those who have described the beliefs connected with the coming of the Mohdy seem sometimes hardly aware how entirely they derive their imagery from the earlier Persian doctrines.

The year 1300 of the Hejirah was commonly expected to be that in which the reincarnate Imâm should appear and the triumph of Islam be secured, and this year coincides with 1882-3 of our era. Many thought that Arâbi Pasha was the Mohdy himself, others believed in the Sudan prophet, others in the Senussi of Tripoli. Yet the orthodox belief points to Aleppo as the scene of his appearance. His coming must be preceded by a time of trouble, with signs and evils of every description. The Earth-beast who supports the world and the incarnate Iblis will appear to oppose him on the plains of northern Syria, and the Sunnee Moslems believe, no less devoutly than the Shi'ah, in this supernatural triumph of their faith, and in the judgment which is to follow immediately. Yet all this imagery can be traced in the Zend Scriptures, probably as early as the time of Cyrus himself, for the antagonist, the Earth-beast, the time of trouble, the future triumphant prophet, are prominent features of the Zoroastrian creed, with the judgment and the wondrous bridge. El Borak is but the Assyrian cherub or the Persian centaur, and the tree of the limit is the tree of Asshur, or Allât. Islam is no new faith, but a syncretic system based on the Mazdeism, the Christianity, and the Judaism which preceded it: in Western Asia it is a religion which has begun to decline, and has almost ceased to be a power capable of uniting men of various race and of distinct aspirations; and those who believe that the green banner could still rally the Indian, the Egyptian, the Arab, Persian, and Turkish Moslems against the civilization of the West, have failed to appreciate the weakness of the bonds which still bind together the various schools and sects of the Muhammedan world.

CHAPTER X.

THE BELKA ARABS.

A RESIDENCE of three months in Moab,* combined with former experience, allows of some degree of familiarity with the tribes of the district, and permits of a judgment being formed at least on those Arab clans which claim to represent in Syria the pure blood of the Nejed and of Yemen.

The recent campaign in Egypt, with its sad accompanying drama in Sinai, has given prominence for the moment to the question of Bedawîn character, and the Nejed Bedawîn have found a champion in Mr. Blunt apparently convinced of the superiority of their race, and of the high destiny which awaits them.

From the little tribes of the Judean desert or of the Jordan valley, and from the impoverished clans round Beersheba and Gaza, or those 'cousins of the gipsies' who represent in Galilee the once powerful

* This chapter is reprinted by permission from *Blackwood's Magazine*.

tribe of Akil Agha, it may not be possible to form a judgment of the Bedawîn at their best; but the 'Adwân, or 'Enemies,' who once held Judea in a continual condition of terror, and who raided as far as Jerusalem, and even to Jaffa, are proud sons of the desert, who yet range over a district of a thousand square miles, and who feign to consider the smaller and older tribes, such as the Ajermeh 'Abbâd or Ghaneimât, as their tributaries or serfs, although they have of late years so decreased in power and prestige that the inferior tribes have now the position of allies and friends, rather than that of dependents.

The 'Adwân own all the Jordan valley and Mount Gilead to the Jabbok, and on the south their influence extends to the Valley of Callirhoe and to Tell M'aîn. Their eastern boundary runs from near this last place to Samik, and thence to Yedûdeh and el Kahf, and east of Ammân to the Kal'at Zerka. On the east and south-east the dominant tribe is that of the Sakhûr or Beni Sakhr ('Sons of the Rock'), superior, if anything, in power to the 'Adwân, whose country they appear to enter at pleasure, at all events in time of peace, to water their camels at the springs of Hesbân 'Ammân and in intermediate valleys. The 'Adwân possess far the richest country, and their chiefs own lands at Kefrein, Nimrîn, and in the hills, which are rudely tilled for them by the Ghawârneh, or 'Men of the Ghor,' and by other Arabs of lower caste. The 'Adwân also own sheep, goats, and cows, whereas the wealth of the Beni Sakhr consists almost entirely of camels.

South of the Zerka M'aîn, or ravine of Callirhoe, dwell various small tribes, known collectively as Hameidi, who have no superior chief, and who are, in fact, dependents of the Beni Sakhr, as are the 'Abbâd and others of the 'Adwân. The proper method of treating the Hameidi appears to be to enter into treaty with the Beni Sakhr chiefs, and visit this district under their escort. The Hameidi are allied to the notorious Sheikh Mujelli of Kerak, and the only hold which the explorer has over them lies in the fact that they often carry corn to Jerusalem, and may there be detained by the Turks as hostages. The Hameidi are a very degraded and turbulent set, and without proper escort the traveller would probably be pillaged in their country.

East of the Beni Sakhr, on the borders of the Syrian desert, are found many tribes of the great nation of the 'Anazeh, or 'Goat' Arabs, who extend northwards east of Haurân. The tribes of Jebel Ajlûn (the Beni Hasan) appear to be scattered and powerless, as the settled population here holds its own. For practical purposes the explorer need, therefore, only deal with the 'Adwân and the Beni Sakhr.

The 'Adwân have two principal divisions—the

elder branch of Diâb, whose present chief is 'Aly, and who live chiefly in the district north of Heshbon, descending in winter to Nimrîn; and the younger branch of the Nimr, those who follow Sheikh Goblân, and who encamp near Heshbon and descend to Kefrein. Both these divisions of the tribe are now very much diminished in numbers and in power, and since they have begun to cultivate the land they have also fallen off in martial reputation. The young chief 'Aly Diâb, a man of perhaps forty, has thrown in his lot with the Turks; while Goblân represents the native opposition, and adheres to the old traditions of independence.

The Beni Sakhr* were until lately a united and powerful tribe, under a famous chieftain, Fendi el Fâîz. He left eight sons, and after his death they quarrelled. The tribe was thus split into two factions, one allying itself with the 'Adwân, the other, under Satm, making a league with the 'Anazeh, once the bitterest of the Beni Sakhr enemies.

In May, 1881, these parties came in collision near the 'Adwân border, and Satm was slain in a skirmish.

* Some one, not apparently a philologist, has suggested that the Beni Sakhr are representatives of Beni Issachar, and represent a 'lost tribe,' but, without considering the question whether the old Jewish notion of 'lost tribes,' which we find perhaps first in 2 Esdras xiii. 40—46, has any foundation in fact, it may be remarked that the words 'Sakhr' and 'Issachar' have only one letter—the final *R*—in common.

Nevertheless, in the autumn of the same year, while we were yet in Moab, the sons of Fendi el Fâiz patched up their quarrels, and were consequently regarded with much suspicion by the 'Adwân. The principal chief, Satâm, brother of Satm, was in league with the Turks, to whom he gave information of our presence; and the malcontents of the Nimr are thus shut up in a corner between Satâm on the east, and the Turks in es Sâlt, aided by their own relatives of the elder branch. Such, roughly sketched, have been the results of Turkish diplomacy beyond Jordan during the last fifteen years; and to these causes of decay among the Belka tribes is added the fear of incursion from the south: for when Ibn Rashid and the Arabs of the Nejed came up in 1880 as far as Bozrah, the Belka Arabs all huddled together in the Jordan valley and the lower hills, and their invading kinsmen feasted joyfully on captured camels of the Beni Sakhr and the 'Anazeh.

The history of the 'Adwân tribe, as related by Sheikh Goblân, is as follows:—About three centuries ago (or nine generations, all known by name), Fowzân Ibn es Suweit, one of the Defîr tribe in the Nejed, fled, in consequence of having slain his cousin, to the Moab plateau, and found refuge with the Korda tribe at Sâmik, east of Heshbon. He afterwards married a daughter of Abu Heider, chief of this Korda tribe, and had two sons—Saleh, from whom descend the elder 'Adwân branch, called 'Ashíret Saleh, of whom 'Aly Diâb is now chief; and Jedid, from whom Goblân claims to be the eighth descendant. The heir of 'Aly Diâb is a boy named Sultan; the heir of the Nimr or younger branch is Goblân's son Fahed, 'the Lynx,' who has a boy named Fowaz. The names of the intermediate generations have no special interest. It may be noted, however, that Jedid and his descendants all married into the Korda tribe (which has now disappeared or become merged with the 'Adwân) down to the time of Goblân's grandfather, Nimr, who took a bride of the Beni Sakhr. Goblân's father, Fadl, married one of the 'Ajermeh, and he has thus in his veins some of the best and oldest Arab blood of the country, for the 'Ajermeh, though now a small and poor tribe, belong to one of the clans which the 'Adwân found in the Belka, when their fugitive ancestor sought hospitality with the Korda in the sixteenth century.

The ease with which Goblân recounted these pedigrees gives a good example of the way in which such knowledge is orally preserved among a people entirely illiterate. It is also remarkable that the tribes which came most recently from the Nejed are those which consider themselves the most noble, and which practically are the dominant class.

The names of the smaller tribes of the Moab plateau we carefully collected, but it would be uninteresting here to enumerate them. The 'Ajermeh, near Heshbon; the Ghaneimât, north of the Zerka M'aîn; the four divisions of the 'Abbâd, round 'Arak el Emîr, and the D'aja, further east, appear to be the most important of the thirty-five tribes whose names, with those of their living chiefs, I collected, in 1881, within the boundaries of the 'Adwân country. The groups of the Beni Sakhr are equally numerous, and we found that there were six principal divisions of this great clan, stretching from near Kerak as far as the Haurân, and including at least twenty-four families or smaller tribes, of which the Fâîz family is the most important, Fendi el Fâîz having ruled the whole of the Beni Sakhr, and leaving eight sons, of whom Satâm, since the death of his brother Satm, has now become the leader.

As regards the numbers of these tribes, it is most difficult to form an estimate. Every father of a family has, however, his tent, and five souls may, as a rule, be counted to a tent. The differences of rank and wealth are shown not by the number of tents, but by the length and newness of the family mansion. The longest tent I ever saw was that of 'Aly Diâb, and his camp consisted of 80 tents, or 400 souls. The smallest camps will consist of perhaps three or four tents, generally found, however, not far from a larger settlement, and their arrangements are constantly changing, as the Arabs seem rarely to remain more than ten days or a fortnight in one place. Goblân estimated the various Beni Sakhr tribes as ranging from 200 to 20 tents, and the average would probably be about 60 tents. The Beni Sakhr, not including those in the Haurân, number, according to his estimate, 1,500 tents, representing a population of 7,500 souls. This is not likely to be an exaggerated estimate, as Goblân would not wish to make them out more numerous than they really are. Taking the same average for the 'Adwân and their allies, we obtain a total of some 2,200 tents, or 11,000 souls, giving a density of 10 persons per square mile, which appears to be a very probable result for such a district as that of the Belka. These figures may not be without value at a time when it becomes important to be able to estimate the probable numbers of various Bedawîn clans, concerning which but little is as yet known.

Although the power of the dominant tribes, 'Adwân or Beni Sakhr, has been materially diminished of late years, such chiefs as 'Aly and Goblân still enjoy the position of great gentlemen in the desert. When crossing the Jordan, in 1881, I was particularly struck by an incident which occurred. Goblân was standing among his retainers, all mounted on strong horses, when a poor Arab, with a wife and daughter, came down to the river from the east, driving a diminutive donkey. The women were afraid to trust themselves in the water, even on its back, and looked hopelessly at the rushing stream; but the man invoked the help of Goblân, with that peculiar mixture of affectionate respect and simple familiarity which is one charm of nomadic society, and his womenkind were promptly hoisted on the two tallest horses, behind two of Goblân's relatives, who went back on purpose to the western shore, and again crossed the ford to the east.

Nor was this the only instance of liberality and courtesy which we remarked among the 'Adwân chiefs. Although most exasperatingly greedy for money, it must be confessed that Goblân spent it with a princely lavishness. The guests of his autumn feast and the poor pilgrim to Mecca alike received a large share of the presents and wages given by the Survey party, and it is by such lordly munificence and hospitality that a great Sheikh retains his influence among poorer and weaker tribes in time of peace.

It is interesting in this connection to mark, among a people entirely unable to write, the way in which the virtues of the dead are recorded, and we found that on the tombs of great chiefs were modelled in plaster the horseman, with his sword and bow, on one side, and on another the coffee-cups, pestle and mortar, jug, and spoon for roasting, the paraphernalia, in short, of Arab hospitality. In this rude manner the prowess and liberality of the dead man were set forth by descendants who could only mark the tribe to which he belonged, and were obliged to commit his name to the pious memory of his children.

As regards Arab character generally, the result of several years' experience is not by any means satisfactory, nor have recent events tended to increase our respect for the Bedawîn. The noble nomad, ranging free as air in the desert, is an original creation of Arab poetry, which has been somewhat clumsily copied by those who see the possibility of turning him to political account. He is represented as naturally high-minded, hospitable, and observant of his word or oath, brave to a fault, and generous to prodigality. But what we have learned of his actual character in Egypt or in Sinai only serves to strengthen the impression made by a sojourn of several months in the Belka. The recluse who would wish to flee from the hard struggle of Western civilized existence, who is disgusted with the insincerity, the jobbery, the schemes and jealousies of European society, the strife and the meanness of public life, and the *banalité* of domesticity, will not find peace in the wilderness. He will find only the same passions, the same objects, the same insincerity and absence of good faith among the mass of the Bedawin which he has deplored at home, and, although exceptions may exist, and men of higher character may be recognised in the desert, the European will certainly find that he has made a change for the worse, and will miss that which is best and noblest among his fellow-countrymen.

A web of petty intrigue is spread all over the Bedawin country. Their quarrels, jealousies, and infidelities are as petty and short-sighted as any in the West. There is but one object which the Arab places steadily before his face, and that is the acquisition of wealth. The influence which a European may exert over them depends, no doubt, in great measure, on personal character, and on knowledge of the language, customs, and ideas of those among whom he dwells. It does so in every quarter of the world; but the mainspring of that influence proceeds from the idea that the Frank is master of untold wealth, to be obtained, if not by terrorism, then by flattery and servility, by an affectation of affectionate esteem, which it is not in Arab nature to feel for a stranger, and also by secret intrigue and petty larceny. The Arab will betray his friend for gold not less readily than the Frank. The Arab will cringe to the rich and powerful, and will be cold or cruel to the poor and helpless, not less than the civilized dweller in Western cities.

Exceptions may, I believe, be found, and I have known Arabs who appeared worthy of trust, and who might, perhaps, be believed, when they spoke, to be telling the truth. But as regards Arab character generally, it seems probable that they may be divided into two great categories—those who have become sordidly avaricious and degraded by contact with civilization, who have acquired some new ideas, such as those of cultivation, of keeping cows and goats, nay, who have even, like Goblân, sent children to school and trod the deck of a gunboat; and, on the other hand, the category of the Arab in all his aboriginal savagery, stalking the desert with nothing but his shirt and his long tuft or pig-tail, a cautious, crafty, not to say cowardly, barbarian, lurking for the stray stranger, filching the camel of his friend, or joining the noble contest of ten against one. Every man, every family, every tribe of the Arabs, has its own character. Some are rich, powerful, and hospitable, of high reputation and great courage. Some are poor and evil, with broken fortunes, flying the consequences of a deed of violence, or joined to the gangs of miserable thieves and outlaws who skulk in the valley in summer, or shiver in mountain caves in winter, and who are shot without mercy if their thieving expedition be clumsily managed. Human nature is, perhaps, at the bottom, not much different in the desert and in the city; but the Arab is without any such incentives to improvement as spring from the religion and civilization of the West, and the idea of the noble dweller in the wilderness, superior in morality and motive to the Western Frank, is an enthusiast's dream, as mischievous as it is unfounded. There are those who seem to believe the camel to be a superior method of transport to the locomotive, the fleet Arab runner preferable to the telegraph, the Bedawi greater than the Briton; but to such there is only one answer, if they wish to study the question fairly and without motive—go to the desert and see for yourselves.

Loving, warring, feasting, singing (but not whistling to Eblis), marrying, and rejoicing over the firstborn; dying under the accursed cairn, or in the foray, or mourned by many friends; hating, backbiting, slandering, envying, quarrelling, cursing, lying, running away; cringing, bullying, flattering, turning the cold shoulder; flirting with maidens, beating (or stoning) wives; weeping over the dead; swearing brotherhood (and forgetting the oath); proud among his sons, scolded by his womankind; happy and irritated, anxious or expectant; grasping, avaricious, untrustworthy, even stupid, but also lavish and courteous, intelligent and full of information; superstitious and sceptical, fearing God and conscience, or without regard to either; rich and poor, good, bad, and indifferent—I can recall the Arab under all such circumstances and aspects, but I never was able to discover that he therein differed from the rest of mankind. I never found a wilderness where peace and goodwill reigned among the whole people, or a tribe where all the moral virtues flourished unadulterated.

The courage of the Bedawîn is one of their most lauded virtues, but one which within the present century has not been conspicuously vindicated. I have seen more than once a tribe on a foray, and have heard more than one tale of Bedawîn battles. As a rule, the bulletin seems to be to the following effect: 'We bravely attacked the enemy, which made its appearance in a force of one to our ten. We took several prisoners, and the enemy lost heavily, two horses and several cows being slain. At length his remaining forces withdrew, and we found our casualties to include one mare hurt in the leg by a spear. We cut off the forefingers of our prisoners in remembrance of those of our tribe whose beards and hair had been burned off on a former occasion, and letting them go, drove off the captured camels, and endeavoured to conceal as far as possible the direction of our victorious retreat.'

Such are the deeds which I have heard recounted, and although men are sometimes slain in battle, and Fahed en Nimr has legs which have been peppered with small-shot, it must be remembered that to initiate a blood-feud is a most serious circumstance in tribe life, and that the whole policy of the leaders will for many years be directed to the healing of the breach thus caused, and to the settlement of blood-money. When a disagreement occurs between two tribes, they will gather their spearmen, concentrate their encampments, and square up, so to speak, towards each other; but they generally contrive, before matters come to an open breach, to find a third party willing to mediate, and a compromise is established, to the great relief of the bold warriors on either side. Such an event as that of Satm's death, slain apparently in hot blood in a quarrel concerning a cornfield, is one of the greatest importance in the annals of the tribes concerned. He was a Sheikh of a most important tribe (the Beni Sakhr), and his death is still, I believe, unavenged, and I found the 'Adwân unwilling to speak on the subject, with exception of the stout Goblân, whose hate of the Beni Sakhr—a tribe sworn to take his life—caused him to gloat with satisfaction over the death of a promising and popular chief. Yet, in spite of this occurrence, one division of the clan of which Satm was leader had allied itself to the elder branch of the 'Adwân within a year of their Sheikh's death or murder.

I have been attacked more than once by Arabs on

the war-path, in their usual proportion of ten to one. On the first occasion I escaped because I was described as being a consul; on another, the horsemen who fell on my native follower rode away rapidly as soon as they saw me turn back and gallop with one companion towards them. On a third, a group of horsemen who were threatening our servants disappeared on seeing a pigeon fall to my gun in the distance. On two or three other occasions, groups of spearmen, who galloped up, brandishing lances and curvetting their steeds, became at first quiet and cautious and then friendly, on seeing that their evolutions produced no visible effect on our conduct. It was the same in Egypt. Gaudy chiefs caracoled in sight of our pickets, but their followers disappeared immediately when one man was hit; and on the morning of the battle of Tell el Kebir, where were the clouds of 5,000 Arab horsemen who were to assist Arâbi Pasha?

It is not, then, on account of his courage that the Arab is dangerous, but rather on account of his crafty strategy. It was at first a wonder to me that our guides should be so much alarmed at the appearance of a single Harâmi, or bandit, when both the guide and the explorer were well armed and mounted; but I learned by experience that the single man is not alone, and that even a single boy may be the fugleman of a whole gang of the worst class of outlaws. The ability of the Bedawi in hiding in folds of the ground, in approaching his victim as the hunter does the stag, in springing suddenly in numbers from behind rocks or gulleys, so that armed men seem literally to rise from the earth; the ambush; the treacherous league with an enemy; the rapidity with which news is conveyed over the desert from hill to hill, by signals and runners—these are the true dangers against which the traveller who trusts himself to the honour of the Arab has constantly to provide. Let it be seen that he has a power behind him, whether political or military, and he is safe in all districts where it is known. Let him even but look over his shoulder as though to observe his distance from unseen support, and he will see the advancing robber checked at once, or behold him suddenly swallowed up by the earth. The eye attains to unusual quickness in the wilderness, where a single head or even a broken bush shows a danger, and where the guide appears to note every imprint on the soil and every shadow in the distance. Silence and solitude are all around at one instant, and at the next moment a rude, inquisitive crowd may have encircled the traveller.

So long as we were able tacitly to countenance the 'Adwân supposition that we were forerunners of an unseen power which had no need to fear the Turk, we were safe: but the great difficulty in our recent

ARAB CIRCLE NEAR HESHBON

To face p. 330.

visit lay in the fact that it became necessary to swagger and to retreat at the same time. The Beni Sakhr had betrayed us, the 'Adwân had deserted us, and intrigues were certainly being woven against our small and unprotected party; it was only the good faith (or political fancies) of Goblân which prevented such an 'accident' as Turkish Governors deplore with satisfaction.

The Arab of the Belka is a shrewd politician. Party feeling runs high, and is divided between the advantages of alliance (temporary, of course) with the Turk, or of stubborn resistance to his will. The patriotic party (if one may so term it) sees its champion in Goblân; the time-servers are the followers of 'Aly Diâb. The Beni Sakhr are divided in the same way; but Goblân, the rebel and outlaw, as he is regarded by the established Government, is far the most popular man in Moab, in spite of his unamiable characteristics.

The power of the 'Adwân lies in their alliance with the Belka Arabs, the smaller tribes already enumerated. Without these their numbers are so few that they would be eaten up by the Beni Sakhr or the 'Anazeh, who dwell in more sterile districts. It was, therefore, considered most ill-advised on the part of 'Aly Diâb to quarrel with the 'Ajermeh concerning certain lands round Hesbân, well known to belong from time immemorial to the older tribe, yet awarded to 'Aly by the Turkish Governor. The dispute caused a mighty gathering of tents at Hesbân, but it was patched up by a mediator. The injustice will, however, probably recoil on the Diâb line in the shape of diminished popularity and influence among their allies, and will yet more widen the breach between the two branches of the 'Adwân family.

During my stay at Hesbân I received visits from many 'Adwân and Beni Sakhr chiefs, but none from 'Aly Diâb. He sent orders that a sheep should be slain in our honour, and he despatched his venerable father to interview the Frank; but he was too wise to compromise himself by a personal visit to travellers not recognised by the Turkish Government, and who were escorted by Goblân. The aged Diâb ('the wolf'), a modern Zeeb, was a little old man of commanding appearance, whom Goblân treated with the respect due to an elder relative. He has either abdicated or been deposed in favour of his son 'Aly, and has a broken leg, in consequence of the barbarity of his captors, when, some years ago, with others, he was trapped by the Governor of Nâblus into a visit to that town. It was the desire of money and Government rewards which led the chiefs of the elder branch into the snare, against the advice of Goblân. They paid dearly for a return to liberty, and their mentor was shown to have been only too correct in his distrust of the enemy, even when 'bearing gifts.'

The conversation on occasion of this visit was most instructive. The old gentleman, who came in a private, not in an official capacity, hobbled in aided by his grey junior, and leaned on his crooked cane, arrayed in a fine white and amber abba, with a warm lambswool jacket beneath. It was not long after the taking of Tunis by the French, and their war with Beni Helal, or 'Sons of the Crescent,' as the 'Adwân term the Arabs of North Africa, for whom they have a great respect. The English, he remarked, had as yet taken nothing in the East. I reminded him of Cyprus. 'No,' he answered; 'you hold that as tributaries of the Sultan.' He then asked if the French would take Tripoli also. I replied that it belonged to the Sultan. 'So did Tunis,' he drily answered. I told him that the English, having a country as fair as that of the 'Adwân, and being a righteous people, did not desire to seize the lands of the Sultan or of anyone else, and this final announcement he received in silence, with an air of courteous incredulity.

The interview was thus of considerable interest. It is not surprising that the Maronites and the Christians of Damascus and Jerusalem should be keenly watching the political horizon—that they should know Lord Beaconsfield and Mr. Gladstone by name, and approve the policy of the latter, because they consider it anti-Turkish; but it was somewhat startling to find in the wilds of Moab an old gentleman with a stiff leg, who had certainly not been over Jordan for several years, yet who understood the nature of our tenure of Cyprus, and dimly foresaw the probability of such an event as the occupation of Egypt.

Another question which greatly excited my interest was that of the religion of the Transjordanic Arabs. West of the river we had often found our guides anxious to pray at all shady streams, rather than to ride fast in the heat. We had seen them kiss the headstones of their fathers' graves, and heard them swear continually 'as the Lord liveth,' but it always appeared that such religion had been acquired through knowledge of cities and mosques, and that the wilder the tribe, the less pious, or, at all events, less orthodox, its members. This view was confirmed by a sojourn among the 'Adwân, for in three months I never once saw Goblân offer a prayer, nor did any of our guides, with the exception of one who could read and write (Sheikh Fellah, the brother of Goblân), ever attempt to recite the fat-hah or go through the ordinary routine of prostration.

But, on the other hand, we found that the more ignorant of our guards were firmly convinced that the dolmens were inhabited by ghouls—an idea at which the sceptical and rationalistic Fahed mocked, saying that educated people knew them to be watch-towers, but that 'some persons had no understanding.' A fine satire, be it remarked, on some civilized opinions; for the dolmen, whether altar or tomb, was certainly not a watch-tower, and was also probably connected with old superstitious worship of demons.

The existence of fairy-tales which we found to be a peculiarity of the Arabs as contrasted with the western Fellahîn, has no direct connection with their religion; but one of the 'Ajermeh pointed out to us the Hajr el Mena, or 'Stone of Desire,' which was a wishing-stone, on which the hand should be placed by those who have a desire to be fulfilled. This also was pronounced by Goblân to be only an ignorant fancy, yet it is probably as much a popular belief as is that in the demon-slave of Solomon who lives in the Valley of Callirhoe, and to whom sacrifices are offered.

On another occasion Goblân, stopping his horse at two little piles of stone, dismounted and brushed away the dust from a slab of rock, where he showed me a natural erosion in the form of a footprint, with a second, smaller and artificially cut, beside it. This is called Mâta et Turkomanîyeh ('The Place of Pressing of the Turkoman Woman'), and tradition says that a travelling prophetess from Mecca here made the mark when alighting from her camel. It is considered pious to clear away the dust, and the relic is greatly venerated by the Arabs.

Trees in Moab are scarce, and this may account for their being sacred. They are hung with rags, and a sacred tomb-circle is often found beside them. In one at Rujm Bel'ath we may perhaps recognise an old Baalath; another is called Sheikh Terki; and a third S'aûr, or 'Flaming,' reminding us of the Tree of Light of the Ghatafan Arabs sacred to Allat, and of the older Assyrian thorn-tree, which was called 'The Tree of the Great Light.'

Cairns or pillars (Meshâhed) are raised along the roads in Moab wherever Neby Musa on the west, or Neby Osh'a on the north, can be seen; and it even seemed that in some cases they had a connection with dolmen groups. But there is another cultus among the Bedawin equally important with the preceding—namely, the veneration shown for the graves of their ancestors. 'Ancestor worship' is no doubt a term liable to misapplication, and the oldest religious ideas are connected with life rather than with the dead. Man has probably never conceived his forefathers to have been when alive materially different from himself, though he may have been afraid of their ghosts after death. But, on the other hand, no student of Brahmin or Chinese creeds can fail to recognise how ancient races have always venerated their ancestors, and have conceived them to be ever present and interested in the welfare of their descendants. It is, in fact, only in the advanced civilization of the West that men have begun to despise ancient birth, and to consider that ancestors are a marketable commodity.

The Arab, then, surrounds the grave of a man of noted sanctity with a circle of stones, and places on one side (almost invariably on the west) a little dolmen altar about 3 feet high, consisting of two stones supporting a third laid flat on the top. Whenever he visits the spot he kisses this stone and invokes the dead man's aid, placing his forehead on the altar, and then depositing a gift—a stick, a bullet, a copper coin, a berry, a piece of blue pottery, or some other memorial of his visit. He faces east as he does so, and mutters his prayer. This cultus appears to be one of the most important rites generally observed by the Belka tribes.

It is true that the Bedawin observe the fast of Ramadan and the ensuing feast. The great day of their year is that on which the Mecca pilgrims visit Mount Arafat, and on this day (as we witnessed in 1881) even the man who has but two or three camels will kill one as a feast for his family and a sacrifice to his God. Then the tents of the chiefs are scenes of unbounded hospitality, and then, for once in the year, even the beggar tastes flesh. But this observance of the great feast by no means proves the Arabs to be strict Moslems. Mecca with its pilgrimage, its sacred stone, its naked pilgrims, was an institution long before Muhammed was born. He purified the Arab Paganism, but he was unable entirely to eradicate ancient superstitions, in some of which he may probably have been himself a believer. We did not, it is true, find moon-worship or sun-worship, such as has been thought to survive in these districts, among the 'Adwân; but what we did find was the survival of the original Paganism of the Jâhalin, or 'Ignorant,' before Islam was preached — stone-worship, tree-worship, the veneration of ancestors, of streams and springs, like that which Herodotus or Porphyry describes, or which is the religion of Dravidians in India. The Bedawîn, as we knew them, were a prayerless people, without mosque, Imam, or even Derwish, superstitiously afraid of the desert demons, and adoring the graves of the dead and the relics of former prophets. They possess also a mythology of most interesting character, and their only approach to Moslem custom is in those points where Islam is founded on ancient Arab Paganism.

The Beni Sakhr and other tribes do, it is true, annually escort the dwindling procession of the Syrian Haj from Damascus, but this is no indication of pious belief in the duty of pilgrimage. The Bedawîn are paid by the Turk, to prevent that inevitable pillage of the pilgrims which would result from the denial of a time-honoured right to levy black-mail as protectors of the Faithful.

In connection with this question the names of the Arabs become important. They are not the ordinary Moslem names of the peasantry, but such as express the qualities most admired. Nimr, 'The Leopard;' Fahed, 'The Lynx;' Dhib, 'The Wolf;' 'Adu, 'The Foe;' Shedid, 'The Strong;' Kablan (better known as Goblân), 'Satisfaction;' Fowâz, 'The Victorious,' are common names. Mr. Drake once heard of a boy who was named Mukt'a, or 'Ford,' because he was born when his mother was crossing a ford. The tribe names are sometimes those of animals, as 'Anazeh ('He-Goats'), Sakr ('Falcons'), etc.; but this is not, as a recent writer seems to have fancied, because any ancient Totem-worship survives, but rather because, as in early mythology, abstract qualities are denoted by the names of animals popularly connected with such qualities by reputation. No trace of the American idea of the Totem seems ever as yet to have been shown to exist among Aryan or Semitic peoples, whose original religious ideas are of quite another order.

The graves of the dead are variously ornamented with sticks, stones, and hair. Of the sticks and the hair of the Arabs a few words may therefore be further added. Sticks are often placed beside the grave of a chief, or hung upon his monument. The Sheikhs, while living, carry such sticks as emblems of authority—rude sceptres, in fact—while the spears and swords are borne by their followers, some of whom may in war-time be seen clothed in chain-mail, with the round steel cap of the Middle Ages; and Crusading arms and armour are indeed yet to be found, with two-handed Crusading swords, taken probably at Hattin in 1187 A.D., and still preserved by Sakhr or 'Anazeh chiefs. As regards the sceptres, we found two forms to be in use, the one a stick, about two or three feet long, with a sort of crutch-head; the other almost exactly resembling the lituus—a crozier or shepherd's crook. It is worthy of remark, that both these forms are recognisable in the sceptres of Osiris or Horus in Egypt. The crutch, the flail, and the lituus are sometimes all held by one deity, but never by a goddess, for the female sceptre ends in the cup or lotus-flower. The crook is also an emblem of Siva and Khrishna in India, and of Ormuzd in Persia. The crutch is found in the hands of Anubis, Seb, Kneph, Ptah, and even of Athor.

The sacrifice of hair as a token of grief is common among the Arab women, who have often long and beautiful locks. Thus at el Kuweijiyeh I found a cemetery with two principal graves inside circles. Beside these were laid sticks and small strips of red and green cloth. Ploughs, coffee-mills, and similar articles of property, were placed within the circles, where no thief would ever dare to touch them. A stick at the head, and another at the foot of the grave, were connected by a string, and from this string depended in one case forty-five pigtails (or plaits of women's hair), and in the other case thirty-three. Similar collections of hair offerings, much bleached by exposure, were found in other instances, and it appears either that the women vow their hair to some departed worthy, or that the female relatives cut off their locks on the death of the head of the family. As regards the wearing of hair in their lifetime, there is some difference among the tribes. The girls have a tangled mop of bleached elf-locks under a simple kerchief. The married women have shining, black, well-combed hair, plaited in tails or concealed under the head-dress, or cut in a fringe over the forehead. Some of the men wear their hair the natural length, but the Arab is much less hairy naturally than the Fellah. Some have a plait like a Jewish lovelock (only the Jews never plait theirs) on either side of the face, but many have the head shaven all but one lock or tuft on the top, which is also worn by the boys. This is a very ancient custom, for Herodotus mentions this lock (the Moslem Shûsheh) among the Arabs of his own day, and it is well-known how in Egypt the young Horus wears the same tuft, and how in India a religious ceremony of shaving the head in the second or third year, leaving only the single tuft, is mentioned in the Laws of Manu, as distinctive of the 'twice-born' castes. The sacrifice of hair by women is also to be traced in Phœnicia in connection with the worship of Ashtoreth, and it is considered by some that Absalom polled his hair annually as a religious duty, the weight in silver or gold being given to the poor (2 Samuel xiv. 26). Lane also mentions that a goat is sacrificed when an Arab child's hair is first cut, and becomes the child's ransom or substitute. On Carmel I have seen the hair of a Druze boy cut and offered to Elijah in the grotto beneath the altar of the Carmelite chapel in the Latin Monastery.

The Belka Arabs are physically a finer and handsomer race than any of the Fellahîn or degraded Arabs west of Jordan. In Moab we actually saw pretty women, a sight only to be noticed west of the river at Nazareth and Bethlehem, or further north, among the Maronites and the grey-eyed Druzes. The men of the 'Adwân who accompanied us were nearly all conspicuous for stature, strength, and fine features. The girls at the springs did not hesitate (when good-looking) to let their faces be seen, and more than once we encountered a beauty with white dazzling teeth, large dark eyes, graceful form, sweeping dark-blue robes, and that peculiar gait which is so much admired that dozens of Arab words have been coined to express its variations. The majority of the matrons are disfigured by the blue under-lip and extensive tattooing, which they seem to consider ornamental; but an 'Adwân maiden, with tangled hair red with henna, delicate aquiline features, eyes blackened with kohl, finger-nails and palms dyed pink, and one or two dots like a court lady's patch on the face, is an extremely picturesque figure. The more beautiful seem to enjoy privileges which will be recognised as most unfair by their Western sisters. They are much sought after in marriage, and fetch a handsome dowry; they are petted and allowed to remain idle in the tent; they are not obliged to toil to the spring with the donkey and the heavy goat-skin bag of water; they lay their commands on the male sex, and they appear occasionally to exhibit a capricious temper, which is, of course, quite unknown to the European beauty. Goblân, who was negotiating his marriage with a princess from the eastern desert while we were in Moab (a bridegroom of more than seventy years of age, with grandsons of his own), appeared to have a general and fatherly interest in pretty faces, which contrasted with the usual grave dignity of his manners among men.

Yet domestic life is not without its drawbacks, even in the desert. I was on one occasion invited to the tent of a minor chief, who was my guide and most humble servant. He concocted for my benefit, and that of several guests from neighbouring tents, a brew of very thin coffee with an immense quantity of sugar, a sort of syrup which had hardly any taste save of sugar ; and, having a small piece of the sugar-loaf left, he gave it to me on our parting, as the only present he was able to offer. We sat in this tent for more than an hour, admiring the 'masterly inactivity' of the Arabs, who can apparently sit silent and quite unemployed for whole days, and who thus appear to await with endless patience the time when civilized races shall have worn themselves out by their struggle for existence, and the Arab survivor shall be left master of the field. This inactivity is, however, delusive, for let it be thought that the guest is dozing in the evening, and he may perhaps see these grave, listless men creeping like cats, or hopping nimbly round his person like birds, feeling his pockets with a delicate touch, or endeavouring to abstract his saddle-bags from beneath his head. The Arab is, indeed, a continual actor. His haughty frowning air, his gravity and laziness, his courage and courtesy, are all assumed as a mask, hiding a soul which is often mean, grasping, cowardly and treacherous. His appearance in the eyes of the European is nothing better than a sham, and it is only his brother Arab who knows how to estimate it at its proper value.

As I sat reflecting on these matters, a noise as of women quarrelling arose on the covered side of the tent. My host assumed an injured air, and went to pacify the contending parties. His brother, sitting by him, manifested on his countenance a disgust and irritation such as I have rarely seen an Arab betray. The Sheikh returned, the quarrelling continued, and I endeavoured to console him by the reflection that women always quarrelled in all countries in the same way; but at length the brother's patience was worn out, and he arose with a large stone in his hand, and looked over the partition dividing the harîm from the open part of the tent in which we sat. Without a word he hurled the stone into the unseen, and a sound of wailing took the place of the angry chatter which preceded this assertion of the rights of a guest to enjoy peace and quiet during his visit.

The head-wife had already appeared with the first cup of coffee, and it may have been on a question of a second chance of peeping at the strange Franjis that the dispute arose. Soon after a spoilt baby of eighteen months appeared, in a dirty shirt and a gorgeous green jacket. It was affectionately kissed by all the men present, and then carried off, with a lump of sugar, by two handsome boys of nine or ten, each with his sling of hair in his hand, with which the young Bedawi is able to perform wonders.

The Arab women enjoy far more freedom and consideration than do the wives and daughters of the peasantry. They salute the traveller with the Moslem formula, 'Peace be upon you, O my brother,' and they rarely hide their faces at all, though some will hold a sleeve or head-veil between their teeth. Goblân would sometimes send his compliments to the mother as well as to the father of any group of children we met. The women ride camels to the spring when the men are employed, and spin the dark wool as they go with an ordinary spindle, but without a distaff, the hank being passed over the hand. They wear bracelets, a signet-ring, and even in some cases a jewel in the nose.

The Arabs are not totally devoid of astronomical knowledge, as was found by Lieutenant Mantell in the course of conversations with his guides. The Milky-way they call 'Derb et Tibn,' 'the Tract of the Chaff;' and the Morning Star and Pleiades (Tereiych) they also pointed out. *N'ash*, or the Great Bear, and *el Mizân*, 'the Balance,' or Orion, seem also to be known; and Aldeboran is called Nejm el Gharârah, 'the Deceitful Star,' because it is sometimes mistaken for the Morning Star. It is of course well known that our astronomical nomenclature is mainly Arabic, but this belongs to the civilization of Baghdad in the ninth century. The early Arabs of Yemen used to worship certain fixed stars in addition to a few of the planets, including *Keis*, or Sirius, *Tay*, or Canope, and *Tasm*, or Aldeboran. The rising and setting of these and others was then supposed (as in Assyria) to be connected with the rain.

It is not proposed here to repeat what has been

written of the Bedawin in 'Tent Work in Palestine,' but something may be said of the riches and possessions of the Belka Arabs, which far surpass those of the small western tribes. The 'Adwân, who own land tilled for them by the Ghawârneh and other inferior tribes, possess also sheep, goats, and cows in numbers, but the Beni Sakhr and 'Anazeh, living in less well-watered districts, have only camels, and in autumn are often obliged to send these more than a day's journey into the 'Adwân lands to drink. Sometimes the camels will remain a day at the spring, and return on the third to camp, when they are obliged almost immediately to travel back again to the water. The number of these camels appeared to be countless, and they were driven like goats or sheep in herds, without either bridle or saddle. To see perhaps five hundred camels in a company, followed by other flocks of equal numbers, descending to the springs, was an interesting sight. The grave elders stalked along with the sulky dignity which their owners seem to copy; the little colts, and sometimes the younger of the full grown, executed the most extraordinary gambols with sprawling legs, which seemed jointless and wooden. The man or boy in charge rode in front, guiding his beast with a switch, and shouting 'Ya-ho, Ya-ho' all day long. The chorus of grunts and grumbles from the flocks of these beasts at the water was ceaseless by day. We once saw a negro woman driving a young dromedary without any bridle. She dropped her spindle, and was obliged to stop. As the beast knelt she jumped off, and ran back like lightning; but before she could get back the dromedary, with many grunts, was on its legs again, and she had only time to seize it by the neck. Here she hung, her toes touching the ground, her wool in her teeth, and was thus carried for some hundred yards, until, by striking with her switch on the dromedary's neck, she stopped it, obliged it to kneel, and mounting with great dexterity, cantered off in triumph.

The Arabs only leave two of the mother-camel's udders for the colts to suck, tying up the others with slips of wood. The colt is weaned at eight months of age, and the rest of the milk is drunk by the tribe. This is the only use ever made, apparently, of the camel, save in moving camp, or when one is killed for the feast. There are many thousand camels belonging to each tribe, and, like sheep or goats, they are in fact a clumsy substitute for money, which is almost unknown in these districts. The Bedawi carries about his capital in the shape of camels, but his wealth is mainly useful for the influence and consideration which it gains him, rather than on account of intrinsic value. The ordinary price of a baggage-camel varies from £12 to £20, and a Hajin, or blood animal for riding, from £30 to £200. Calculated on this proportion, the money value of the herds we saw in Moab was very considerable.

We were much disappointed with the horses of the 'Adwân, and I only saw two or three colts of pure blood. The Belka tribes seem to have hardly any horses, but it is possible that the Ruala or the 'Anazeh may still possess fine mares. As a rule, however, the breeding of horses among the Arabs seems to have declined, and donkeys are extensively used—a sure indication of decay in warlike character.

The camels and other property are marked or branded on the neck and flank with the *Wusm*, or 'sign' of the tribe. We collected a great many of these signs, and found that each had a distinctive name. The original 'Adwân mark is a vertical stroke; but the younger, or Nimr branch, bear two; and the 'Abbád, a yet younger offshoot, have three, thus approaching the system of heraldic differences. This mark is called the Mut-luk. The original Beni Sakhr mark is the Mihmasah, or 'spoon' for roasting coffee —a circle with a vertical stroke below. The Fâiz family bear this, with two short strokes on the right extending horizontally from the vertical stroke; and this variation is called Tuweikeh (the 'little bracelet'). The Kurshân have a circle with a dot; and one family of this subdivision of the Beni Sakhr has also two strokes by the circle. The Khadir have a mark not unlike the Cheth in square Hebrew, called el Bâb ('the door'). They are a subdivision of the Beni Sakhr. The Jibbûr, another division of the Beni Sakhr, use a cross, and also the 'Raven's Foot,' a rounded trident like the Indian Trisul caste-mark. All these marks are simple enough, but it should be noted that the Mihmasah is exactly like the Himyaritic Yod; the Mut-luk is the Himyar numeral one, and the subdivisions of each tribe are marked by numerals which are vertical strokes; the 'Raven's Foot' is the Samech of the same alphabet. The door is the Himyarite Beth, the bracelet is the Tza, the Cross is the Tau. The Lam, the 'Ain, the Jim, the Tzadi of this same alphabet are also used by other Belka tribes. The traveller is liable to make the mistake, into which at least three careful observers are known to have fallen, of diligently copying what he supposes to be a Himyaritic inscription, but which is really a collection of various tribe-marks scrawled either by shepherds when idle, or deliberately placed on stones in buildings and elsewhere where treasure is believed to lie hid, which is thus claimed by the tribe in whose territory the spot may be included.

This identification of the tribe-marks agrees with the history of Arab immigration from Yemen, and it is interesting to find tribes totally illiterate still preserving unconsciously their ancient alphabet. The Azdites, who migrated northwards about 120 A.D., were descendants of Kahlan, brother of Himyar. The Beni Ghassan (Zenobia's Arabs), in Syria, were migrants also from northern Arabia. The discovery of Himyaritic inscriptions at Madeba shows the early presence of similar tribes in the Belka; and there are ruins named after the Himyarites, and Himyaritic legends and words to be found in Moab even to the present day.

The Arabs are subject, as are the Fellahin, to the depredations of thieves, even when no foray from a distance need be feared. We found that the valleys near the Dead Sea swarmed with these bandits, outlaws of every tribe, who are obliged to migrate to the mountains in winter, when the camps are in the valley. Sometimes they are found dead of hunger in the snow, and on one occasion two of them were seen by our party enjoying a feast off a fox which they had shot. Goblân used nightly to perambulate the great Hadânieh circle at Wâdy Jideid, within which we were encamped, addressing in stern tones imaginary or unseen robbers with these words: 'Come out, you cowards! May Allah destroy you! There are no goats or cows here, but only men and bullets.' He erected a pillar of stones six feet high as a dummy guard or 'bogey' at night, and, generally speaking, he and his men seemed to live in great fear of these thieves.

This apprehension was not by any means groundless, for during the moonless nights we were constantly attacked by thieves, who endeavoured to steal our animals. More than once we pursued them and fired small shot at them; but our immunity from loss was due chiefly to the vigilance of our dogs, and to the defensive arrangements of the camp. The straying donkeys of one careless muleteer were snapped up before we had been a week in the country.

Near the Jordan valley Goblân showed us a cairn erected over the body of a thief, who was shot at night, near the camp, some quarter of a mile or more below, and found in the morning lying dead. Such cairns are common in Moab, as well as the larger ones which cover the dead slain in some foray on the spot. Women also seemed to be buried in a common grave, by laying them together on the ground and heaping stones over them. Corpses, bones and fragments of clothing could often be seen beneath the cairn, so that in some cases at least it was clear that no excavation had been attempted.

Goblân also showed us a sort of depression in the ground which he said was used in the punishment of thieves who had stolen corn. They were laid in it, and sacks of barley placed over them. It was not clear whether they were induced thus to confess where the corn was hidden, or whether the punishment was merely a revenge. On asking, however, how long they were kept, the answer was, 'Sometimes we leave them there.'

The old custom of the ordeal is also still in use among the Arabs. The man who swears innocence of any accusation is made to drink boiling water with flour in it. If this does not appear to hurt him he is judged to have sworn truly, and the natural deduction appears therefore to be that the Bedawi's inside must be constructed of iron or his forehead of brass.

The Arab cannot afford generally to expend shot in hunting, although he makes his own gunpowder, as we discovered by finding the little mills in the rocks. The sling is much used, and partridges are knocked down with sticks. I once saw an Arab hunting with a shield, composed of a white skin, painted with circles and spots, so as to resemble a stone heap, and stretched on two cross sticks in X shape. It folded up like an umbrella, and was five feet high. From behind this he shot, but missed his aim. The hunting of gazelles with the sluki, or greyhound, and with the falcon, which flies at the head, and, settling between the horns, flaps its wings in the victim's face, thus impeding its flight till the dog drags it down, is also said to be still practised.

The Arabs on a raid generally take a woman with them as cook. The old practice of placing one of the beauties of the tribe in a kind of palanquin made of ostrich feathers, on a gaily caparisoned camel, and putting her in front of the party, is said still to survive among the Ruala and the 'Anazeh. One of the black slaves of the 'Adwân was considered a great hero, in the last generation, because he succeeded single-handed in cutting off a camel with his Utfa, or ostrich-feather palanquin, and brought the captured beauty to his master's camp. The slaves still are found in numbers among the 'Adwân, but their valour is not what it was of old.

The palanquin called Mahmal, which conveys to Mecca the so-called 'Holy Carpet,' or new covering for the Kaaba, is akin to the Utfa, or 'hoop.' It appears to be an institution older than Islam, and answers probably to the arks of Egyptians and Dravidians. A camel with a Mahmal not only accompanies the Haj from Damascus and Cairo, but also forms part of the procession on such occasions as a circumcision of the richer Moslems. In Egypt it is traditionally connected with the somewhat mythical princess called 'Moon of the Age.'

And now, at length, we must bid farewell to the Arabs of the Belka; not, let us hope, with the feelings which the 'Adwân aroused in my mind when it was discovered that, after protestations of the most lofty sentiments of courtesy and gentlemanly feeling, one great chief had placed our pewter tea-pot in his saddle-bag. The Arab is an unimprovable savage, with all the craft, the cruelty, the deceit and the cowardice which are usual among savages, and with all the affectation of courage, nobility, and honesty which is equally common to the wilder races. When civilization is at a low ebb, and government is weak, the Bedawî chief flourishes and spreads terror; before a strong settled population he retreats to the howling wilderness, which he does not love, or sinks to the level of a poor cultivator or despised 'cousin of the gypsies.' Yet it must not be forgotten that he has his rights also. The fields in the Jordan valley have distinct owners and are rudely tilled. The 'Adwân are acknowledged by the Turk to be proprietors of the lands in which they dwell, and the colonist must buy them out if he wishes for their country. The 'Adwân are on a downhill path, and with the death of Goblân and his generation, their future seems to be that they will either become tillers of their own lands or else sink to the ignoble position of tourist guides, abused and perhaps ill-paid by the Dragoman, who as yet hardly ventures over Jordan. The 'Anazeh and Beni Sakhr are wilder, and more capable of living in the desert; they must either fall back as the settled population spreads from Sâlt and the Ajlûn villages, and confine themselves to the eastern hills, or they must be ground between the Pasha on the west, and other fiercer 'Anazeh clans on the east, and, like the

'Adwân, finally disappear. Much as one may regret all that is romantic and picturesque in decaying Bedawîn life, it is the fate of wild races so to yield to the more energetic and civilized; and the material for a future conquering and progressive race is not to be discovered among the Semitic nomads of Syria or Arabia.

CHAPTER XI.

ARAB FOLK-LORE.

SEATED on the edge of the cliff of Minyeh, beside the seven circles with altar-stones, we looked down on the brown and utterly arid plateau which runs to the top of the eastern cliffs, beyond which the Dead Sea lies calm and shining.

In this plateau is the black basalt outbreak called Hammet Minyeh; and not far below us, on the slope, is the spring-well of Minyeh, with its stunted thorn. It was here that Abu Wundi, the hale and cheerful old Sheikh of the Awazim Arabs, began to tell us the first fairy-tales we had heard beyond Jordan. The black natural fortress, he said, was once the city of 'Antar, the black hero whose woes and dolorous love-songs are said to fill forty-five volumes of Arab poetry. To the spot on which we sat came once the wandering 'Aly, 'the Lion of God,' son of Abu Taleb, and husband of the Prophet's daughter Fatimah, one of the first converts to Islam, whose claims to the Khalifate originated the great schism of Shi'ah and Sunnee. He has become in Persia, and even in Syria, a mythical hero whose name is often substituted for that of Moses, Joshua, or Samson in perverted versions of Old Testament histories. 'Aly, riding his horse Maimûn, reached Minyeh in a state of exhaustion, and prayed to Allah that he might die. He was, however, commanded to strike the earth with his spear, when at once the fountain of Minyeh welled up, and 'Aly drank and was refreshed. Minyeh signifies 'desire' or 'wish,' and the wishing-well was here so named, according to the Arabs, because it arose at the desire of 'Aly.

Further instructed by Allah, 'Aly descended to the Hammet Minyeh and cried out for 'Antar ('the Spearer'),* when suddenly fifteen hundred black men rose up, each saying, 'I am 'Antar! We are all 'Antars!' 'Aly, again divinely instructed, asked for the 'Antar whose father was Shadid ('the Strong One'), and his mother Zebibeh, or the 'Sea Foam,' and this host he at length found, and was invited to enter his house. Here he perceived a woman hanging to the beam of the roof, to which she was tied by her long eyelashes, and, being astonished at such cruelty, he demanded who she was. 'She is my mother,' said 'Antar, 'and I hung her up because she hates and curses strangers.' 'Aly begged that she might be taken down, which was no sooner done

* Perhaps connected with the Egyptian Nutar.

than she began to revile the guest at whose asking she had been released. 'Hang her up again!' said 'Aly; and this was also done, after which 'Aly and Maimûn were alike courteously treated, and he remained the guest of 'Antar for three days, according to the law of the Prophet.

'It was after this,' said Abu Wundi, 'that he went forth and took the City of Copper'—a legend we had already heard at Jericho. Here (as I have previously related) stood the copper or brazen city of the infidels, where now the single enormous tamarisk marks the site of Gilgal. Round the brazen walls (as the Abu Nuseir Arabs told us in 1873) 'Aly rode on Maimûn seven times, and, blowing upon them with his breath, they at once disappeared, and the faithful pursued the infidel westwards to Koruntil. The sun was about to set behind the cliff of that mountain, when 'Aly cried to it, 'Return, O blessed one!' and the sun stood still until the infidels were slain.

This tale differs from others about to be mentioned in one respect, that it presents affinities to three Old Testament episodes—namely, the Rock of Rephidim, the fall of Jericho, and the miracle of Gibeon; while many others of its features are clearly akin to the Persian mythology. It cannot well be supposed that the tradition preserved is indigenous, because the Arabs, to whom alone such tales are peculiar (none of the same class being known to the Fellahin), are a people who emigrated in post-Christian times from the Hejaz and from Yemen into Syria. There is, however, a very simple explanation possible of the existence of Bible stories among the Bedawin, and one which appears to be supported by the fact that a mediæval monkish legend is certainly preserved among the Abu Nuseir. The 'high mountain' of the Temptation was shown in the twelfth century at the curious peak called 'Osh el Ghurâb, or 'Raven's Nest,' north of Jericho, although its summit is 300 feet below the level of the Mediterranean; and this place is still called 'The Ascent of Jesus' by the Bedawîn. East of Jordan, also, we must not forget that a Christian colony founded by the Crusaders still survives at Kerak; and it was, no doubt, from the priests or monks of this fortress that the Arabs first learned the history of Moses and Joshua, which they have gradually confused with legends of 'Aly and 'Antar, although retaining some indistinct remembrance of the localities which led to their belief in a city of brass or of copper, which they place at the true site of Israel's camp, and not far from the Jericho whose walls are related to have fallen before the blast of Hebrew trumpets.

Leaving, then, aside the Biblical aspect of the legend, we may consider the purely mythical elements of this and other tales. A little further north is the spring of Wâdy Jideid, on the south side of

Mount Nebo. Beside it lies the lintel-stone of a little chapel, which was once perched on the cliff, and on the lintel is a well-cut Byzantine cross. There is a rock not far off with a rude Arab inscription scrawled upon it, recording apparently the names of various persons. Tradition says that a beautiful maiden called Ghareisah ('the Little Palm') used here to meet a youth named Zeid, or 'Increase,' who belonged to a tribe unfriendly to her own. They were a Bedawîn Romeo and Juliet, and their fate was equally sad. She consented to flee with her lover, whom she concealed in a box (apparently placed on a camel); but her relations became suspicious in consequence of certain movements in the box, which she failed to conceal, and, discovering her lover, they became furious, and caused both to be slain. Ghareisah, say the Arabs (who cannot read), scrawled the inscription on the rock before she died to tell her kinsfolk of the murder; and as she fell her hand rested on the lintel, and its impress remained as the cross now visible.

Down in the Jordan valley, south of Kefrein, stands the extraordinary stone which is called the 'dish of Abu Zeid.' It is 10 feet in diameter and $3\frac{1}{2}$ feet high, with a hole through the middle 2 feet in diameter. It lies flat like a great cheese beside a thorn tree, and is much too large to have been a millstone. The Arabs say that Abu Zeid, another of their famous black heroes, here slaughtered a camel, and made of the entire animal a huge pilau on this stone, while the melted butter ran down from the cone of rice into the central perforation. It was thus that he feasted the local Arabs before his departure, for it is a rule that the stranger, when quitting a territory in which he has received hospitality, should thus feast his hosts before leaving.

From Abu Wundi also we gather a story, reminding one of a fable of Æsop, and connected topographically with a site near Tell M'ain on the Moab plateau. Here dwelt a chief with two wives, Hâna the elder, and Bâna the younger. The younger pulled out all the grey hairs from her lord's beard to make him look young; the aged wife pulled out all the black hairs to increase the venerable appearance of the Sheikh; and thus at length between them he had no beard left at all—a disgrace which is much felt by a man of dignity among Arabs. Hence arose the proverb, which appears to be known in the Lebanon and elsewhere, as well as beyond Jordan,

'Bein Hâna wa Bâna
Râh Lahâna.'*

That is, 'between Hâna and Bâna our beard went.'

* It seems not impossible that Hâna may be the Zendic Hana, 'an old man,' and Bâna, made to rhyme with it, be derived from Ben, a son. In this case the wives are personifications of age and youth.

It answers to our 'falling between two stools,' or to the 'redding strake' which he who stands between two contending parties must expect. We must not here diverge to speak of Syrian proverbs, for they are innumerable. Many have been published by Captain Burton, and others have been kindly collected for my information by residents, but they have little connection with the present subject.

A legend attaches to the great ruined Palace of Hyrcanus at 'Arâk el Emîr, and is preserved in the name applied to that palace, Kasr el Abd, 'the black slave's house;' and in the Mutull el Hisân, or 'place of the appearance of the Horse,' which is a hill east of the palace. The Emîr, from whom the site in question is named 'Arâk el Emîr, or 'Prince's cliff,' had a beautiful daughter whom he left in charge of the black slave when he himself departed on a pilgrimage. The princess was loved by the slave, and during her father's absence consented to marry him if he would first (like Aladdin) build her a beautiful palace. The black one at once began to erect the great building, with stones of enormous size, whose ruins still bear witness to his superhuman strength; but before he had finished it, the 'horse appeared,' the angry Emîr was seen coming over the hill from the east on his steed; the black slave slew himself in despair, and his body was burned with fire by the Emîr, and afterwards buried beneath a stone. What became of the princess history says not.

North-east of this site, on the plateau above, is a low rounded hill with a single bush, which is called Dhahr el Hamâr, or 'the donkey's back.' Twice I heard the same legend related concerning it, once by Goblân en Nimr and once by his brother, Sheikh Fellah. It was so-called, they said, because, when father Noah was sailing by in his ark, this hill, alone of all in the world (or, at all events, within the district), was visible above the waters, like the back of an animal. 'See the donkey's back,' cried the patriarch, and the name has adhered to the spot ever since. Thus Noah's flood is as well known to the Arab of Moab as to the western peasant of the Sharon or Hittite plains.

A yet more elaborate legend is that of the history of Zir, one of the greatest of the black heroes of Arabia. His name is known in Moab, in Galilee, in Philistia; and it appears that his history (though not related by Lane) must be among those which the public story-tellers of Egypt read to the Moslems, for it is said that a printed copy has been brought from Egypt to Lebanon, where it amuses the Maronite youth and children of the mountain.

The name Zir is from the root Zor, 'to visit,' or 'go round'; it is connected with Mazâr, a shrine, and with Ziâra, a pilgrimage or visit to a sacred place. Zir, then, was the great pilgrim, the perambulator who goes round, or revisits sacred spots. Traditionally he was one of the sons of the Beni Helâl, or 'Children of the Crescent,' the most famous of Arab traditionary tribes. His brothers are said to have been called Kuleib, 'the little dog,' and Jerro, 'the whelp,' and from the first of these descended the great tribe of the Beni Kuleib, of mythical renown, of whom a remnant still appears to exist south-east of the Sea of Galilee. Near Nimrîn, in the Jordan valley, are a row of pits large enough to hold a horseman, and said to have been used as places of ambush by Zir and his men, whence they pounced on the foe. There are similar pits (probably remains of an old system of irrigation) near Phasaelis, west of the river; and these are called Habej ez Zir, 'the tryst of Zir,' showing that the same legend attaches to them.

Near Nazareth is the open place called Meidân ez Zir, 'Zir's Racecourse'; and further west, at M'alûl, is (or rather was) a fine masonry tomb of Ionic style, used as a Greek chapel, but called Kasr ez Zir, or 'the tower of Zir'; further west, again, are acacias, said to have grown from his tent pegs, a legend which applies also to certain thorn trees in the Valley of Elah, near Philistia. Zir is believed to have migrated from Palestine to Egypt, and thence to

Tripoli, but many of his men were slain by the Emir of Gaza.

Zîr, then, was perhaps a real chief of the days of the Moslem conquest under Omar; but the favourite legend of his life is full of wonders. In his youth he was an enormous feeder, and drank more than ten other men, both of wine and water. He was reproached by his relations with sloth and cowardice, because, when his brother was slain, he remained a whole night without doing anything, after which he arose and avenged him. Later, however, he was seized by his foes and cut into small pieces, which were placed in a box, and the box thrown into the sea. The waves carried the coffer to Beyrout, which was then ruled by King Hakmûn ('the wise'), who was a Jew. The fishermen in the bay fished up the box in their nets, and, supposing it to hold a treasure, began to quarrel over it. They were, therefore, brought before King Hakmûn, and when the chest was open Zîr was found inside, whole, but covered with scars. He was revived, and became a groom in the King's stable, where he was again regarded as a poor foolish creature, just as before his murder.

Meantime a war broke out, and Hakmûn marshalled his forces, leaving only women and boys at home. Zîr was, of course, not considered capable of fighting; but the King's daughter saw him seated on a wall with a pole in his hand, dashing his bare heels against the stone till they bled, and brandishing his pole like a lance. This having happened thrice, the Princess told the King of the strange behaviour of his groom, who was at once brought in and asked the meaning of his folly. He replied that he wanted to go and fight with the rest, and was trying to imagine himself on horseback in a battle. The King, pleased by such eagerness for war, took Zîr at once to the stable, and bade him choose a horse; but it was then discovered that no beast was able to bear the extraordinary weight of the champion, save one heroic horse, a foal by the immortal sea horse of an Arab mare.

On the next day the battle was again arrayed, and Zîr rode off with the King. A great defeat of the enemy followed, and Zîr was seen killing right and left; but when the evening came, the chiefs were boasting of how many they had each slain, and the groom stood silent, as though ashamed. They mocked him, and asked where his prisoners were: and at length he bade them follow him to a huge stone, which he recommended them to raise. This all the united strength of the warriors was unable to accomplish, and at length Zîr, unaided, like the young Theseus, rolled away the stone, and beneath it were found fifteen hundred bridles and fifteen hundred tongues of men whom Zîr had slain, and whose steeds he had captured. After this his power was at once recognised, and he became a mighty prince, and married the Princess, and lived happy ever after.

Such, then, are a few of the legends which are known to the Arabs beyond Jordan, and to other Syrians. Such stories are not found among the Fellahin west of the river, who only know the tales repeated to them by Europeans or by educated natives. The young study of comparative mythology teaches us to set store by such traditions, which, when genuine, serve to assist the antiquary in tracing the history of a race. Arab folk-lore has, however, as yet received less attention than Aryan mythology, partly because it is unknown, and partly because it is less ancient or important. The myths of Islam form a fascinating study which yet awaits its full development.

The story of Zir seems without doubt to be a solar myth. The great hunger and thirst, the humility and small repute of the hero in his youth, remind us of the insatiable hunger and thirst of Indra, which is the preparation for his great contest with the dragon, and of the small repute of 'Boots,' the younger brother of Western folk-lore. Zir slain by his enemies, Zir the wanderer, Zir in the coffer on the sea, recalls Osiris and Perseus and Dionysus, the sun-gods of Egypt and Phœnicia, who are rocked on the deep as infants, or cut to pieces by the dark winter, and apparently slain. Zîr who delays to avenge his brother is akin to the Persian hero Khai Khosru, who in like manner bewails his lost brother Firûd all night: for the sun's victories are only won by day. Zîr the groom reminds us of countless heroes in adversity, as shepherds, grooms, scullions, swineherds, but finally raised to honour. The bridle of the horse is most important in all myths which relate a hero's conquests; and the heroic horse of Agnis, the Pegasus-twin of Bellerophon, is an inseparable companion of the sun-warrior in Persia and elsewhere. It is impossible to doubt that the basis of the Zir legend is a regular myth, and that the 'wandering hero' is the sun.

The same origin may be attributed to several of the stories above related. Thus the prince on the horse, who burns the black slave when he rises above the hill on the east, is clearly once more the sun on the sun-horse. The black slave is the night-demon; the princess delivered from him is probably the blushing dawn. When, again, we find 'Aly on his heroic horse, riding west from the black city of 'Antar the 'transfixer,' we recognise in the mythical Imâm the same great horseman who is so famous in Persia. The city whose walls fall before his breath is a cloud-city like those which Indra destroys, and the sun which he stays in heaven reminds us that Hushedar has power to stop the swift horses of

Mithra, who refuse to be stayed at the command of the evil spirit.

There are other legends which have no apparent solar meaning. The magic well, the living box, the donkey's back seen in the Flood, are more obscure stories, which may have a different derivation; and Hâna and Bâna seem to belong to the somewhat cynical wisdom of old observers, not of the heavens, but of human weakness and folly. A very curious circumstance may, however, be noted concerning the heroes, for Zîr was black, Abu Zeid was black, and 'Antar, the warrior and poet, was also black. Moses even was black according to Arab tradition. In India Khrishna, the sun-god or Apollo of the Puranas, was also black, though shining. The sun is often black in Asiatic myths, but whether because the legends are derived from the old dark Cushite race, or because the adventures are those of the sun by night, when (in Persia) his dark face was supposed to be turned towards the earth, does not seem to have been discovered.

A great many of the familiar Arab stories related by Lane, or to be found among the 'Thousand Nights and a Night,' are generally recognised as of mythical origin. Such is the story of Sinbad, which can be traced far back in India, and even to the Sixth Dynasty in Egypt. Such is the wondrous Palace of Aladdin, the magic flying horse, and many other

tales. In Lane's wonderful account of Moslem
manners in Egypt, several mythical tales are given
in full, although he does not offer any suggestion as
to their origin.

Thus Abu Zeid ('the father of increase') is related
to have been born black, though his parents were of
pure lineage—Rizk, or 'food,' and Khadra, 'the
green one,' being his father and mother, a Prince and
a Princess of the Beni Helâl. He was disowned and
cast out, but became a hero in his mother's country,
and returns to fight his father, whom he defeats, but
is not allowed to slay; and his name is changed to
Barakât, or 'blessings,' in the days of his prosperity.
Then again, among the Beni Kelâb in the Hejâz, we
find el Hâris, a chief whose name recalls the old
Hebrew term for the rising sun, and also the Hârit,
or 'yellow' sun of India. His wife dreams, like
Althea, that she becomes the mother of a flame, and
is sent away by her husband, and slain by a black
slave. Her helpless infant is found, miraculously
fed and guarded by the swarm of locusts, who hover
over him in a black cloud. He is thence named
Jundubah, 'the locust man,' and he grows to be a
great hero—a horseman who attacks the witch
princess esh Shamta, or 'the Grizzle,' and who
wanders over the earth, and finally marries a moon-
faced maiden.

Similar stories have a greater antiquity in Persia,

and the Arab tales approach so closely to those of the Shah Name, dating from 1000 A.D., and to the earlier notices of the Bundahish and the Yashts, that our attention may for a moment be turned to the Sassanian mythology.

In Persia we have the famous Feridun, or Thrætona, the Vedic Trita, or 'third' brother; and his descendants are all famous heroes. Among them Sal, the son of Sam, is nourished on the boundary mountain, Alborz, by the mythic Simurgh, an eagle which suckles its young like a bat. He is aided by the more celebrated Rustem to fight the Turanian infidels, and Rustem has a heroic horse which slays a lion when it attacks his sleeping master. Rustem conquers also a dragon woman, and kills a demon at sunset in a cave, bringing back to earth and to light the blind King Kawus. The son of Rustem is Sohrab, who destroys the white palace of an evil princess, and who wounds his father Rustem, and is finally slain by him, although the pain of each wound is felt by the other who deals the stroke: that is to say that Rustem and his son, like Osiris and Horus, or Abu Zeid and Rizk, are but one and the same.

In Khai Khosru, again, we find a hero who is exposed, like Cyrus, on a mountain, and who can cross water without any boat. His brother Firûd is slain in a burning castle in the evening, is bewailed at night, but avenged at sunrise on the following morning.

These affinities between the Arab and the Persian tales are not accidental; a few of the latter have been mentioned to show the kind of relationship, but the history of the diffusion of these myths has long since been traced by Max Müller; and, though the variants here given may, perhaps, be interesting, the subject is one already well understood.

In the days of the Khalif el Mansûr (754-775 A.D.), Abdallah ibn el Mokaffa, the Persian, translated into Arabic, from Pehlevi, certain tales which were known to be at least two hundred years old, and attributed to a certain Barzuych of the time of Khosru Nushirvan, the contemporary of Justinian. The Arab collection was known as Kalila wa Dimnah; the Pehlevi original was derived from certain stories collected by Barzuych, who was commissioned by the Persian monarch to travel to India, whence he brought back stories for his master's amusement. These tales are recognised as belonging to some ancient Indian collection, of which the Pankatantra is a survival; and there is thus an historic connection through Persia between the Arab fairy tales and the myths of the Aryans in India. A Syriac version of the Kalila wa Dimnah has also been discovered at Mardin; and in the same way the tales of Lokmân, the Arab Æsop, whom the Koran commentators identify with Balaam, have a common origin with the Greek fables in the earlier Indian parables, such, for instance, as the Buddhist Jataka, or 'birth stories.'

This historic genealogy of Arab stories, derived from a Persian and Aryan source, appears to account in a satisfactory manner for the circumstance already mentioned, that such tales are not found among the Moslem peasantry of Western Palestine. The influence of Sassanian civilization on the hordes led by Omar and early Moslem Khalifs was very remarkable. The science, the literature, the architecture, even in great measure the religion, and also most of the mythology of the Arabs, were based on the Iranian civilization, which is traced back to the days of Cyrus. Ibn el Harith pronounced the tale of Rustem to be better than the Suras of his enemy Muhammed. There was little that was original in the creed of Islam, nor did the wondrous culture of Baghdad originate from an Arab source. The student who compares the Koran with the Zendavesta will find that all Moslem eschatology, and many of the noblest Moslem ideas, existed much earlier in Persia. The schism of the Shí'ah and the Sunnee is that between the Moslem under Iranian influence on the east, and under Semitic influence on the west; and Islam is nowhere found in Asia as a really original system of faith. Persian influence has never affected the older population of Canaanite stock still found west of Jordan ; and therefore it is that the stupid superstitions of the Fellahin of Palestine are replaced on the east by the more fanciful and poetic legends of the Bedawîn of Moab.

APPENDICES.

No. I.
SCRIPTURE GAZETTEER OF EASTERN PALESTINE.

THE following will, it is hoped, be found to be a complete list of the places mentioned in the Bible in Bashan, Gilead and Moab. The author would, however, be obliged if the reader can point out any errors or omissions. The more important sites are mentioned in the text of the volume, and the authors of several of the more recent identifications are therein noticed by name.

Out of about ninety-six names, forty-nine were known before the recent commencement of the Survey beyond Jordan. To these I have now added thirty proposed identifications, leaving seventeen sites still to be identified. It is satisfactory that (supposing the new suggestions to stand criticism) we now know a proportion of eight-tenths of the ancient Biblical sites of this country, and of these we owe two-fifths to the recent explorations, including several of importance, such as Peor, Bamoth Baal, Mizpeh, Penuel, etc.; while of the unknown sites, Cherith and Mahanaim (placed by some at Mânch) are the most important, if Ashtaroth Karnaim be at Tell 'Asherah. The remaining fourteen are obscure places of no importance.

SCRIPTURE TOPOGRAPHY BEYOND JORDAN.*

1. *Abarim* (Mountains), Deut. xxxii. 49.—The chain east of the Dead Sea, including Nebo.
2. *Abel Shittim*, Num. xxxiii. 49.—The plains of Kefrein as far as Nimrim on north, and the Dead Sea on south (see p. 152).
3. *Alema*, 1 Macc. v. 26. 'Alma, south of Edrei (Merrill).
4. *Almon Diblathaim* = Beth Diblathaim (see p. 269).
5. *Aphek*, 1 Kings xx. 26.—Now Fik, east of the Sea of Galilee.
6. *Ar of Moab*, Isaiah xv. 1 = Rabbath Moab. Rabba north of Kerak.
7. *Argob.*—Apparently the present Lejja or Trachonitis. The Targum of Jonathan reads Terakina.
8. *Arnon* (River).—Now Wâdy Môjib.
9. *Aroer*, Deut. ii. 36.—'Ar'aîr, on north bank of Mojib.
10. *Aroer*, Josh. xiii. 25.
11. *Ashdoth Pisgah*, Deut. iii. 17.—Now 'Ayûn Mûsa (see p. 131).
12. *Ashtaroth Karnaim.* — Doubtful; perhaps Tell 'Asherah.
13. *Ataroth*, Num. xxxii. 3, 35.—Jebel 'Attarûs.
14. *Baal Meon*, Num. xxxii. 38.—Tell M'ain (see p. 143).
15. *Baal Peor.*—Probably the same as Beth Peor.
16. *Bajith*, Isaiah xv. 2.—Unknown.
17. *Bamoth Baal*, Joshua xiii. 17.—El Maslûbiyeh (see p. 145).
18. *Beer*, Num. xxi. 16.—Near Dibon.
19. *Bela* = Zoar.
20. *Beon*, Num. xxxii. 3 = Baal Meon.
21. *Beth Diblathaim*, Jer. xlviii. 22.—Probably = Almon Diblathaim (Num. xxxiii. 46), south of Nebo. It means 'house of the two discs.' Possibly the name Deleiyât may

* See Conder's 'Handbook to the Bible.'

be a corruption of Diblah, as the situation seems appropriate, south of Tell M'ain.

22. *Beth Gamul*, Jer. xlviii. 23.—Probably Jemâil, east of Dibon.

23. *Beth Haran*, Num. xxxii. 36.—Tell Râmeh.

24. *Beth Jeshimoth*, Num. xxxiii. 49.—Suweimeh.

25. *Beth Nimrah*, Joshua xiii. 27.—Tell Nimrîn.

26. *Beth Peor*, Deut. iii. 29.—Minyeh (see p. 145).

27. *Betonim*, Joshua xiii. 26.—Possibly the Butein district.

28. *Bezer*, Joshua xx. 8.—Possibly Abu Ser, west of Dibon.

29. *Bosor*, 1 Macc. v. 26.—Busr, south of Edrei (Merrill).

30. *Bozrah*, Isaiah lxiii. 1.—Probably Bozrah, south of the Haurân. = Bosora, 1 Macc. v. 26.

31. *Bozrah*, Jer. xlviii. 24.—Probably the same as Bezer.

32. *Camon*, Judges x. 5.

33. *Casphor* or *Casphon*, 1 Macc. v. 26.

34. *Cherith* (Brook), 1 Kings xvii. 3.

35. *Dathema* or *Dametha*, 1 Macc. v. 9.—Probably Dâmeh, in the Lejja.

36. *Dibon*, Num. xxxii. 3.—Dhibân.

37. *Dibon Gad*, Num. xxxiii. 46.—The same as the last.

38. *Dimon* (Waters), Isaiah xv. 9.—Possibly Medeineh, near the stream of Wâdy Themed. Possibly = Dibon.

39. *Edrei*, Num. xxii. 33.—Edr'a, in Bashan.

40. *Elealah*, Num. xxxii. 3.—El 'Al.

41. *En Eglaim*, Ezek. xlvii. 10.

42. *Ephraim* (Wood), 2 Sam. xviii. 6.—Near es Salt (see p. 185).

43. *Ephron*, 1 Macc. v. 46.

44. *Gadara*, Mark v. 1.—Umm Keis.

45. *Galeed*, Gen. xxxi. 47.—See Mizpeh.

46. *Golan*, Joshua xxi. 27.—In Gaulonitis, the modern Jaulân.

47. *Havoth Jair*, Num. xxxii. 41.

48. *Heshbon*, Num. xxxii. 3. Tell Hesbân.
49. *Holon*, Jer. xlviii. 21.—Perhaps 'Aleiyân, north-east of Dibon.
50. *Horonaim*, Isaiah xv. 5; Jer. xlviii. 3. Possibly Wâdy Ghûeir (with ancient road). The Hebrew and Arabic have the same meaning, with a slight change of guttural.
51. *Iim* or *Ije Abarim*, Num. xxi. 11; xxxiii. 44.—'The ruins of the regions beyond,' near south end of Dead Sea.
52. *Jabbok* (River), Deut. iii. 16.—Now Zerka Shebîb.
53. *Jabesh Gilead*, 1 Sam. xi. 1.—In Wâdy el Yâbis.
54. *Jahaz*, Num. xxi. 23.—Probably Rujm el Makhsiyeh, north-east of Heshbon.
55. *Jazer*, Joshua xiii. 25.—Beit Zer'ah.
56. *Jegar Sahadutha*, Gen. xxxi. 47.—See Mizpeh.
57. *Jogbehah*, Judges xxxii. 35.—Jubeihah.
58. *Judah upon Jordan*, Joshua xix. 34.—Probably should read Horah of Jordan = el Ghôr.
59. *Kedemoth*, Joshua xiii. 18.
60. *Kerioth*, Jer. xlviii. 24 = Kiriathaim.
61. *Kir* (Heres, or Haraseth, or Haresh, or of Moab).—The Targum reads 'Kerak.'
62. *Kiriathaim*, Jer. xlviii. 1.—Kureiyât, north of Dibon.
63. *Kirjathaim*, Num. xxxii. 37.—The same as the last.
64. *Luhith* (Ascent), Isaiah xv. 5.—Tal'at el Heith (see p. 144).
65. *Madmen*, Jer. xlviii. 2.—Probably Medeineh, north-east of Dibon.
66. *Mahanaim*, Gen. xxxii. 2 (see pp. 182—186).
67. *Medeba*, Num. xxi. 30.—Mâdeba.
68. *Mephaath*, Joshua xiii. 18.
69. *Minnith*, Judges xi. 33.—Possibly Minyeh.
70. *Misgab*, Jer. xlviii. 2.—'The high place.'
71. (1) *Mispeh of Moab*, 1 Sam. xxii. 3. Perhaps = Shophan.
72. (2) *Mispeh*, Gen. xxxi. 49.—Probably Sûf (see p. 181).

73. *Nahaliel*, Num. xxi. 19.—The Zerka M'ain (see pp. 145, 148).

74. *Nebo* (Mount).—Jebel Neba (see p. 132).

75. *Nimrah* and *Nimrim*, Num. xxxii. 3.—Tell Nimrin.

76. *Nophah*, Num. xxi. 30.

77. *Peniel* or *Penuel*, Gen. xxxii. 30 ; Judges viii. 9.— Possibly Jebel Osh'a (see pp. 183—186).

78. *Peor* (Mount), Num. xxxii. 28.—Minyeh (see p. 147).

79. *Pisgah*, Deut. xxxiv. 1 = Nebo.

80. *Rabbath Ammon*, Deut. iii. 11.—'Ammân.

81. *Ramath Mizpeh*, Joshua xiii. 26.—Possibly = Mizpeh (2), or possibly Remtheh, west of Bozrah.

82. *Ramoth Gilead*, Deut. iv. 43.—Probably Reimûn (see p. 180).

83. *Raphon*, 1 Macc. v. 37.—Rafeh, three miles west of Edrei (Merrill).

84. *Salchah*, Deut. iii. 10.—Salkhâd.

85. *Shaveh Kiriathaim*, Gen. xiv. 5.—Possibly the valley at Kiriathaim of Moab, which see.

86. *Shibmah* or *Sibmah*, Num. xxxii. 38 ; Joshua xiii. 19.— Probably Sûmieh.

87. *Shittim*, Num. xxvi. = Abel Shittim.

88. *Shophan*, Num. xxxii. 35.—Sûfa, east of Baal Meon.

89. *Succoth*, Gen. xxxiii. 17.—Probably Tell Deir 'Alla (see p. 183).

90. *Tob* (Land), Judges xi. 3.—Taiyibeh.

91. *Tophel*, Deut. i. 1.—Tufileh.

92. *Trachonitis*, Luke iii. 1.—The Lejja district.

93. *Zaphon*, Joshua xiii. 27.—'Amâteh, south-east of Sea of Galilee.

94. *Zareth Shahar*, Joshua xiii. 19.—Zâra, on shore of Dead Sea.

95. *Zered* (Brook), Deut. ii. 14.—Probably Wâdy Siddiyeh.

96. *Zoar*, Gen. xiv. 2.—Tell Shaghûr (see p. 154).

97. *Zophim* (Field), Num. xxiii. 14.—Tal'at es Sufa (see p. 133).

No. II.

ON THE MOSLEM RELIGION.

THE study of the faith of Islam becomes constantly more important and interesting to the Englishman as our relations with the Moslem world become more intimate, not only in India, but in Cyprus, Syria, and Egypt. It may, therefore, not be uninteresting to enlarge somewhat on the suggestions offered in Chapter IX. respecting the very mixed character of Muhammadan beliefs and the syncretism of Islam. In all countries, no doubt, is traceable in peasant superstition the survival of a Paganism which the existing creed of the nation condemns; but in the doctrines even of the Korân, and yet more in the traditions of the Moslem world, an extraordinary survival of early Asiatic Pagan ideas may be recognised as intimately bound up with the faith of even the most pious and best educated Moslems. We may consider then, first, vulgar superstitions of the lower class; secondly, traditions of the faith; thirdly, tenets and tales found in the Korân itself.

The peasant superstitions of Syria have been sketched in the body of the present work. It would, no doubt, be possible to trace in Egypt superstitions founded on the old faith of the land of Khemi; but as yet few of these have been collected. The Fellahah women are known still to visit the famous Temple of Athor at Denderah; and the Moslem belief that an angel brings a drop of water from Paradise every year, which causes the Nile to rise, is founded no doubt on the old Egyptian idea of the 'tear of Isis,' which had the same result. It is traceable to the old mythology, which thus symbolized the fact that the Nile is fed by the waters of heaven falling on the Abyssinian hills. The famous Seiyid el Bedawi and other Derwish saints will no doubt be found to present points of comparison with old Egyptian divinities, and the question would be one very interesting to investigate.

In India, in the same way, the Shaf'aî sects have been much influenced by Parsee, Hindu, and Buddhist ideas. The belief in astrology, in magic, and in charms, which is so universal among the Moslems of India, is opposed to the spirit, if not to the wording, of the Korân. *Buddee ed Din*, the wandering celibate, who is so revered near Cawnpore, though believed to have come from Syria, is clearly connected with Buddha; and the name of Buddha figures with those of Moslem heroes on the magic diagrams and charms of the faithful in Hindustan. The use of cow-dung ashes by the Moslems of India seems also clearly derived from the Hindus or the Parsees, and the digging of holes filled with food resembles a Persian practice; while the entry of the *Murîd*, or 'candidate,' into the 'path' of the Derwish orders seems a mere imitation of the entry into the 'path' of Buddha, or of earlier Indian ascetics. The saints, the customs—nay, many of the beliefs—of the Indian Moslems are entirely different from those of the Arab and African sects; and although Sunnees by profession, the Indian faithful are often nearer to the Shi'ah in belief and practice than to the Sunnees of Western Asia.

Turning from the unauthorized customs and beliefs of the Moslem world to those which are sanctioned—not, indeed, by the words of the Prophet, but by tradition generally received—it is curious to note how many ideas are founded on Magian and Chaldean stories. In illustration of this view we may glance at the belief in the Mohdy, at the lamentation for Hosein, at the Night Journey, at the Sirât Bridge, at hair-cutting and black heroes.

The idea of a future return to earth of el Mohdy, or the 'Guide,' who was the twelfth Imâm, a descendant of Imâm 'Ali, is common to the Shi'ah and the Sunnee sects, but is not countenanced by anything in the Koràn, although Muhammad seems to have expected the future appearance of our Lord Jesus and of 'the Green One' (Elijah) with himself at the end of the world. The Shi'ah make of 'Aly and his descendants to the twelfth a series of incarnations of the Deity. The twelfth Imâm, el Mohdy, retired to a cave near Baghdad, whence he is to return to oppose *ed Dejal*, the Moslem Anti-Christ, in a time of great trouble. The 'earth-beast' who supports the world will assist ed Dejal, who will ride on his ass, accompanied by the Jews, from Irak to Syria, and the final battle is to take place at Aleppo.

All these ideas are traceable to the Zendavesta, and were certainly incorporated in Magian literature four centuries before the time of Muhammad. The future Prophet of Persia is to have two forerunners, and will be opposed by the powers of evil. The Geus Urva, or 'soul of the bull,' in Persian mythology, is exactly the counterpart of the Moslem earth-beast, and a battle predicted in the Yashts is the same as the Moslem triumph which fanatics expected to witness at Tell el Kebir.

The lamentations for Hosein are of an extravagance which seems quite unaccountable. The Prophet's grandson was beheaded at Kerbela by order of Yezid, grandson of Muhammad's old Meccan enemy, Abu Sofiân, and his head was carried to Kufa. But round this historic fact has grown up a wealth of legend and myth which may easily be traced to early Pagan sources. It is very curious that the head of Hosein is shown in the Mosque of Damascus, where Christians believed the head of John the Baptist to have been interred; but when we remember how the Phœnician women mourned over the head of Adonis at Byblos, and reflect on the Greek myth of Kephalos ('the head' of the sun), we may perhaps be nearer the origin of the extravagant lamentations and lacerations which annually celebrate the death of Hosein, and which exactly reproduce the practices of the priests of Osiris recorded by Herodotus. It is said that the detested Shamer, who encouraged the executioner to slay Hosein, had tusks like a boar; and he is thus connected with the boar which slew Adonis. It is said also that Jaffur Ibn Tiâr, King of the Jan, offered to assist Hosein; and he was a centaur, with a man's head and horse's body. In him we recognise the Gandharva of the Persian myths, sometimes the sun's enemy, sometimes a golden-footed man-horse who assists the sun-hero, a relation of Pegasus and of the hero-horse of Rustem. Thus the traditions connected with Hosein seem to be clearly myths of the older Asiatic religions, and the tale of Hâris and the sons of Muslim bears a wondrous family likeness to the English story of Hop-o'-my-Thumb in the ogre's castle.

The Sirât bridge, which will stretch from Olivet to the Temple, has long been recognised as identical with the old Persian 'Bridge of the Gatherer;' but the legends of the Night Journey are quite as clearly traceable to Persian or Indian mythology. In the Korân there is a mere hint of a vision, or actual translation from Mecca to Jerusalem, but tradition supplies the wondrous beast *el Borak*, and states that Muhammad ascended to the seventh heaven, beyond the 'boundary thorn tree,' into the invisible presence of God. This wondrous beast—a kind of cherub with a shining face, a lion's body, peacock's wings and tail, and called *Borak*, or 'lightning,' on account of its swiftness, is but another of the centaur class, already mentioned in connection with Hosein. The retreat of Muhammad to a cavern, his concealment with Abu Bekr behind a spider's web (as in the story of Bruce), his ascent to heaven, are legends which must be compared with those of Zoroaster's retreat to the cave on Alborz, and of his ascension thence to Ahuramazda. The wondrous Alborz, the boundary mountain of the horizon, is also reproduced in the Moslem Mount *el Kaf*, which surrounds the world, and stands on the great emerald which gives colour to the sky.

The sacrifice of a goat for a child as a substitute, 'skin for skin' (cf. Job ii. 4), is a Moslem custom, in which we trace a reminiscence of human sacrifice, and until the time of Muhammad all Arabs buried their daughters when born, as sacrifices to their idols. The cutting of the child's hair, which is accompanied by this sacrifice, is followed by offering to religious mendicants the weight of the hair in silver, and this is a practice which is probably traceable in the Bible (2 Sam. xiv. 26), where Absalom is said to have weighed his hair.

The black heroes of Arab folk-lore have been already mentioned (chap. xi., p. 370), and it is very curious in this connection to notice that even Moses, according to Moslem tradition, was black. Why great heroes should be credited with this hue, among a non-Negro people, it is very difficult to understand.

Turning from Moslem tradition to the contents of the Korân itself, we shall not find that we have escaped from the regions of myth and pagan superstition; and, indeed, it is impossible to read the Suras without seeing how deeply imbued with superstitious ideas the Prophet of Islam must himself have been.

It is true that moderate writers have long ceased to regard Muhammad as an impostor, and the tendency has indeed of late been rather to over-estimate the character of the Moslem religion. As a reformer among pagan and barbarous Arab tribes, the courage and superiority of the eloquent but 'unlearned' Prophet can hardly be over-estimated; but as an original and more enlightened religious system, Islam, when compared to the three faiths on which it is based, may easily be placed in too exalted a position until its nature and derivation are fully examined. The Moslem creed is indeed only original where it is negative; it differs from Judaism and Christianity mainly in denying important dogmas, and its one new tenet is couched in what Gibbon has called 'a necessary fiction compounded with an eternal truth,' namely, the addition of the dogma that Muhammad is the messenger of God, to the doctrine, even then so ancient in Asia, which declares the unity of the Deity.

Before his quarrel with the Jews of Medina, Muhammad's teaching as a *Hanîf*, or disciple of Abraham, seems to have been fundamentally indistinguishable from Judaism. The great offence which he gave to the Jews by acknowledging 'Our Lord Jesus' as a Prophet, led to the change of the Kibleh from Jerusalem to Mecca, and to the charge which he formulated against the Jews of calling Ezra a son of God. No doubt in the sense in which every son of Abraham was considered a child of a Heavenly Father, the Jews may have applied this title to their second lawgiver; but amid the most extravagant eulogisms of the Rabbis, it is impossible to find a single attribution of a divine nature to the Scribe who restored the Law.

Muhammad warns his followers in the Korân that the Jews will be their most bitter foes, but in order to make a marked division between his own teaching and that of the Rabbis, he seems to have been forced to press a false charge against a purely monotheistic religion.*

In reading the Korân we soon become aware of the poverty of its materials, and of the wearisome repetitions of its verbose descriptions. The new faith, which added our Lord to the list of Jewish Prophets, was inferior not merely to the Semitic religions which preceded it, but even to the Persian and Buddhist creeds which had already existed at least 1,200 years. The beautiful imagery and endless fancy of the Magian hymns find only a feeble echo in the literalism

---

* For the benefit of those who believe in the possibility of contracting friendship with Moslems, it should be noticed that Muhammad, though he considers the Christians as less unfriendly to Islam than the Jews, yet *forbids* the faithful in most positive manner to contract friendship with either Jew or Christian. A pious Moslem cannot, without violating a direct command, enter into any relation with a European beyond those which are unavoidable.

of Muhammad's adaptations, and when we consider the five cardinal points of Islam—faith, prayer, fasting, alms, and pilgrimage, we miss a yet more noble command, which Buddha made the very basis of his teaching—the duty of love to fellow-men.

Islam is, indeed, the creed of a savage race, the highest conception to which the wild Bedawin mind can attain. Muhammad found his fellow Arabs worshipping stones and adoring local pairs of divinities, male and female, slaying their sons as a bloody sacrifice to the menhir, burying their infant daughters alive : living, like the wild tribes of Beluchistan, on fish or on reptiles, without moral laws, without letters, their only delight in bloodshed, and in the amatory strains of their wine-loving bards. It was no small triumph to persuade barbarians, who were exactly what the wilder Arab tribes still remain, to renounce their idols, to save the lives of their children, to observe the more simple rules of social morality, to express (if not to feel) a belief in one spiritual God, and in a future life of happiness or woe.

That Muhammad countenanced the preservation of many superstitions is clearly shown in the Korân itself. He did not forbid the visiting of Safa and Merwah—he himself perambulated the Kaaba—and while removing Hobal and the 360 menhirs, he left untouched the stone of Allât. It must also be remembered that he inculcates the retaliation of the blood-feud as a duty second only to that of giving alms, and that he commands the faithful in the Korân to punish thieves, even when they are women, by striking off the hand. These last injunctions illustrate those connected with the superstitions which he countenanced, and seem to show that it was not through any cynical intent to incorporate in his system rites which he was powerless to put down that he permitted such customs to be still observed, but rather because, being himself not far removed above his fellows—a barbarian who conceived murder and mutilation to be religious duties—he was unable entirely to shake himself free from the beliefs in which, as a son of the Koreish who guarded the Kaaba, he had been brought up in the very centre of universal Arab adoration. Muhammad gloried in the epithet of 'unread,' and perhaps insisted upon his own ignorance in order to guard himself from the suspicion, which his enemies carefully fomented, that he had read and borrowed from the books of Jews, Christians, and Magians. It is impossible to read the Korân without perceiving that its legends are based on oral tradition and not on books. The Suras were written, it is said, on palm-leaves and tablets, but when they were first collected, after the Prophet's death, many were taken down from 'the minds of men,' and who shall say what additions were made to the Canon revised by Othman twenty years after Muhammad had ceased to speak? Although Cufic was not unknown in Medina, it was Othman or Zeid, and not Muhammad, who wrote down the inspired songs, and the boast of the Prophet, that he was, like most of his fellows, 'unread,' becomes the basis of a just condemnation of Islam as a religion of the uncivilized.

It has been well said by a great writer, that the man destined to sway the masses is he 'qui sait conter'—who can speak or sing, and who can put in eloquent words the thoughts which lie without expression in the hearts of his fellows. This is what Muhammad did, and in his eloquence, his enthusiasm, and his personal influence, lay the secret of his astonishing success, far more than in any originality of teaching or ritual. The Jews had settled in Arabia seven centuries before Islam was first preached. The Magian songs and myths were known even as far as Yemen, and were then at least twelve centuries old. The Beni Hârith, Beni Hânifa, and Beni Tai, in Arabia, and the Beni Ghassan in Syria, had embraced some form of Christianity four hundred years previously. The Collyridian heresy, the Nestorian and Jacobite monophysite doctrines, were known also in Arabia, both in Yemen and in the kingdom of Hira. Muhammad was not the first to propose the idea of the *hanif*, or 'puritan,' founded on the so-called 'Religion of Abraham,' and, whatever be the truth as to the influence of a single monk on his teaching, the stories of the patriarchs, the apocryphal accounts of the Virgin and her Son, were popularly known in Arabia before the poet of Islam was born; and the syncretic system of which he became the most famous teacher already existed, as it were, 'in the air,' when first he sang his earliest and most beautiful Suras. Had Omar been defeated in Syria, had the Sassanians repulsed the wild Arab hordes in Persia, we should have heard no more of the Moslem faith than of the earlier Hanif system from which it sprang.

The indebtedness of Muhammad to Rabbinical Judaism, and to Oriental or Gnostic Christianity, is too well known to need any lengthy mention in this note, but it is important to mark how much there is in the Korân which can be found in the Zendavesta, though absent from Jewish or Christian writings. Muhammad once mentions the Magians, and speaks often of the Sabei, who (if he refer to the 'baptizing' sect of Lower Mesopotamia) combined Christianity with Persian or Buddhist dogmas. A rapid glance will enable us to appreciate how much he depended on the Persian system for his ideas of the future and of the remote past, although such doctrines must have been obtained from oral tradition, rather than from any acquaintance with Zend literature.

Muhammad in the Korân repeats again and again his version of certain Old Testament episodes, mingled with stories of the patriarchs which are found exactly reproduced in the Talmud, and with other legends of purely Arab origin. Hûd and Sâleh stand side by side with Abraham and Solomon; stories are told of Moses of which the derivation has not yet been discovered, and Jethro attains to an importance (as also does Ishmael) for which it is difficult to account.

The stories of the birth and infancy of Christ, of the early history of Mary, and of the phantom Crucifixion, betray acquaintance with legends of the Nestorians, the Ebionites, and various Docetic sects, which are preserved in the apocryphal Gospels of the fifth century, which, though condemned by Popes and Councils, remained popular, and were firmly credited, even as late as the days of the English knight, Sir John Maundeville, who cites these stories in the fourteenth century as though equally credible with the accounts in the Canonical Gospels.

In all these episodes the vagueness of the Korân version shows that Muhammad was indebted to oral tradition, and not to literature. He confuses the stories of Saul and Gideon, of Moses and Jacob, of Pharaoh and Haman: he makes Israel to be misled by a Samaritan in the wilderness, and he confounds the Virgin Mary with Miriam, the sister of Moses. Such confusion is natural, if we consider that he sang from memory, and did not write from reading; and the modest claim which is put forward in the Sûras represents the Korân as a 'cry' made plain for ignorant men among the Arabs, by an Illiterate Prophet of their own kin—an Arabic version of the 'mother of the Book,' the eternal and divine volume in heaven, which in the creed of Zarathustra becomes so important as the Word of Ormuzd.

A few of the ideas borrowed in the Korân from early Paganism, both Magian and Chaldean, may be enumerated as showing one of the important bases on which the faith of Islam rests.

The idea of a guardian angel belonging to every soul is Persian. The balance in which the soul must be weighed is found represented in Egyptian paintings. The seven solid firmaments were believed in by the Assyrians, and are enumerated in the Zendavesta and in the Talmud: the bitter food eaten in hell, where grows the zakkum tree, reminds us equally of the language of Accadian tablets, of Zend hymns, and of the Book of the Dead, where the balsam tree of Neith is shown in Amentu. The 'thorn tree of the boundary' in Muhammad's heaven is the Assyrian *Samulti*, the tree of light, which becomes the Haoma tree of the Zendavesta. The waters of Tasmîn, which flow from the Paradise of the Korân, are the same 'waters from on high' which proceed, according to the Yashts, from the springs of light.

'Alexander of the two horns' has a long legend devoted to him in the Korân, and is invoked with offerings of pottery horses in India. He appears as a sun-hero in Persia, with many national heroes, and the Greek conqueror has thus become almost a divine person to the Moslem. The jinns who scale heaven in the Suras are but the hosts of Ahriman, who assault the heavenly palace of Ormuzd. The faithful are exhorted not to worship Satan, just as the Zend hymns exhort the Medes not to worship Ahriman. The *Ansâr*, or 'helpers,' of Islam recall, in like manner, those who in Persian hymns are exhorted to 'help the future life.'

Many curious remnants of yet older Paganism may also be noted, for, although Muhammad condemned the *Ansâb*, or Menhirs, of the Arabs, together with games of chance and divining by arrows, he yet long hesitated to renounce the three great goddesses of Mecca—Allât, 'Azzi, and Menât: while Kifl, or the 'divider by lot,' seems to have been an old god of fate; Khudr, or the 'green one,' is a personification of fertility; and Dhu en Nun, or the 'fish man,' is quite as likely to be Oannes or Dagon as to be the Prophet Jonah. All these strange characters hold, in the Korân, a rank hardly inferior to that of Hebrew heroes.

The story of the Deluge in the Sûras is peculiar. The waters appear to have been boiling hot, and issued from the Tannûr, or 'Oven,' which swallowed them again. The waters of hell are also said to be boiling, and in the Talmud the same idea of a deluge of hot water is found. The original Tannûr was the Zemzem well at Mecca, made by Ishmael as a child when he struck his heel on the sand (a legend also related of Job in the Korân); but, as we have seen in the text, other Tannûr springs occur in Syria, and the relation suggested by Professor Sayce with the chasm at Bambyce is no doubt sound, while the sacred cave-springs of Aphek and Banias, and other places, have also a connection with the idea of the Tannûr.

Even Muhammadan writers admit that the *Towâf*, or perambulation of the Meccan Kaaba, had a symbolic meaning connected with the worship of the stars. The running to and fro between Safa and Merwah is said to symbolize the distraction of Hagar, but it is more probably derived from the old idea of the sun's journey backwards and forwards between the mountain of the east and that of the west. Throwing stones at Eblis, in the Valley of Mena, is sanctioned by the words of the Korân, and attached to a legend of Abraham; but, as has been noted in the text of this volume, it has a much older origin in the Paganism of Syria.

It would be tedious further to array the evidence of Persian and pagan influence observable in the Korân, although many other confirmations might be cited; but at a time when many Englishmen seem tempted rather to over-estimate the purity of Moslem teaching, and, as if fascinated by the gravity of Moslem manners, to extol the followers of the Prophet at the expense of the Christians of the West, it may not be without interest thus to point out the true nature of the belief of the Prophet of Islam.

Muhammad was a poet who had gathered a scanty crop of materials from sources almost inexhaustible: these ideas he clothed in language which cannot compare for force and beauty with that of the originals, and he repeated them with wearisome iteration. His ideas were essentially narrow, and without originality, as compared even with the teaching of Zoroaster and Buddha; and, however great his triumph among Arabs, who were mere savages in a boundless wilderness, the power of Islam has been consolidated by men not of Arab race, and it is impossible for the civilized European, unless led astray by enthusiasm or by interest, seriously to maintain that the barbarous fatalism of Islam is the religion of the future.

INDEX.

Abel Shittim, 152.
Abu Zeid, 361, 371. ?
Adonis, 79, 80, 81.
  ,, River, 78.
'Adwân Arabs, 315, 318, 331.
Afka, 2, 40, 80.
'Ain, 11.
'Ain el 'Asy, 8, 11, 12.
  ,, Hesbân, 128,
Alborz, 384.
Alexander, 309.
Alignments, 199, 209, 211.
Altars, Phœnician, 89.
Aly (Imâm), 357, 368.
Amairo (Amorites), 21.
Amanus (Mount), 9.
Ammân, 158, 167.
  ,, Dolmens, 253, 254.
Amûd el Benât, 6.
'Anazeh Arabs, 316.
Ancestor Worship, 336.
Anseiriyeh, 290.
Antar, 358, 369.
April Fools, 294.
Aqueducts (mud), 16.
Arab Civilization, 166.
  ,, Paganism, 338.
Arâk el Emir, 169, 177, 363.
Architecture, Arab, 165.
    ,, Byzantine, 164.
    ,, Jewish, 174, 175.
    ,, Roman, 160.
Arjûn, 36.
Arka (Arkites), 63.
Arks, 36, 231.
Armour, Arab, 339.
Asâf and Naila, 219.
Ascent of Jesus, 360.
Ashtoreth, 23, 65, 80.
Assassins, 289.
Astronomy, Arab, 346.
'Ayûn Mûsa, 131.

Bamoth Baal, 145, 146.

Bath Rabbim, 128.
Batrûn, 77.
Bektashi Derwishes, 297.
Belka, 144.
Belkis, 131.
Beni Hasan Arabs, 316.
  ,, Sakhr Arabs, 315, 317.
Berothah, 9.
Beth Meon, 143.
Beth Peor, 145, 146.
Black Heroes, 370.
Bridge of Gathering, 287, 310.
Bronze Tablet from Palmyra, 84.
Bubale, 128.
Byblos, 78.
Byzantine Architecture, 164.

Cadytis, 26.
Cain and Abel, 148, 307.
Cairns, 241, 242, 264.
Callirhoe, 145, 149.
Camels, 347.
Caves, Sacred, 295.
Character, Arab, 323, 327.
Ciccar Plain, 185, 188, 189.
Circassians, 167, 168.
Circles, 220-223, 227, 234, 265.
Cities of the Plain, 153.
City of Copper, 359.
Cook, Mr., 361.
Courage, Arab, 327-329.
Courtesy, Arab, 321.
Crac des Chevaliers, 52, 56.
Crusading Castles, 52, 60.
  ,, Rule, 61.
Ctesiphon Palace, 163.
Cup Hollows, 235-237.

Dancing Derwishes, 67-74, 299.
Daphne, 74.
Dead Sea Geology, 125.
Debir, 185.
Deir Ghazaleh Dolmen, 250.
Derwishes, 67, 296, 382.

INDEX.

Diblathaim, 229.
Disc Stones, 264, 269.
Dish of Abu Zeid, 264.
Distribution of Dolmens, 200.
Dolmens, 228, 275, 337.
Dome of the Rock, 164.
Donkey's Back, 364.
Dragon Fountain, 307.
Druzes, 288.

Elagabalus, 44.
Elealah, 142.
Eleutherus River, 50, 64, 66.
Elijah, 286.
Emesa (Homs), 43.
Esau, 307.
Evil Eye, 293.

Fables, Arab, 362.
Feasts of Arabs, 337.
Field of Zophim, 133.
Fikieh, 10.
Fires, 294.
Fish, Sacred, 66, 103, 300.
Flowers, 194.
Footprints, 302.
Frescoes, 76.

Gad, Border of, 157.
Gebal Giblites, 78, 79.
Gerasa, 190.
Ghareïsah and Zeid, 361.
Gilgal, 227.
Goblân, 112-119.
Gomorrah, 153.
Grackle Bird, 127.

Hadânieh Circle, 257.
Hair Offerings, 340, 385.
Hajâret en Nasâra, 249.
Hajr ed Dumm, 249.
,, el Hubleh, 249.
,, el Mansûb, 260.
,, el Mena, 263, 338.
,, Munkeia, 249.
Hamath, 7.
,, Inscriptions, 24, 25, 26, 49.
Hameidi Arabs, 316.
Hammon, 89.
Hâna and Bâna, 362.
Hand of Might, 283.
Har or Khar, 7, 10.
Hazar Enan, 7, 8, 10.
Heshbon, 142.
Himyaritic Letters, 350.
History of the Survey, 4, 106-122.
Hittites, 17, 20, 23, 27, 34, 35.

Homs (Emesa), 43-49.
Horses, Arab, 349.
el Hosn, 52.
Hot Springs, 150.
Human Sacrifice, 102, 157, 218, 219.
Hunting, 352.
Hyrcanus, 168, 169, 175.

Identifications, 144.
Inscriptions, 45, 53, 176, 177.
Ism'aileh, 289.

Jabbok River, 190.
Jebel Osh'a, 186.
Jehoshaphat Valley, 286.
Jerâsh, 190.
Jewish Superstitions, 280-286.
Jews, 287.
Jibeil (Byblos), 78.
Job's Fountain, 305.

Kabr 'Abdallah, 137.
Kadesh on Orontes, 18-35, 66.
el Kaf (Mountain), 384.
Kamû'at el Hirmil, 12-15.
Kareiyah, 1.
Kasr el 'Abd, 171-174, 363.
Kefr el Wâl, 251.
Kefrein, 152, 258.
Kenites, 148.
Kerâd Goblins, 305.
Khar, 7, 81.
el Khudr, 308.
Kiosk at 'Ammân, 162-167.
Kodeshoth, 26.
Korân, 310-313.
Koteineh, Lake, 27, 28, 36, 41, 50.
Kurmiyeh Dolmens, 253-255.
Kuseir, 18.

Lebweh Leboa, 6, 8, 11.
Libben (bricks), 16.
Lilith, 283.
Litâny River, 11.
Living Stones, 204.
Luck Marks, 293, 294.
Lucky Days, 293.

Machærus, 149, 151.
Mahanaim, 182, 184, 185.
Mahmal, 353.
Malawiyeh Derwishes, 67-74, 299.
el Mareighât, 260, 262.
Marina, 75.
Marks on Dolmens, 233.
Mar Marûn, 11, 13.
Maronite Superstitions, 292.

Mashita Palace, 166.
Masons' Marks, 57.
Mâta et Turkomanlyeh, 335.
Medeba, 142.
Melearth, 91-93, 99, 101, 308.
Menhirs, 199, 203-209, 260-262, 265.
Mensef Abu Zeid, 263.
Meshâhed, 212, 336.
Metzebah, 215.
Minyeh, 147, 357.
  ,,   Dolmens, 259.
Mithræa, 290.
Mizpeh, 180.
Moab, 123-125.
el Mohdy, 41.
Moslem Myths, 296, 310.
Mosque of Light, 44-48.
Mount Pilgrim, 65, 66.
Munker and Nakir, 310.

Nahaliel, 145, 148.
Nahleh, 5.
Nail Parings, 282.
Names, Arab, 338.
Nebo, Mount, 132-141, 256.
Neby Duhy, 308.
  ,, M'ashûk, 94, 308.
  ,, Mendeh, 14, 19, 29, 30.
  ,, 'Othman, 11.
  ,, Osh'a, 188, 189.
  ,, Samat, 278.
  ,, Shit, 307.
New Moon, 283, 293.
Nimrod, 307, 310.
Noah's Ark, 36, 37, 306.
  ,,   Tomb, 306.
North Border of Holy Land, 7.
Numbers of Arabs, 320.

Og's Bedstead, 160, 252.
Oiled Stones, 204, 215.
Oleander, 174.
Ordeals, Arab, 352.
Orontes River, 8, 10.
Ostriches, 128.
Ovens, 17.

Palæ-Tyrus, 97.
Palm, Sacred, 308.
Passing through, 301.
Penuel, 182-185.
Périetié Collection, 83-85.
Philadelphia, 157.
Phœnicians, 81.
Pisgah, 132, 145.
Politics, Arab, 317, 337.
Pomegranate Offerings, 305.

Pseudo Traditions, 279.

Rabbath Ammon, 157.
Railways, 50.
Ramath Mizpeh, 180.
Ramoth Gilead, 179.
Raymond of St. Gilles, 65.
Red Heifer Bridge, 286.
Reimûn, 180, 192.
Religion, Arab, 333, 334.
Riblah, 7, 10, 13, 16.
Ring Hill, 258.
Roebuck, 127.
Roman Architecture, 160.
Rude-Stone Monuments, 16, 153, 160, 181, 196, 274.
Rustem, 372, 374.

Sabbatic River, 54.
Sacred Stones, 197-207, 215-218.
Saklb, 192.
es Sâlt, 185.
Samaritan Legends, 287.
Samson, 278, 282.
Sannin, Mount, 2, 6.
Sassanian Architecture, 163.
  ,,   Myths, 371.
Secret Passage, 161.
Seisebân Plain, 152.
Sentinel Stones, 233.
Set, 23, 81, 104, 148, 306.
Shabatuna, 21, 55.
Shedim (demons), 287.
Shoes, Sacred, 303.
Sidd, 43.
Sitt Eslâmiyeh, 308.
Solomon's Servant, 151, 336.
Sodom, 153.
Springs, Sacred, 303.
Sticks, 339.
Stonehenge, 199.
Stylites, 6.
Sûf Mizpeh, 180, 250.
Sûk Sairi, 247.
Sûnia, 129, 256.
Sun Worship, 225, 337.
Swastica, 233.

Table of Christ, 250.
Tahtun Hodshi, 26.
Talmud, 282.
Tammuz, 78.
Tannûr, 33, 37, 305.
Tashlich, 282, 283.
Tear of Isis, 381.
Tell el Kady Dolmens, 247.
  ,,   Shagûr, 154.

INDEX.

Tells, 243.
Templars, 299.
Theouprosopon, 75.
Thieves, Arab, 351.
Thresholds, 302.
Tob, Land of, 181.
Tombs, Amman, 157-161.
    ,,   Arab, 322.
    ,,   Phœnician, 95, 96.
    ,,   Prehistoric, 267.
Topes, 243.
Trade of Tyre, 98.
Trees, Sacred, 42, 302, 336.
Tribe Marks, 350.
Tripoli, 65.
Turkomans, 15, 17.
Typhon River, 8.
Tyre, 90-103.
Tyrus, 169.

Umm el 'Amûd, 88, 89.
Utfa Palanquin, 353.

Valley of Figs, 101.

Wishing Stones, 263.
Wood of Ephraim, 185, 186.
Women, Arab, 342-346.

Zahleh, 3.
Zedad, 7.
Zeid, 361.
Zenobia's Garden, 130.
Zerka M'ain, 148.
  ,,   Shebib, 190.
Zikr Ceremonies, 73.
Zir, Legends of, 364-369.
Zoar, Site of, 156.
Zoology of Moab, 128.

THE END.

BILLING AND SONS, PRINTERS, GUILDFORD.

www.ingramcontent.com/pod-product-compliance
Lightning Source LLC
Chambersburg PA
CBHW050850300426
44111CB00010B/1206